John B. Carwile

Reminiscences of Newberry

Embracing important occurrences, brief biographies of prominent citizens and historical sketches of churches: to which is appended an historical account of Newberry college

John B. Carwile

Reminiscences of Newberry

Embracing important occurrences, brief biographies of prominent citizens and historical sketches of churches: to which is appended an historical account of Newberry college

ISBN/EAN: 9783337419523

Printed in Europe, USA, Canada, Australia, Japan

Cover: Foto ©ninafisch / pixelio.de

More available books at **www.hansebooks.com**

OF

NEWBERRY,

EMBRACING

IMPORTANT OCCURRENCES, BRIEF BIOGRAPHIES
OF PROMINENT CITIZENS AND HIS-
TORICAL SKETCHES OF
CHURCHES:

TO WHICH IS APPENDED

AN HISTORICAL ACCOUNT OF NEWBERRY COLLEGE.

BY

JOHN B. CARWILE.

CHARLESTON, S. C.
WALKER, EVANS & COGSWELL CO., PRINTERS.
3 & 5 Broad and 117 East Bay Sts.
1890.

TO

ROBERT LUSK McCAUGHRIN,

WHO STANDS PRE-EMINENT AMONG THE BENEFACTORS OF

NEWBERRY,

THESE REMINISCENCES AND SKETCHES

ARE RESPECTFULLY DEDICATED

BY HIS FRIEND AND ASSOCIATE OF MANY YEARS,

JOHN B. CARWILE.

NOTE.—In addition to acknowledgments already made in the body of the work, the author desires to express his grateful thanks to, J. F. J. Caldwell, Esq., Silas Johnstone, Esq., Dr. O. B. Mayer, Sen., Rev. E. P. McClintock, Hon. Y. J. Pope, John A. Chapman, Esq., Mrs. Dr. James McIntosh, Mrs. J. M. Baxter, Miss O. E. Garlington, Mrs. Dr. Sale and Mrs. Nancy Moon of Newberry, the Hon. Samuel McGowan, Associate Justice of the Supreme Court of S. C., the Rev. S. T. Hallman of Augusta, Ga. and Mrs. William Hood of Due West, S. C., for valuable aid and assistance most cheerfully given him in the prosecution of his labors.

INTRODUCTION.

IN the following pages it is attempted to give some account of the principal persons who have resided in the town of Newberry, South Carolina, and of the prominent occurrences in that town during the past half century, as these persons and occurrences are known to the author. His design has not been to write a history of that town, or of the surrounding section, but to present to the public, and especially to those who are acquainted or connected with the individuals and events and institutions described, the author's knowledge of these persons and things. He has no religious, social or political theory to advocate, no personal interest to advance; he simply records his own reminiscences and his own experiences, and leaves the reader to draw his own conclusions.

The reach of such a work is, as I have more than once suggested to my friend, far beyond his purpose in writing these sketches, and far beyond what he is willing to claim for them. For, as has been said, history is little more than the biographies of prominent men; when, therefore, the lives of the principal men of a community have been correctly delineated, there has been written, at least for the period in which they lived and acted, the history of that community. Nor is this history limited to the duration of those men's lives, for what they were and what they did constitute the result and expression of thoughts, sentiments and customs transmitted to them from past generations, and are also the producing cause of much that follows them. And thus their lives are both a history of the past, and a forecast of the future of their people. Moreover the inhabitants of a town or county are so like those of the surrounding section, that a truthful account of one neighborhood will present at least a tolerably accurate description of a considerable territory about it.

Judging from our experience of men, we can scarcely expect that a book of this character, professedly local in its scope, should have much interest for persons far removed from the scenes described, for such persons usually take it for granted that it contains nothing which at all concerns them. Yet, it is for those very persons that it should have the greatest interest, for while to the vicinity it is but a narrative of things already pretty well known there, to one at a distance it is a history of a people to him hitherto almost utterly unknown. While therefore, I may commend this work to the people of Newberry and of this State, on account of its truthfulness and accuracy in describing persons and things already known, and to some extent appreciated by them, I may especially commend it to persons outside of the State because of its affording such a description of our customs, sentiments and modes of thought as they are not likely to find elsewhere. To us the book is a narrative: to

Introduction. ix

the foreigner it is a painting of the life and thought and sentiment of Southern people.

The author has resided in the town of Newberry for somewhat more than fifty years. In his occupations as merchant and banker, he has been pretty well acquainted with almost all of our prominent men, and more or less concerned in all movements of interest in that community during that period. He has spared no pains in collecting accurate information; he has cheerfully corrected every error, even the least material of his first views or narrations, whenever it has been shown or suspected. I have examined his manuscript with the closest scrutiny, and I must say that if there is a misstatement in the work I am not able to name it. And the taste and tone of the volume cannot be to highly praised. While entirely frank and fearless in handling the matters under investigation, the author has written nothing which is not consistent with the most elevated morality, and has written of nothing in any other manner than that which the most refined sensibility must approve.

I take pleasure in commending the work to the people of America, not only as an accurate historical narrative, but as a truthful picture of Southern thought and life.

J. F. J. CALDWELL.

Newberry, September, 1889.

CONTENTS.

CHAPTER I.

Early Recollections—Schools and School Masters—Rev. S. P. Pressly—Miss —— Clark—Simeon Pratt—James Divver.. 1

CHAPTER II.

Old time Domestic Economy — Polly Goulding—Schools and School Masters again—McGovern—Dick Cahill—Old Billy Cahill—Rencounter between McGovern and Bill Pearce—Rolly Hughes—Death of Albert Johnstone—Rev. J. Galloway—"Shinney"—Rev. Mr. Chaplain and Mr. Wiley, both New England Teachers—New Methods of Teaching and Discipline Introduced—Daniel A. Dobson—His wonderful Attainments and early Death... 10

CHAPTER III.

Bird's-eye view of Newberry fifty years ago—Dr. M. T. Mendenhall—Robert Stewart—A typical old time store—M. W. Gracey—A celebrated race horse—The Old Shoe Store—Gouveneur Thompson—Circus and Menagerie show bills—Why the Circus and Menagerie were combined—Antoine Gilbal—Mystery of his former life—His excentricities—His horsemanship—Solomon's Song.................. 25

CHAPTER IV.

Manners and Customs—Everybody on horseback—The people all of one political party—Personal appeals for suffrages unknown—"Treating" almost universal—Merriman Clocks as badges of prosperity—Marriages—Funerals—Mail Coaches—Postoffice—A trip by stage coach—Some reflections and some advice to young men which the reader may skip if he chooses—Publications received at the Postoffice in 1840—Horse Racing—Scenes on a Race Course—Gambling Hell............ 37

CHAPTER V.

The Old Locust—Dr. Burr Johnston—He removes to Alabama—Affecting scenes on the day of his departure from Newberry—Memories of the old Locust—Paul Johnstone—Howard H. Caldwell—Dr. William H. Harrington—Major Christian H. Suber—Thomas Pratt—His journey to Philadelphia on horseback in 1813, to purchase goods—Priestly Pratt—John W. Stewart, Richard C. Carwile, John C. Higgins and Priestly Pratt Volunteer for the Mexican War—The last Farewell—Only Higgins lives to return—Guzman—His noble conduct and death in Mexico.......................... 53

CHAPTER VI.

The Old Court House—A Day in Court—Genl. H. H. Kinard, Sheriff—Judge O'Neall on the Bench—Y. J. Harrington, Clerk—James J. Caldwell, Solicitor—Rapid Dispatch of Business—Flexibility

PAGE.

of the Old Judiciary System—L. J. Jones—His Remarkable Career of Fifty Years as a Lawyer—John Caldwell—Member of the Legislature—Cashier of Bank of the State—His Eloquence at the Bar and before the People—P. C. Caldwell—Member of the Bar—of the Legislature—of Congress—of the Senate—Silas L. Heller—Lawyer—Member of Legislature—Teacher—Henry Summer—Attorney—Member of the Legislature—Elected to Southern Congress in 1851—Member of State Convention, 1865—Enthusiastic Lover and Collector of Books—Graphic account of the Perils and Sufferings of the Family during Sherman's March (1865) Narrated by his Wife, Mrs. Frances Summer—Adam G. Summer—His Short Career at the Bar—Devotes himself to Agriculture and Literature—His Sad Death—Geo. F. Epps—His promising Professional Career cut short by Death. 72

CHAPTER VII.

Great Religious Awakening—Organization and History of Baptist Church—Picture of a Church Edifice fifty years ago—Rev J. M. Barnes—Rev. N. W. Hodges—Rev. D. Mangum—Rev. Thomas Frean—Rev. Samuel Gibson—Rev. Jno. G. Landrum—Rev. M.C. Barnett—Rev. Richard Furman, D. D.. 97

CHAPTER VIII.

Methodist Church—Organization and History—Rev. Angus McPherson—Rev. G. W. Moore—Rev. Saml. Dunwoody—Rev. C. S. Walker—Rev. S.

Townsend—Rev. J. R. Pickett—Rev. W. A. McSwain—Rev. A. W. Walker—Rev. C. McLeod—Rev. Bond English...... 114

CHAPTER IX.

Aveleigh (Presbyterian) Church—Letter of Chancellor Johnstone's—Organization and History of the Church—Rev R. C. Ketchum—Rev. J. McKittrick—Rev. E. F. Hyde—Rev. A. D. Montgomery—Rev. E. H. Buist...... 122

CHAPTER X.

St. Luke's (Episcopal) Church—Service in Court House and Female Academy, in 1836, by Rev Cranmore Wallace—In 1845, by Rev. R. S. Seely, followed by Rev. E. T. Walker—Consecration of Church Edifice in 1855—Rev. C. R. Haines—Rev. Lucian Lance—Rev. Maxwell Pringle—Rev. E. R. Miles—Rev. P. F. Stevens—Rev Jno. Kershaw—Rev. S. H. Gallaudett—Rev. F. Hallam—Rev. W. F. Dickinson—Rev. W. H. Hanckel...... 135

CHAPTER XI.

Luther Chapel (Evangelical Lutheran Church)—Organization and History—Rev. T. S. Boinest—Rev. Wm. Berly—Rev. Theophilus Stork, D. D—Rev. J. P. Smeltzer, D. D...... 142

CHAPTER XII.

Thompson Street (Associate Reformed Presbyterian Church)—History—Rev. E. P. McClintock—Rev. H. L. Murphy...... 151

CHAPTER XIII.

Some Living Ministers Formerly Pastors in Newberry—Rev. John J. Brantley, D. D—Rev. H. W. Kuhns, D. D—Rev. R. A. Fair 156

CHAPTER XIV.

Biographical Sketches—Chief Justice O'Neall—Chancellor Job Johnstone—Chancellor J. J. Caldwell 165

CHAPTER XV.

Biographical Sketches Continued—Simeon Fair—Thomas H. Pope—J. M. Baxter—A. C. Garlington 192

CHAPTER XVI.

Biographical Sketches Continued—Y. J. Harrington—John S. Carwile—F. B. Higgins—Drayton Nance—James D. Nance 225

CHAPTER XVII.

Biographical Sketches Continued—Rev. Samuel P. Pressly—Remarkable Scene in a Court House—Story of a Celebrated Trial (Foot Note)—Rev. Luther Broaddus 258

APPENDIX.

Historical Sketch of Newberry College 275

Reminiscences of Newberry.

CHAPTER I.

EARLY RECOLLECTIONS.—SCHOOLS AND SCHOOLMASTERS.—
REV. SAMUEL P. PRESSLY.—MISS CLARK—SIMEON
PRATT.—JAMES DIVVER.

"A wonderful stream is the River of Time,
As it runs through the realms of Tears,
With a faultless rhythm and a musical rhyme,
And a broader sweep and a surge sublime,
As it blends with the Ocean of years.

"How the winters are drifting like flakes of snow,
And the summers like buds between,
And the year in the sheaf—so they come and go
On the river's breast, with its ebb and flow
As it glides in the shadow and sheen."
BENJAMIN F. TAYLOR.—"*The Long Ago.*"

I PROPOSE in an unostentatious way to present some reminiscences, chiefly of the town of Newberry in the olden time, without much regard to chronological order, and as it will be necessary to have something with which to bind them together, I shall use the thread of my own life for that purpose. This is unavoidable, and will I trust be accepted as an apology for frequently introducing myself.

In taking a retrospective view of my life, I have sometimes endeavored to ascertain how far back my memory would lead me. In this effort the following somewhat ludicrous incident which must have occurred when I was about four or five years of age, invariably appears to be the earliest impression left upon my mind which can be recalled.

On a sunny spring day, in a shady back yard, I was busily engaged in damming up a little stream of water which ran from the pump, in order to provide a comfortable retreat for a bevy of young ducks. In this absorbing occupation I was assisted by several small "darkies." I was dressed in a loose flowing garment, which in shape if not in color must have resembled the one presented by Jacob to his beloved son, Joseph.* From the duck puddle I could see through the main hall out into the piazza of the dwelling. Hearing some lively conversation and laughter I looked up and saw a young girl, (leading by the hand a boy larger than myself and in full dress) passing out of the hall followed by my eldest sister to whom she had just paid a visit. All oblivious of the condition of my hands and face, not to speak of my apparel, I ran through the hall and peeped cautiously around the frame of the front door.

The young girls were taking leave of each other. They kissed and said good bye. When my sister's young friend had descended the steps leading from the piazza, she suddenly turned round and came back, the little boy following, to say something to my sister, and they again entered into a spirited conversation. This manœuver was repeated several times, varied only by my sister sometimes going out to

---

*It is uncertain when the art of dyeing became known to the Hebrews: the dress worn by Joseph (Gen. xxxvii, 3, 23) is variously taken to be either a " coat of divers colors" or a tunic furnished with sleeves and reaching down to the ankles. The latter is probably the correct sense. *"Smith's Dictionary of the Bible."*

her friend. So that they did not separate until long after the first farewell kiss had been exchanged.

I digress here to remark, that the habit of lingering, and renewing conversation again and again, after formally taking leave, appears to be universal among women and is a phenomenon which I have never heard explained.

Meantime, in my eagerness to get a good look at the boy, I incautiously leaned too far into the doorway. The little fellow saw me, and pointing with a finger of one hand towards me, and giving a tug at his sister's skirts with the other hand exclaimed. "Is that a white boy"? An explosion of laughter from the girls, sent me flying through the hall with my "Joseph's coat" fluttering in the wind. I landed pell-mell on my hands and knees in the midst of my dusky companions, who stood grinning at the back-door.

After this very unsatisfactory reconnoisance, I resumed my labors at the duck puddle.

The next incident recalled is of quite a different character; I am standing in a large room, with a capacious fireplace, above which there is a tall mantle-piece, adorned with objects of virtu. On one side of the room there is an antique clock fastened to the wall, on the opposite side there is a curiously fashioned chest of drawers, surmounted by an elaborate book-case, called by the maker a "Secretary". In one corner of the room there is a walnut buffet, dark and rich in color from age, behind the glass doors of which are to be seen my mother's treasures of china and glass-ware. It is a warm summer day and the windows are all thrown open to admit the air. From the rear windows there is a pleasant view of green grass and trees, and some tall lagerstroemia's in full bloom just beyond the entrance of the garden. A humming bird with his brilliant livery of green and gold flashing in the sunlight, flits to and fro across the windows as he regales himself from the blooming climbers, trained against the wall of the house outside. A child's crib in which my youngest brother, less than one year of age, is breathing his last, has been placed in the center of the room. Around this the family have gathered. I see my mother, with the tears streaming down her cheeks; my father calm and composed but exhibiting marks of a severe inward struggle, while a dear sister who has always been my guardian angel has her arms around me; and thus we watch the little sufferer as his life ebbs away.

In the long record of the years which lie between these incidents of my childhood and the present:

> "What tragedies what comedies are there:
> What joy and grief, what rapture and despair,
> What chronicles of triumph and defeat,
> Of struggle, and temptation, and retreat."

There are scenes which stand out boldly against the background of the past. There are others only dimly shadowed forth; and many more which appear to be almost obliterated.

I have never kept a diary, and only a few of the friends of those about whom I propose to write, have been able to furnish me with records of value. I must therefore depend chiefly upon my memory. Only those who have undertaken similar work, can appreciate the difficulties which lie before me.

DeQuincy observes: "what else than a natural and mighty palimpsest* is the human brain? such a palimpsest

---

* A parchment (used by the ancients) on which the original writing has been effaced and something else has been written. When parchment was not supplied in sufficient quantities, the monks and others used to wash or rub out the writing in a parchment and use it again. as they did not wash or rub it out entirely, many works have been recovered by modern ingenuity.

is my brain; such a palimpsest, Oh! reader is yours. Everlasting layers of ideas, images, feelings, have fallen upon your brain soft as light. Each succession has seemed to bury all that went before. And yet in reality not one has been extinguished."

Now while all this may be true, and that under certain conditions, such as the consciousness of the near approach of death, or while under the influence of fever, or opium; "all the mysterious hand-writings of grief or joy which have inscribed themselves successively on the brain, may be revived," yet we know that under ordinary circumstances the memory is very capricious, and often refuses to respond to the demands which are made upon it.

Sometimes it is obedient and prompt, at other times obstinate and rebellious and then again tyranical and oppressive compelling the mind to dwell upon some unpleasant and painful incident and refusing to allow it to be dismissed.

Those of my readers who may miss some things which they expected to see in these pages will now, I trust understand why they do not appear.

In the year 1832, I began my school life. This was my first great trial. I was a diffident child, fond of home, and never so happy as when following my mother, as she went about her daily tasks; watching her busy fingers and listening to her sweet voice as she sung some old familiar song. The night preceding the day on which I was to enter school, I went to bed with a heavy heart, and sobbed myself to sleep. In the morning when the sun came peeping in at the window I did not welcome his appearance. Until that morning,

"He never came a wink too soon,
Nor brought too long a day;"

but his arrival that day brought back all my forebodings of trouble.

Very soon a servant came in and proceeded to array me in a new suit, made for the occasion. The house cat followed, purring and pressing her sleek sides against my legs, looked up into my face and said, as plain as a dumb thing could, "what is the matter with my little master, that he does not stroke my back and carry me in his arms down to the breakfast room?"

After breakfast with a "blue backed" Webster's Spelling Book in my hand, a biscuit in each of my jacket pockets, and with a heart heavier far than the combined weight of the book and the biscuits, I was led away to school by a sister older than myself, who was to be my companion, and who had always watched over me with tender solicitude.

How strangely changed everything appeared that morning. There before my eyes were the woodbines and yellow jasmines which I had helped my mother to train against the wall of the house, the old apple tree under whose spreading branches I was accustomed to retreat from the heat of the sun ; and the soft green turf beneath the locust trees where I had so often rested from my play, but all the light and beauty of them seemed to have disappeared. Alas! how often in maturer life, do we not, under the shadows of grief and disappointment, experience such sad transformations.

> "Seldom when life is mature, and the strength proportioned to the burden.
> Will the feeling mind, that can remember, acknowledge to deeper anguish
> Than when, as a stranger and a little one, the heart first ached with anxiety,
> And the sprouting buds of sensibility were bruised by the harshness of a school."

The schoolhouse to which I was sent stood on the corner of Caldwell and Boundary streets, diagonally opposite the Baptist Parsonage. The school was taught by the Rev. Samuel P. Pressly, an Associate Reformed Presbyterian minister, assisted by Miss Clark a " Yankee school marm." The first floor, one large room, was occupied by the primary department, presided over by Miss Clark, who was a stern disciplinarian; the second floor by higher classes, under the tuition of Mr. Pressly. But what they did "up stairs," or how that part of the house appeared, I do not know to this day. I could hear the tramp of feet and the murmer of voices over my head, but was never allowed to go up, indeed I had no desire to go, the first floor had terrors enough for me.

The terror of my childhood was a thunder storm, whenever one came up, I did not feel safe until I had buried my face in my mother's lap and felt her hands resting on my head.

One warm spring day while at Mr. Pressly's school a dark cloud arose in the west accompanied by much lightning and thunder. I began to sob and cry piteously. The thought of my absent mother filled me with a new horror. Miss Clark heard my sobbings and sternly ordered me to cease crying at once, or she would punish me. To convince me of her determination, she sent out a boy larger than myself to bring in a switch. The boy who was sent out was my honored friend Simeon Pratt, so well known in Newberry. When he returned he had in his hand a branch, with some blossoms left on the small end, broken from a peach tree in full bloom. With that peculiar gentleness of manner, and softness of tone in speaking, which has always characterized him; he said to me as he passed by, on his way to deliver the twig to Miss Clark: "See! my dear

John what a beautiful switch I have brought for you to be punished with." I did not at the time perceive the beauties of the switch nor appreciate the motive of my friend, whose intention no doubt was to divert my thoughts from the thunder storm. I have long since forgiven him however for his share in the matter, but have never been able to find excuse or justification for the stern cruelty of Miss Clark in seeking to quiet the fears of a terror-stricken child by a resort to threats of punishment.

Anything ludicrous which has actually happened under my observation, has generally made a more lasting impression on my memory than other things of a more sober and serious character. I cannot account for this and have sometimes had cause to regret it.

A ludicrous incident which happened at Mr. Pressly's school I have never forgotten.

A long bench without a back, placed about midway in the schoolroom, was occupied by a class of small boys to which I belonged. I sat near one end of the bench. One day while Miss Clark was busily occupied, and had her back turned towards us, we became very much interested in a whispered discussion about watermelons. One boy said "I wish I had a watermelon as large as my head;" another boy said "I wish I had one as large as the water bucket." Not to be outdone I got astride the bench, and sliding back as I measured it, began to mark out the size of an imaginary watermelon which was to be larger than all others, suddenly there was a crash, and I found myself on the floor, with my heels in the air. The next moment I was grasped by the collar of my jacket, and lifted upon my feet by Miss Clark and made to "see stars" by slaps inflicted upon my cheeks with her broad palms.

My next teacher was James Divver who taught in a house

which stood upon the present site of the county jail. At that time there was a bold spring of refreshingly cool water, a few rods west of the schoolhouse, surrounded by some large beech trees. In addition to the schoolhouse Mr. Divver owned and lived in the house which still stands on the north west corner of Harrington and ——— ——— ——— streets now occupied by Mr. Knighton.

Very little is known of Mr Divver's early history. He emigrated from Ireland and landed in New Brunswick sometime previous to the year 1819. In that year he came to Newberry on foot, with all his worldy possessions tied up in a bundle and slung across his shoulders. He was at once employed to teach a country school somewhere in the district. In 1820 he was a pupil in the Newberry Academy, and afterwards attended a school in Laurens District. In 1822 he entered the junior class of the South Carolina College, and was graduated in 1824. Upon his graduation he he was elected tutor of mathematics in his alma mater. Judge O'Neall in his Annals, says of Mr Divver: "Such unexampled success attending the course of a stranger indicated rare qualities of head and heart, such had James Divver. He was one of the best mathematicians ever graduated in the South Carolina College; he was a true Irishman generous and devoted. But an unfortunate habit, too much indulged in, of using intoxicating drink made it necessary for him to resign his position in the College."

Mr. Divver came back to Newberry in 1828, and took charge of the Academy. In December, 1833, he removed to Charleston, S. C, where he died in 1847.

It affords me much pleasure to say that my respected teacher, for several years previous to his death, abstained entirely from the use of intoxicating drinks, and led a consistent, Christian life.

CHAPTER II.

OLD TIME DOMESTIC ECONOMY—POLLY GOULDING—SCHOOLS AND MASTERS AGAIN—MCGOVERN—DICK CAHILL—OLD BILLY CAHILL—RENCOUNTER BETWEEN BILL PEARCE AND MCGOVERN—ROLLY HUGHES—DEATH OF ALBERT JOHNSTONE—REV. J. GALLOWAY—"SHINNEY"—REV. MR. CHAPLAIN AND MR.—WILEY, BOTH NEW ENGLAND TEACHERS—NEW METHODS OF TEACHING AND DISCIPLINE INTRODUCED—DANIEL A. DOBSON, HIS WONDERFUL ATTAINMENTS AND EARLY DEATH.

> "Oh ye who teach the ingenuous youth of nations,
> Holland, France, England, Germany or Spain,
> I pray ye flog them upon all occasions,
> It mends their morals never mind the pain."
> *Don-Juan.*

MY mother was a staunch believer in the value and economy of home products. Until I was probably fifteen years of age, all my suits of clothing except some special ones reserved for "Sunday wear" were made of cloth woven from thread spun by her servants. The weaving was all done by Miss Polly Goulding who lived "all alone" in a little cabin about two miles from the village.

Polly was a frequent visitor to our house. Every one on the premises except my parents were afraid of her, and even they permitted her to have her own way in everything.

In appearance she bore a strong resemblance to the

pictures of old women riding on broom-sticks across the face of the moon, which we sometimes see in children's toy books. She always spoke in sharp, quick tones, and was seldom seen to laugh. She would generally come in through the back door without knocking, walk into my mother's room, and deposit on the floor a bundle which she always brought with her, and after lighting her pipe and sitting some time with her elbows resting on her knees and her hands supporting her chin, would begin to inquire after the family, making comments as she went along, and giving my mother directions about the management of her domestic affairs. She came in one day and found me in the act of taking some quinine to ward off a chill. She railed out against such folly, and denounced in unmeasured terms all sorts of "doctor truck" and declared that if I did not send out some of the "niggers" to get some "pine tops and mullen" and have them "biled" and drink the tea, I never would get well. One of her eccentricities was, that she always reversed her position in bed. She entertained some superstitious notion about this, which she never would disclose. Her life and character illustrated the fact that it is possible for some persons to spend a lifetime in a civilized and enlightened community, and never change in their habits nor make any progress in intellectual improvement. She knew no more when she died at a good old age, than she did when she was twenty years old. Nothing that the family could do, would induce her to change her style of dress, her habits or her views of life. But with all her eccentricity she was scrupulously honest, truthful and faithful, and in her simple way served God to the best of her ability. While she never said so much as "thank you," for any kindness rendered, I believe there was no sacrifice she would not have made for my parents.

Polly was never married. I suppose she was young once but it must have been in years only. I think she never knew anything about the hopes and joyful anticipations of girlhood, I never heard any one speak of her youth, nor did she ever refer to it herself, she had a great contempt for men, and with a few exceptions, heartily despised them all. She honored and trusted my father.

It is quite probable that the cost per yard of Polly's cloth was more than the price asked for goods of equal value in the village stores. Doubtless my father with his clear head for business knew this, but he was too wise to hint such a thing to my mother. It would have shaken her faith in her wonderful industrial system, by which, under the guise of receiving compensation for services rendered, Polly and other poor women were really the recipients of her bounty I now return to my school life.

The next teacher who comes to view in the dim vista of the past is Mr. McGovern, a squint-eyed, irritable, tyrannic Irishman, who was the terror of the small boys in the school.

> "Well had the boding tremblers learned to trace
> The day's disasters in his morning face;
> Full well they laughed with counterfeited glee
> At all his jokes, for many a joke had he;
> Full well the busy whisper circling round,
> Conveyed the dismal tidings when he frowned."

Where he came from to Newberry or what became of him after he left I do not know. He first taught in what was then known as the "Red House", (a two story building with one end on the street,) which stood on the north side of Boice street about midway between Caldwell and Adams streets.

I entered McGovern's school during the exciting days of "Nullification". I wore a suit of clothes made from the product of Polly Goulding's loom ; the jacket of which was profusely ornamented with brass buttons upon which the coat of arms of the State was stamped. These buttons were generally worn by the, so called, nullifiers, in the centre of cockades on the outside of their hats. My mother had ornamented my jacket with them to please my father who belonged to the "Nullification Party."

Among the larger boys at McGovern's school, Dick Cahill was a conspicuous character. He was the butt of the school, against whom the boys of his set, constantly directed their ridicule, and whenever he exhibited too much resentment, they did not hesitate to pummel him into submission. Poor Dick ! I can see him now as he appeared after one of these "scrimmages," his shirt front torn open, disclosing a fearful bruise on his chest, his hair disheveled, and the tears streaming down his cheeks, while he upbraided his comrades with their lack of manliness and fairplay.

Notwithstanding all his harsh treatment Dick never seemed to harbor a spirit of revenge, and was always ready to take the lead, and become the scape-goat in any frolicsome adventure that might be proposed. He wandered away in his early manhood, and after leading a wild, dissipated life, returned to Newberry just before the recent war, and died in a room adjoining Julius B. Smith's drinking saloon. Poor fellow ! I cannot think of his sad end without regret. With all his faults, he had a warm place in my heart. He always stood forth as the champion of the oppressed, and at school would never allow a small boy to be bullied or hectored by one of superior growth and strength.

Old Billy Cahill, (generally called Carroll,) the father of Dick, was a simple-hearted, ignorant Irish laborer, very honest and faithful. He was often employed by Chancellor

Job Johnstone, and very kindly treated by the Chancellor's family. One evening he was sitting with the family listening to the Chancellor as he read some amusing Irish stories. When the time for family prayer arrived, the Chancellor exchanged the book from which he had been reading, for his Bible, and after a short pause, began to read the fourth chapter of the Gospel by John. Old Billy who sat looking into the fire, did not observe the change, and as he knew very little of the contents of the Bible, naturally supposed that he was listening to another Irish story, but did not seem to be much interested until the Chancellor read the reply of the Saviour to the woman of Samaria, who had just said I have no husband: "Thou hast well said I have no husband, for thou hast had five husbands, and he whom thou now hast is not thy husband: in that thou saidst truly." Here Old Billy nudged one of the Chancellor's sons, who was sitting near, and giving him a knowing wink, remarked in a very audible whisper, "Be-gonney that was cute." It is needless to say that it required all the self-control and parental authority that the Chancellor and Mrs. Johnstone could exercise to carry them safely through the evening service.

At McGovern's school I began to study arithmetic. We had no series of books then, conveniently arranged for primary, intermediate and advanced classes. All pupils used Stephen Pike's Arithmetic. This book, like Webster's "blue backed" spelling book was always bound in one style of binding. It was printed on dingy, bluish paper and bound in some material of a pale brick-dust color. The edges of the leaves were sprinkled to correspond with the color of the binding. Even a new copy had a fossiliferous appearance. It almost made one thirsty to look at it.

I was furnished with a copy of Pike and a new slate, and

without previous instruction or explanation, was directed by "Old Mack," one Monday morning to "begin ciphering." Under the excitement of the occasion I found it well nigh impossible to work out a solution of the first example in addition.

Dick Cahill, seeing my embarrassment kindly offered to assist me. This he could do, as we were not immediately under the eye of the teacher at the time. After adding up the columns of figures and writing down the result underneath, Dick directed me to carefully remove his figures with the moistened end of my finger, and substitute my own in their place. I followed his instructions and then marched up to exhibit my work to the teacher. Unfortunately, as the sequel proved, I overlooked one of Dick's figures.

Old Mack looked at my slate for a moment and then with a fierce scowl on his face demanded: "Who did this sum for you my boy?" Quaking with fear and smarting under a sense of humiliation, I determined at once to imitate George Washington with his little hatchet, by making a "clean breast of it." With a meek and quavering voice, I answered; "Dick Carroll did it sir." Now my boy "replied Old Mack; "If I catch you at such a trick again, I'll make those nullification buttons fly from that coat of yours."

With this brilliant start and under the stimulating encouragement of my teacher I began to ascend the arithmetical ladder.

McGovern sometimes came to the school-room in the afternoon about "half seas over" and on such occasions he had an alarming way of propounding unheard of questions to the scholars. On one of these afternoons he had a number of us—composing the primary class, standing before him and reciting by turns the multiplication table. When the boy at the foot of the class had reached the bottom of the last column and called out in clear confident tones twelve times twelve are one hundred and forty four," we breathed more freely, and congratulated ourselves that our troubles were over for that afternoon. But we soon discovered our mistake. McGovern looked at us for some time through his half closed eyes and after rolling a large quid of tobacco from one side of his mouth to the other, asked; "How much is quadruple times fifteen : " We looked at each other for some time in blank amazement, but no one of us ventured to reply. He then said "Well if you can't answer that question tell me how much is sextuple times twenty" By this time we were reduced to a condition of mind bordering on despair and the hair on our heads was well nigh standing on end. The very sound of those two tremendous words the meaning of which, we did not in the remotest degree comprehend, filled us with consternation. But to our great relief he presently dismissed us with the remark that we were a set of dullards."

We wondered at the time why he let us off so easily. It must have been because he was shrewd enough, even with some whiskey in his head, to understand; that while he could with impunity punish his scholars for failures in their recitations, he would not be sustained by his patrons in punishing them for not answering questions, which were not in their books."*

One day near the Fourth of July it was whispered around in McGovern's school that there would be an important

---

* In those early days, the authority of a teacher was, by common consent, almost unlimited. Parents considered it of the utmost importance to support his authority, and except in extraordinary cases would not listen to complaints from their children. On the contrary if they did complain, would rebuke them for "telling tales out of school."

meeting of the scholars after dismission. After the school closed Dick Cahill proposed that, on the next day, we should "turn out" the teacher and demand a week's holiday. This proposition was unanimously agreed to. The next day when McGovern came, he found the door of the school room closed, and while attempting to force it open, was hailed by Dick Cahill, (who as usual occupied the post of danger, and was standing in a door which opened on the street from the upper story,) and informed of the demand of the school for a holiday. At least half of the male population of the village, had by this time assembled in the street in front of the schoolhouse, to enjoy the fun. McGovern raved and threatened dire punishment on the whole school as he walked back and forth in front of the door, leering at Dick and charging him with being the instigator of the diabolical plot. But Dick defied him and stood his ground, while the crowd in the street laughed and jeered. Finally McGovern ordered every boy to be at his post the next morning at the usual hour, and walked off. The next morning McGovern found the door open, but the boys, led on by Dick would not yield their demand. After a long parley "Old Mack" succumbed and we had our holiday. This was probably the last exhibition of the time honored custom of "turning out a teacher" witnessed in Newberry.

After leaving the Red House, McGovern opened a school in a house which stood on the northwest corner of Holman and Johnstone streets. In that house I began to study English grammar. I do not remember how I managed to get through the early chapters of "Lindley Murray," but I have a vivid recollection of terrors by day and disturbed dreams by night from apprehensions, of the application of McGovern's rod to my shoulders.

L—— G———— a member of our grammar class was a very dull boy ; spoke in a slow, drawling manner, often played truant, and had brought down upon himself McGovern's stern displeasure.

At one of our recitations, L——was examined in Gender. "What is gender" ask McGovern.

"Gender is the distinction of sex," replied L——

" How many genders are there ?"

" Three."

" Name them."

" Masculine, Feminine and, and"

"Out with it! Out with it! Sir!"

" Masculine, Feminine and, and

Here, McGovern took down from two nails driven in the wall, a long, keen switch, and brandishing it over L's head, ordered him to answer the question at once, or be flogged. In a desperate attempt to escape the dilemma, L made a leap across the floor, and exclaimed at the top of his voice, "adjective!" This brought down the house. Old Mack himself could not refrain from laughing, and even the small boys who had been very much frightened ventured to laugh behind their books. L very unexpectedly escaped punishment, and McGovern predicted that he would surely become a great man. Like other tyrants, McGovern was destined to meet with a downfall.

Among his scholars, there was a stalwart young fellow named Bill Pearce. Bill's parents were poor, and he had received very little education, he was therefore assigned to a class of boys much younger than himself. For some reason McGovern entertained a special dislike to this boy. One day while the class of which Bill was a member were sitting on a bench together, some boy, who was probably learning to chew tobacco, had soiled the floor near Bill's feet. As soon as McGovern discovered this he caught up his switch, and coming up to Bill, charged him in an angry manner with the offence, and threatened to "larrup" him if he repeated it. Bill declared he was not the offender. McGovern insisted that he (Bill) was not only the offender, but was adding to his disgrace by attempting to lie out of the difficulty, and brought down his switch heavily across his shoulders. The next moment Bill sprang to his feet, and striking out vigorously with his right arm, planted a blow on McGovern's temple that sent him spinning over the floor, and landed him with a crash across a desk which intercepted his fall. Bill quietly put on his hat and left the house. McGovern recovered himself with some difficulty from his prostrate position, and sitting down in his chair, spent some time in chafing his temples, and feeling for bruises on his arms and legs.

Their encounter naturally created great excitement among the scholars. The larger boys chuckled behind their books, but "we small boys" were too much alarmed to think of laughing. Our consternation knew no bounds. We could think of nothing more frightful than the tragedy we had just witnessed, except the end of the world. How any scholar could have the courage to knock down a man clothed with the mighty power of a teacher, and such a stern and implacable teacher as "Old Mack" was, we could not understand.

Bill returned in a few days, and took his accustomed seat. McGovern eyed him askance for some time, then said, "Well, William, have you come back to school?" "Yes, sir," answered Bill. "Well now, William," replied McGovern, "behave yourself, and we will let by-gones be by-gones."

Whatever the opinion of the reader may be in regard to the conduct of Bill Pearce, candor compels me to say, that it had a most salutary effect upon McGovern. It made him far more considerate of the rights of the boys ever after

During this period of my life, I was made very sad, by the departure from the village of one, and the death of another, of the best beloved of my schoolmates.

Mr. —— Hughes (who came from Kershaw District) kept the Newberry Hotel. He had a son whom we called Rolly. I do not remember what his real name was. I became warmly attached to this boy. He was kind-hearted, gentle and confiding.

During Mr. Hughes' short sojourn in Newberry, he lost by death several members of his family including his wife.

On the day that Mrs. Hughes died, while I was walking along the street in front of the Hotel, I heard my name called, and looking up saw Rolly at a window. Never can I forget his look of grief and despair as he stretched out his hands toward me, and with tears streaming down his cheeks, exclaimed, "Oh ! John, my mother, my dear mother is dead." I could not find words with which to give expression to the sympathy and compassion I felt, and could only look with tearful eyes and in silence upon the spectacle of my unhappy schoolmate, until he slowly sank upon the floor, and disappeared from my view. Rolly left Newberry shortly after his mother's death, and I never saw him again.

I cannot account for it, yet amid all the vicissitudes of half a century, that sorrow stricken face of Rolly Hughes, just as I saw it the day his mother died, has never forsaken me, and I am sure it will go with me to the end of my life.

Shortly after Rolly's departure, Albert Johnstone, the son of Chancellor Job Johnstone, the other schoolmate to whom I have just referred, died at the early age of eleven years.

Albert was greatly beloved by all his schoolfellows and I may add feared by some of them; not on account of his superior physical strength, nor because he was unjust or overbearing in disposition, but because of his ready wit and wonderful satirical powers. His wit was as keen as a Damascus blade, and woe betide the boy who became the object of his satire. But while he could vanquish an opponent he never exulted over him. He had a keen sense of humor, and would often have his companions convulsed with laughter, but seldom laughed himself. He was the embodiment of truth and honor and was frank and generous. He was one of the brightest and noblest boys I ever knew.

Among other teachers from whom I received instruction I shall only speak of the Rev. Jonathan Galloway, Rev. A. J. Chaplain, Mr.——Wiley, and Daniel A. Dobson.

Mr. Galloway was an Associate Reformed Presbyterian minister, and the father of the Miss Galloway, who a few years ago went as a missionary to Egypt, and died there.

In person Mr. Galloway was tall, lean and angular, his figure and deportment suggesting to the mind an ideal Scotch Covenanter. He was of the stuff that martyrs are made of. He would, no doubt, have died in defence of his religious principles. He was quiet and imperturbable in manner, and a firm believer in the doctrine, that to spare the rod is to spoil the child. His use of the rod was vigorous and impartial, he applied it alike to all who disobeyed his rules, respecting neither size nor age.

At Mr. Galloway's school, some boys, who had just returned from the celebrated school of Dr. Waddel at Willington in Abbeville District, introduced a new game called "Shinney." This game was played with a small ball and stout sticks about three feet long, with one end bent like a shepherd's crook. Two squads of small boys armed with these sticks ranged themselves on either side of a long narrow plot of ground chosen for the purpose. At a given signal the leader of one of these squads would drop the ball and then the struggle began. The squad which first succeeded in sending the ball through wickets set up at a given distance from the centre of the ground, by striking it with their sticks, won the game. If a member of one squad, in his efforts to strike the ball with his stick, got on the opposite side of the ground, any member of that side had the right, after warning him, to strike him on the shins with a stick, if he did not at once retreat to his own side.

It was a dangerous game. Many an awkward blow was struck in the skurry and excitement of the play, but its very danger made it the more attractive to school boys.

It was not uncommon for boys to go home in the evening with half closed eyes, or with blue streaks on their shins, from the effects of thwacks received in the game.

The Rev. Mr. Chaplain (a Baptist minister) and Mr. Wiley both came from New England, in response to applications made by the Trustees of the Newberry Academy, for teachers, to some Educational Bureau or Teacher's Agency in Boston. I do not remember which of them came first. They were both thoroughly educated but had very little experience as teachers. They both undertook to introduce an entirely new system of teaching and discipline. They addressed the boys as young gentlemen, pronounced the use of the rod a species of barbarism, and left everything to the honor of the boys. Among other reformations they required us to pronounce our a's broad. How we laughed at each other when we first began this, and what wonder and astonishment we created when we began to use our broad a's at home.

Some boys who were ambitious and studious made

very good progress under the tuition of these New England teachers, but for the most part the scholars had a jolly time. They did as they pleased, knowing that the worst that could befall them would be to receive demerit marks, and hear a lecture on the moral aspect of their conduct. This was all wrong of course, but I have no doubt, that release from the unnecessary stern discipline of former teachers, influenced their conduct in no small degree.

Neither Mr. Chaplain nor Mr. Wiley tarried long in Newberry. I suppose they found Southern boys too much for them.

Dr. Daniel A. Dobson, my last teacher, was a native of North Carolina, and was graduated from Chapel Hill College in that State. He had charge for some time of an academy near Dr. Geo. W. Glenn's, and came from that place to take charge of the Newberry Academy, (probably in 1840 or 1841.)

Dr. Dobson was a ripe scholar, and with the exception of Paul Johnstone, Esq., was the most thorough mathematician of his day, in Newberry. Irritability of temper interfered somewhat with his success as a teacher. But for this infirmity, he would have been the most admirable instructor of youth I ever knew.

After teaching some years, he entered the office of Dr. Benjamin Waldo at Newberry; pursued a course of reading, and was graduated from the Medical College of Charleston, S. C. After his graduation, he entered upon the practice of medicine in Newberry.

In 1848, at the request of his friends and patrons, Mr. and Mrs. Robert Stewart, he went to Mexico to superintend the removal of the remains of their son, Lieutenant John W. Stewart, of the Palmetto Regiment, to Newberry. Soon after his return from Mexico, he died at the house of Mr. Stewart.

Dr. Dobson was an omnivorous reader, he read all sorts of books, and extended his enquiries into every department of human knowledge, he was a diligent reader of the Bible. His wonderful memory seemed to retain and hold ready for use every thing that he had ever read or heard. He was a walking cyclopedia, and his knowledge was not superficial, but thorough. His usual habit was to spend the whole of one night, at least, in every week in reading.

Dr. Dobson was extremely sensitive, and his temperament quite variable. He was often despondent and melancholy, and would imagine that his best friends were not as considerate of his feelings as they should have been. All this influenced him at times to take a pessimistic view of human affairs and tended to make him unhappy. I came in for my share of his frowns, but would not let him break with me. I was too grateful for the thorough instruction which he gave me at school, as well as the more valuable instruction and advice he gave me afterwards, especially with reference to my reading. Beside I could not deny myself the benefit derived from his brilliant and entertaining talks; indeed I am sure that all of his friends, while they regretted his infirmities of temper, believed that he had no malice in his heart, and remained faithful to him.

I always look back with sorrow and regret upon his unhappy life and untimely end. With his brilliant talents and wonderful attainments in knowledge, he should have been a prominent and distinguished man.

He died on the 8th day of August, 1848, not having lived out half the allotted time of man's brief existence. His body is sleeping in the old Aveleigh Cemetery near the present residence of J. A. Crotwell.

CHAPTER III.

BIRDS-EYE VIEW OF NEWBERRY FIFTY YEARS AGO—DR. M. T. MENDENHALL—ROBERT STEWART—A TYPICAL OLD TIME STORE—M. W. GRACY—A CELEBRATED RACE HORSE—THE OLD SHOE STORE—GOUVERNEUR THOMPson—CIRCUS AND MENAGERIE SHOW BILLS—WHY THE CIRCUS AND MENAGERIE WERE UNITED (anecdote)—ANTOINE GILBAL—MYSTERY OF HIS FORMER LIFE—HIS ECCENTRICITIES—HIS HORSEMANSHIP—SOLOMON'S SONG.

"Ah me! the fifty years since last we met,
Seem to me fifty folios bound, and set
By Time, the great transcriber, on his shelves
Wherein are written the histories of ourselves."
LONGFELLOW.—*Morituri Salutamus.*

Fifty years ago, the town of Newberry contained probably not more than three or four hundred inhabitants, nearly half of whom were negro slaves. There were only two or three residences north of the northern branch of Scott's Creek. West of the track of the Columbia and Greenville Railroad, only the old Nance Mansion, recently destroyed by fire; the Male Academy, and one other building were then standing. Southward the town did not extend beyond the old Cemetery, while its eastern limits did not extend beyond the present line of Calhoun street.

The only brick buildings in the town, were the Court House, Robert Stewart's store-house on the south side of

Court House Square, the old Newberry Hotel, one or two buildings on the north side of Pratt street, between Caldwell and Adams streets; and a two-story dwelling which stood on the present site of the Crotwell Hotel. The old jail just in rear of the Court House was built of stone. The western wall of the terrace, upon which the Soldier's Monument now stands, embraces a part of the rear wall of the old jail. All the other buildings of the town were constructed of wood.

Pratt, (then called Main street,) did not extend beyond Thomas Pratt's storehouse, which stood opposite the southern door of the present Court House. The hotel now called the Fallaw House was owned and occupied as a dwelling by Mr. Thomas Pratt. The ground now covered by buildings on the south side of Pratt street, between Nance and McKibben streets, was then a part of Mr. Pratt's vegetable garden. McKibben street ended where it now intersects Pratt street. A broad, deep gully, impassable by vehicles of any kind, began near the western end of Mr. Pratt's storehouse, and winding around below the public well, (then an open natural fountain called the public spring) continued on until it reached Scott's Creek. Friend street ended where it now intersects McKibben street. There were no buildings in that part of the present town embraced within the space bounded by McKibben, Friend and Harrington streets, and the track of the Columbia and Greenville Rail Way, except a servant's house, and stables belonging to Mr. Pratt, a small cottage perched on the side of the hill near the site of the Rail Way water tank, and occupied by Mrs. Esther Moore, a very intelligent, but somewhat eccentric Irish widow, and a cabin near the site of Taylor's blacksmith shop, occupied by Hannah Mike, an old free negro woman, who was a sort of factotum to many families of the village, and reigned supreme in the kitchen at wedding feasts and at " hog killings."

The principal business houses stood on three sides of the Court House Square and on Pratt street between Caldwell and Adams streets. Most of them were of one story, with piazzas in front. Of all the houses which then composed the town there remain only about twenty, and most of these have been remodeled.

Upon the present site of the "*Herald and News*" office, at the northeast corner of Friend and Caldwell streets, stood a small two story frame building, occupied by Marmaduke Thomas Mendenhall, M. D., as an office. The Doctor also built, and during his stay in Newberry, resided in the house on the south side of McKibben street, now owned and occupied by Mrs. Martha Harp. At the time of its erection this building was the most spacious and costly private residence in Newberry.

Dr. Mendenhall was born in Guilford County, North Carolina, on the 8th of December, 1798. His parents were members of the Society of Friends. He was graduated in medicine from the University of Pennsylvania in 1822, and entered upon the practice of his chosen profession in his native State.

He was married on the 18th of March, 1824, to Miss Phœbe Kirk, of Newberry District, (whose parents were also members of the Society of Friends,) and soon after removed to the valuable farm, about four miles south of the village, which his wife had inherited from her father.

In 1830 he removed to the village of Newberry. During his entire residence in Newberry he continued, successfully and with growing reputation, in the practice of medicine, a profession for which he was eminently qualified, and adapted, and which many of his friends thought he never should have abandoned. In 1837 he gave up the practice of medicine, and removed to the City of Charleston to engage in mercantile business, which he pursued with varying fortunes until 1847, when he was elected Judge of the Court of Ordinary for Charleston District. I think he continued in this office until his death, which occurred on the 2nd day of November, 1852.

Through a somewhat checkered commercial career, extending over ten years, and ending in disaster, as well as throughout his entire and very successful professional and official career, Dr. Mendenhall's character as a man of integrity was unblemished. He was one of the most amiable and polished gentlemen of his day. He was modest, pious, humane and magnanimous. "So genial was his spirit, that he seemed to live in an atmosphere of perpetual spring, and he never failed to breathe a sort of blandness over the companies in which he mingled. * * * * He exhibited the sincerity of his disposition in his willingness to render favors. He never wearied in obeying the requests, however whimsical and unreasonable, of friends and strangers even. Nothing but a genuine virtue could have endured a test so severe. * * * * The mental endowments of Dr. Mendenhall were such as to fit him for the widest usefulness. * * * His views on all subjects were comprehensive, such as indicated a large mind and a liberal heart. * * * With a respectable early education he had acquired a decided literary taste, and a fondness for reading and scientific investigations, which remained unabated amidst all those cares of business, which are apt to destroy such a relish. He was extensively acquainted with books of a theological and miscellaneous character, a judicious critic, and an easy and graceful writer. * * * His piety was cheerful, equable and calm, flowing on like a placid river that spreads fertility and gladness in its noiseless course."*

The storehouse of Robert Stewart stood on the south side of Courthouse Square, on the corner of Pratt and Caldwell streets. It was a one story brick building with a broad piazza in front, and an annex built of wood running back on Caldwell street. The ceiling was very low and the windows quite small. Even in the brightest days, there were nooks and corners within the old building, into which the light of the sun never penetrated. In this house Mr. Stewart carried on his business most successfully for nearly half a century. What Noah's Ark was to the animal kingdom Mr. Stewart's establishment was—in a somewhat limited sense—to the realm of man's ingenuity.

Mr. Stewart could have fitted out a blacksmith, a wagon-maker, a carriage-maker, a builder, a carpenter, a shoe-maker, a miller, a tanner, a cabinet-maker, or a painter. He could have furnished all the implements required for the farm and garden, beside harness, saddles, bridles and household effects. He sold clocks, watches, jewelry, cutlery, guns, fishing tackle, millinery, medicines, perfumery, stationery, hats, shoes, paints, oils, all kinds of groceries and hardware, musical instruments—consisting mostly of jews harps, mouth organs, and fiddles, all sorts of dry-goods from the coarsest fabrics to the most elegant and costly silk and lace worn by the wealthiest and most fashionable ladies, and so on " *ad infinitum.*"

Whenever a customer called for an article he did not have he immediately entered it upon a memorandum book kept for that purpose to be included in his next purchases. He was a sagacious, persevering man of business, who studied

---

*Discourse by Rev. J. R. Kendrick, D. D., delivered in the 1st Baptist Church, Charleston, S. C., November 28, 1852.

the wants and tastes of his customers more closely than any other merchant of his day, and always sold the best quality of goods.

He constantly overlooked every part of his business. His watchful eye seemed never to slumber nor sleep. On one occasion he saw one of his customers, a young man of respectable standing, slily abstract a fine pocket knife from an open package and drop it into his pocket. Mr. Stewart said nothing to him at the time, but quietly ordered the book keeper to charge the knife to the customer's account. At the close of the year the young fellow called for his bill, and while reading it over was intently watched by Mr. Stewart. Presently the young man said : "Sir you have charged a pocket knife to me in this bill. I didn't buy one." "No," replied Mr. Stewart (in a sharp and somewhat discordant tone in which he spoke when angered), "you didn't, but you stole one!" The young fellow paid the bill without another word, and left the store. It is probable that Mr. Stewart's heroic treatment of his case saved him from a life of shame and disgrace into which he might otherwise have drifted.

Mr. Stewart was emphatically a merchant of the "old regime." In common with most of the merchants of Newberry, he probably lost all of his estate by the disastrous termination of the recent war, and found it well nigh impossible to adapt himself to the changed condition of affairs. He struggled on manfully however to the end, but death overtook him before he succeeded in extricating himself from the difficulties which surrounded him. He died on the 24th of August 1869. He was married early in life to Miss Eliza R. Ward, of Laurens District, who survived him and died in 1879. Mr. Stewart was a member of the Legislature of South Carolina for one term during the recent war.

West of and adjoining the store of Mr. Stewart, was the store of Minor W. Gracey, who came from North Carolina. His establishment was a popular resort with the ladies of the village. Mr. Gracey was one of the finest specimens of physical manhood I ever saw. He was full six feet in height, with a full chest and well turned limbs. His head was massive but well formed, and with the exception of a slight tendency to obesity, and a scarcely perceptible stoop of the shoulders, his figure was almost perfect. The habitual expression of his face denoted sincerity, good-humor and cheerfulness, his manner, though somewhat stately, invited rather than repelled familiar intercourse. He dressed elegantly and in excellent taste, and was probably the handsomest man who ever lived in Newberry. It is needless to say that he was very popular in the community, and much admired by the ladies.

Mr. Gracey was a great lover of horses, and always owned one or more of these noble animals. During his residence in Newberry, he at one time owned a handsome gray mare which he sold to a horse trader from Kentucky, who carried her to that State, where she afterwards became the dam of Gray Eagle, one of the most celebrated racers of his time. Some of my readers will doubtless remember the great four mile race between Gray Eagle and Wagner, which took place at Louisville, Ky., in 1839, and created almost as much excitement, especially in the South, as an ordinary Presidential election.

Mr. Gracey was twice married. His first wife was Miss Mary Wadlington, of Newberry District, who died in a few years after her marriage. His second wife was Mrs. ——— Patterson, of Abbeville District. He removed to Alabama many years ago, and died there, leaving no descendants.

On the east side of Court House Square, at the intersection

of Pratt and Caldwell streets, stood an old one-story frame building, known as the "Shoe Store." It was elevated about six feet from the ground, with a basement built of stone underneath. It had the usual broad piazza in front, facing the square, and flights of steps leading up to the piazza, and to a door which opened on Pratt street. It was occupied for many years by Gouverneur Thompson, a New England shoe merchant, who afterwards removed to Columbia, S. C. Mr. Thompson was familarly known as "Guv. Thompson." His disposition was lively and cheery, he had a pleasant word for every one, and was celebrated for his humorous stories and anecdotes of which he possessed a rich store.

The piazza in front of his place of business was surrounded by a balustrade; there were benches nailed to the floor inside the balustrade and against the wall of the house. Here the "grave and reverend signiors" of the village would assemble on pleasant afternoons to interchange views on subjects of public interest, and to enjoy Guv. Thompson's stories.

"We boys" would often "drop into" this piazza in the afternoon after school hours, to listen to the conversation and laugh at Mr. Thompson's stories. But there was another, and far more fascinating attraction which the old piazza sometimes had for us. It was there that the advance agents of menageries and circuses put up their show bills. Ah, me! the happy hours spent, sitting on those benches with my schoolmates, contemplating and analyzing those show pictures. One thing only marred our enjoyment, that was the dismal apprehension we sometimes felt, that we might not be able to coax our parents to give us their consent to attend the show, and to furnish us with the needful quarter before it arrived. We always took courage, however, when we read on all the bills, in large type, the announcement that the approaching show was to be a "strictly moral exhibition."

We had no flaming colored show bills then pasted over hundreds of square feet of board walls erected for the purpose. Our pictures were plain wood cuts tacked upon the wall of the house. But we had the same glorious showman's vocabulary, there has been no improvement in that. We had the same "Colossal Combinations of Aggregated Wonders" and "Stupendous and Bewildering Features" which are advertised now.

Menageries and circuses were not united then, they traveled separately.

Two friends, J. F. H. and S. J., once attended an exhibition of a circus and menagerie at Newberry. The menagerie was very inferior, the animals were few in number and in poor condition. After entering the tent, the two friends, while waiting for the circus performances to commence, spent the time in looking at the animals. When they had made the circuit of the cages, the following colloquy ensued:

J. F. H. "Silas! why under the sun do the circus people haul these poor old half starved beasts around with them."

S. J. "Is it possible, Jim, that you do not know why they do it."

J. F. H. "I do not, and cannot imagine."

S. J. "Well, I can inform you. It is to ease the consciences of church members."

I am inclined to think that S. J. had discovered the original cause of the combination of the menagerie with the circus

On the east side of Court House Square at the intersection of Caldwell and Boyce streets, there was a one story building very similar to the shoe store. There was a small yard in rear of it enclosed by a board fence within which there were several smaller buildings. These premises were occupied as a residence and place of business by Antoine Gilbal, (G pronounced soft), who made and sold candy and confections, and also kept a bar-room.

Gilbal was a native of France. Very little was known of his previous history as he was very reticent on that subject. From some hints, however, which he had incautiously dropped, or from some reports which had followed him to Newberry, it was asserted and believed by some persons that he had been engaged with Lafitte, the celebrated pirate of the Gulf of Mexico, whose career gave rise to so many romantic stories, and who secured for himself and his men a pardon from President Madison, for all their past misdeeds, by entering the service of the United States, and fighting gallantly under Jackson at the battle of New Orleans.

Gilbal had an ugly seam across one of his cheeks, such as a gash made by the point of a cutlass would be likely to leave, and a maimed hand. These marks of conflict with some deadly foe served to confirm the belief that he had been a rover of the seas. However this may have been, there was undoubtedly some mystery connected with his previous life, which rendered him very restless, and which he never would disclose. His heavy overhanging eyebrows partially concealed his dark piercing eyes, in which there was an ever restive, furtive expression as if he was expecting an attack from some unseen enemy.

He could never master the English language. He would sometimes reverse the position of words in a sentence and syllables in words, and often use a word in a directly opposite sense from its true meaning. When he would call one of his servants, he would say, "Bob, come dere (there)," instead of "Bob come here." He called the plant commonly known as "Bone set," "Set bone," and it is said on one occasion when he supposed one of his ribs was broken by a fall from a horse, he drank, by the advice of Guv. Thompson, a quantity of "Set bone" tea in order that it might repair his broken bone.

Mr. Gracey owned a very fast pacing horse, which had been trained to bear heavily against the bit. Gilbal or "Gil," as he was familiarly called, was once persuaded to take a ride on this horse. The rapid motion of the animal soon bounced Gil out of the saddle and landed him astride the horse's shoulders. In order to avoid falling to the ground, he dropped the reins and seized the mane. The horse finding the pressure of the reins removed from his mouth came to a halt. Some one who was passing assisted Gil to dismount. He returned, leading the horse, and in answer to the inquiries of the crowd, which had assembled to see him ride, exclaimed: "Bigar, I see nevair one horse like dese. The more I push 'im the bridle the faster he go, and when I no push 'im the bridle at all, bigar, he stop." This defect in language, together with his mercurial temperament and irritable disposition, made Gil a target for all the wags and mirth-making people of the town.

There was an old negro fiddler, named Solomon, who frequented the town in Gil's time, and sometimes sang songs—chiefly of his own composition, to a fiddle accompaniment. His tunes never had more than two strains, and his songs never more than two lines to a stanza. He always sang to the first strain of his tune and played the last strain as an interlude. I believe I could re-produce some of Solomon's tunes, but all of his songs appear to have escaped from my memory, except a stanza of one which he composed in honor of Gilbal. Here it is:

"All them ladies jes from France,
    Come for to see Mr. Gilbal dance."

Nothing ever enraged Gilbal so much as this song. Whenever Solomon began to play and sing before his door, he would rush out into the piazza, and with violent gesticulations and grimaces, threaten him with terrible punishment if he did not desist; but Solomon was always accompanied by some of Gil's tormentors, who came to enjoy the fun and protect the musician as well.

Gilbal furnished much amusement to the people of the town. It was not so much his humor, as his broken English, his facial contortions and his grotesque manner that excited merriment and laughter. His candy, kisses, sugar plums, indeed all his confections, surpassed anything of the kind that has been seen in Newberry since his death. They were all made by himself out of pure sugar. Tables at weddings or other merry-makings were never considered completely furnished until they were supplied with his delicious confections.

Gilbal died in 1842, in a house on the north side of Court House Square, to which he had removed.

CHAPTER IV.

MANNERS AND CUSTOMS—EVERYBODY ON HORSEBACK—ELECTIONS—PEOPLE ALL OF ONE PARTY—PERSONAL APPEALS FOR SUFFRAGES UNKNOWN—"TREATING" ALMOST UNIVERSAL—MERRIMAN CLOCKS AS BADGES OF PROSPERITY—MARRIAGES—FUNERALS—MAIL COACHES—POST OFFICE—A TRIP BY STAGE COACH—SOME REFLECTIONS AND SOME ADVICE TO YOUNG MEN WHICH THE READER MAY SKIP IF HE CHOOSES—PUBLICATIONS RECEIVED AT THE POST OFFICE IN 1840—HORSE RACING—SCENES ON A RACE COURSE—GAMBLING HELL.

In the days of my boyhood, life in Newberry was very quiet and free from excitement. People from the surrounding country did not come into the town in considerable numbers except on sale-days, court weeks or upon the advent of a menagerie or circus. But on these and similar occasions, everybody came, and came on horseback. Very few persons owned pleasure carriages of any kind. There were a few gigs or chaises, but not a buggy in the county.

On sale-days, and during court weeks, that part of the plaza or public square as it was commonly called, in front of the Court House, would be filled with people, while every available space on both sides was occupied by tobacco wagons, apple wagons and the carts of the venders of "ginger cakes and cider."

The people of that time had great respect for courts and the authority of judges. When "His Honor" was seen approaching the Court House, accompanied by the sheriff, arrayed in cocked hat and sword, every one respectfully gave way for him to pass. The strictest order was enforced in the Court room, and, if at any time during the sessions of the Court, there was a disturbance in the Public Square caused by drunken men, or otherwise, the sheriff was ordered by the judge to go out and arrest the offenders. Whenever an unlucky fellow was arrested, he would be followed into the Court House by a crowd to hear the judge's lecture.

The culprit, after receiving admonitions from the judge, was generally discharged upon the condition that he would go home at once. At other times, especially if he was very drunk, he was sent to jail to remain until he was sufficiently sobered to realize his situation.

As the people of the district, and indeed of nearly the whole State, belonged to the same political party, and as the Governor, and all other State officers, and Presidential electors were elected by the Legislature, there was usually very little political excitement. The most notable exceptions were, the campaigns and elections during the "Nullification excitement" from 1832 to 1835; and in 1851 to test the question as to whether the State should secede from the Union alone or await the co-operation of other States.

There were no regular party organizations, no nominating conventions or primary elections; contests for seats in congress, the State Legislature and District offices, were merely personal. Every man who desired office announced himself as a candidate. Candidates were expected to appear at all places of public assemblings, in order to make the acquaintance of voters; but the custom of riding over the county and of making personal appeals to citizens for their suffrages, which has prevailed to a considerable extent in more recent years, was then unknown.

I have heard gentlemen who had been candidates for office in those early days say, that if they had made personal appeals to citizens for their votes, they would have been condemned for violating the public conscience. Yet the custom of offering intoxicating drinks, free, to voters or "treating" as it is called, was almost universal.

I remember, one election day, seeing people constantly going in and out at the door of an old house (generally unoccupied) which stood on the south side of Pratt street near the present site of Singley's building, and with other boys going in to find out what was the attraction. We found inside an extemporized barroom, the bar tender would now and then—pointing to certain decanters labeled with candidates' names—say: "This is A's treat," "This is B's treat," and so on. Each voter would help himself according to his choice of candidates.

There were social distinctions then as there are now, but the lines were not so sharply drawn, you could sometimes hear the term aristocrat applied to some citizen who was more prosperous than his neighbors, but for the most part fortunes were accumulated slowly and the people were contented and happy.

A very peculiar but sure mark of prosperity was the possession of a "Merriman clock." When a man had succeeded in accumulating considerable property, and began to feel that he was growing independent he usually purchased one of these clocks, the cost of which was about one hundred dollars. They were made by Reuben Merriman at Cheshire, Connecticut, and brought to Charleston by sail and from the city transported in wagons to various points in the State. The clock work was contained in a somewhat elaborate mahogony case, about eight feet high, and each clock had attachments to indicate the changes of the moon and the day of the month. One of these old "time-pieces" which formerly belonged to Mr. Robert Stewart, and has been running for more than a-half a century, is now in the possession of the National Bank of Newberry, where it still tells off the passing hours with unfailing regularity.

In the social life of the people there was less of mere etiquette and ceremony than at the present time, but there was more hospitality, a loftier homage paid by men to the gentler sex and certainly not less of genuine politeness and courtesy.

When a marriage was to be celebrated, even in the wealthiest and most prominent families, it was made an occasion of general rejoicing, and every honest and respectable person in the town was invited to the marriage feast. These invitations did not of themselves imply complete social recognition, but were rather understood to be expressions of the prevailing spirit of abounding hospitality.

A very pretty custom was sometimes observed at these marriage feasts: Two young girls, tastefully arrayed in white, preceded the bridal procession into the parlor, and stood during the ceremony on the right and left of the officiating minister, bearing in their hands long silver candlesticks containing lighted wax candles.

When a death occurred (as there was no hearse), the body was borne to the cemetery by strong men, who passed their silk handkerchiefs under the coffin, and grasping the ends, walked with slow and measured steps to the grave, followed by the assembled company on foot. The absence of vehicles, and the bustle and confusion sometimes produced by them, together with the solemn quietness of the people, rendered these funeral processions profoundly impressive·

Religious services were generally held at the house in which the body lay. For a period of probably fifteen years, dating from my childhood, I never saw a corpse carried into a church.

The only regular channel of communication with the "outside world" was through a tri-weekly line of stage coaches which ran between Columbia, S. C., and Asheville, N. C. The arrival of these coaches, with their freight of passengers and the mail, was looked for with as much interest then as the arrival of the railway train is now.

For many years the Post-Office was not kept in a separate building. The postmaster was usually a merchant, and kept the office at his place of business.

Thomas Pratt was the first postmaster I remember. The next was Wm. P. Butler, now living in Edgefield, then came Reuben Pitts, the father of the Rev. John D. Pitts, of Laurens, S. C. During Mr Pitts' term the Post-Office was kept in a store room (under the old Newberry Hotel), on the southeast corner of Pratt and Caldwell streets, then occupied by Mr. Pitts and Z. W. Carwile, as dealers in general merchandise.

Although quite a lad, I was employed by Mr. Pitts as mail clerk. This occupation was very agreeable to me. From my childhood I had a great admiration for stage coachmen. I suppose every one has at some time in his early boyhood wrestled with the all-absorbing question as to what he will do with himself when he becomes a man. After much thought over this question I had made up my mind to become a stage coachman. To my youthful imagination stage coachmen were such jolly, happy fellows. As a matter of fact, I do not remember to have seen more than one who was lean and melancholy, all others that I have known belonged to the class of which Tony Weller is the immortal type.

Every one paid homage to the talismanic words "United States Mail" emblazoned on the bright, gilded panels of a stage coach, and made all haste to get out of the way when one came dashing along the highway or through the streets of the town. The prevailing idea was, that a mail coach was entitled to the right of way at all times.

As the mails arrived in the evening, I could attend school during the day and go on duty in the Post-Office after school hours. My young schoolmates regarded my promotion to the position of mail clerk as a piece of good fortune, but, dear fellows, they were too generous to envy me. They would often assemble at the Post-Office door in the evening, and when the coach arrived, look on in wondering admiration to see the coachman tip his hat to me, or hear him "crack a joke" as he handed down the mail bags. I was the only night-clerk, and occupied a room in the rear of the store. Part of my duty was to get out of bed every other morning at two and at four o'clock, to deliver the mail bags to the departing coaches.

During mid-winter the roads became almost impassable. At that season, often the coaches would not arrive before midnight, then the coachmen would barely have time to refresh themselves, and look after their jaded horses before they would be compelled to start on their return trip. Yet I never heard one of these fellows complain of his lot, nor did I ever see one of them drunk.

I cannot at times repress a feeling of regret that the spirit of progress has, banished the old time stage coach:

> "Over new roads that men lay,
> Rush we with rattle and roar,
> Only sweet memories stay;
> Gone are the driver and four!"

Notwithstanding some discomfort there is more real pleasure to be had from a journey by stage coach than by a railway train. The opportunities afforded for observing the country as you pass along are so much more favorable, and then you can converse with your fellow passengers without bawling at them as you are compelled to do, amid the din and roar caused by a railway train in motion.

I retain vivid impressions of my first trip by stage coach, which was made from Newberry to Asheville, N. C. At Greenville on my way I met for the first time young C. H. Suber, (who though a native of Newberry County, had seldom visited the town previous to that time,) and together we made the journey on to Asheville. S. was then a student in the South Carolina College. It was during the summer of 1846.

We left Greenville on a delightful summer day. Fleecy clouds were floating above us, and a brisk breeze tempered the atmosphere, and produced a feeling of exhilaration, as we were bowled along; catching glimpses, here and there, through forest vistas or across open fields, of the soft blue outlines of the distant mountains.

I soon found myself attracted by S's handsome appearance, and admirable conversational talent He proved to be a most interesting and entertaining traveling companion. I could have forgiven him for being more fashionably dressed, and so much handsomer than I was; but fear I felt some pangs of jealousy when I discovered that his intellect was being cultivated and expanded, by a college training, of which I had deprived myself by yielding too early to the allurements of a commercial career.

Early in the forenoon we made the toilsome ascent of the Saluda Mountains (a spur of the Blue Ridge), and looking back from the summit, could see the zigzag road over which we had traveled, lying, like a huge serpent across the side of the mountain ridge. After descending the other side, we passed the famous Poinsett Spring, crossed the beautiful Green River, ascended and descended another ridge, and in the afternoon arrived at Flat Rock, a name given to an elevated, rolling section of the country near Hendersonville, N. C., embracing hundreds of acres, encompassed by mountain peaks, and diversified by clear bold streams of water (here and there converted into artificial lakes,) and the picturesque summer residences of many families, from the sea coast of South Carolina.

At the Flat Rock Hotel, we took on additional passengers; among them two elderly ladies, with prim curls adorning their temples, and smelling bottles in their hands, from the contents of which they frequently stimulated their noses; and an old gentleman with a florid face, a ruffled shirt front, the gout and an enormous snuff box. From their conversation which chiefly revolved around their native city, and their family trees, we learned that they came from Charleston, and that each of them had always lived in a state of single-blessedness. Having surrendered our places on the back seat to these good people; S. and myself were compelled to occupy the middle seat, but finding it, after a short trial somewhat uncomfortable, we took refuge outside; I occupying a seat on the box beside the driver while S. reclined upon the coach top among the carpet bags. (Every respectable traveler was a "carpet bagger" then). Our conversation having been in some way turned to the subject of music, S. mentioned that he had recently had the pleasure of hearing Sloman sing the beautiful old song, *Tubal-Cain*; and as I had never heard it, he sang it for me with excellent effect, though in a somewhat subdued tone, in order that he might not disturb our friends inside. I have since that time heard *Old Tubal-Cain* sung by Sloman himself and by others; but never heard it with more pleasure than when sung by S. seated on the top of the stage coach.

But extremes are sometimes said to meet. Almost before the echo's of S's song had died away, and while we were drinking in the invigorating mountain air, and silently watching the deepening shadows creeping up the sides of the everlasting hills, as the sun dropped behind them, leaving their summits fringed with a brilliant setting of purple and gold; the driver took his bugle, and after giving us a lugubrious imitation of *Old Rosin the Bow*, wound up his performance, by sounding nine prolonged notes, which he informed us was to notify the hotel people at Asheville of the number of passengers on board. In a few minutes more we were safely landed at the Eagle Hotel.

My employment in the Post Office, while it interfered somewhat with the prosecution of my studies, by filling up hours which should have been devoted to my school books, was not without its benefits. It gave me my first lessons in business, and in order to while away the lonesome hours of the long winter nights while waiting for the arrival of the mails, I began to dip into the newspapers and magazines, of which a number were always remaining in the office. This gave me a love for reading which has followed me through all the years of my life since, and contributed greatly to my happiness.

I shall never cease to regret that I did not go through a collegiate course of education, which I might have done, but my father who was a thorough man of business, and a (so called) self made man, was not unwilling to allow me, at my own solicitation to enter into commercial pursuits at the age of sixteen years. After spending more than forty years in business pursuits, I can truly say that whatever of knowledge I have acquired, is largely due to the reading I have done, in such hours as I could spare from daily toil, and the consequent improvement and development of my powers of observation.

I do not wish to be understood as holding myself up as an example to be followed, nor do I feel that I deserve to be so held up by others. But I do wish to hold out some encouragement to any young man who may read these pages, and who, because the benefits of a college education, and it may be even a thorough high school education have been denied him, is disposed to neglect the improvement of his mind. If you, my reader, are among this number let me urge you —whatever your surroundings, your occupation or your profession may be—to read even if it be only for a half hour or an hour each day; and be sure that you read good books. Perhaps you will say: "Shall I not read novels at all?" Yes, you may read the works of Hawthorn, Cooper, Irving, Sims, Goldsmith, Sir Walter Scott, Dickens and Thackeray.

There are a few other novelists whose works you may read; but do not read a novel until you have first ascertained from some trustworthy and judicious authority whether it is worth reading or not. Let your attention be chiefly given to books that will make you think, and "*widen out* your mind so that you can take broad views, instead of being narrow-minded; so that you can see the different sides of a question, or at least can know that all questions have different sides."

Above all, do not fail to read the Bible constantly. Do all this and you will find that your position in society will be improved, the labors of life lightened and sweetened, and if at any time you are laid aside from the active duties of life, by old age or loss of health, you will find that you have something to fall back upon; that books are friends which never desert you, and that they will brighten many an hour that would otherwise be full of restlessness and discontent. But I am about to forget that I am writing reminiscenses, and must return at once to the Post-Office.

Our postal arrangements were quite primitive and simple. When the mail was received we closed the door of the store, and after distributing the contents of the bags, spread out all the letters and papers for the people of the village on the counter, depositing those for the country in cases alphabetically arranged to receive them. The door was then opened and the crowd, which had in the meantime assembled outside, came in and received their mail matter from the counter.

The rate of postage on letters was six and a quarter, twelve and a half, eighteen and three-quarters and twenty-five cents each; according to the distance to be sent. The postage was not required to be paid in advance, and was generally paid at the place of destination. There were no daily papers received at the office. Of newspapers received the *South Carolinian*, edited and published by A. H. Pemberton, and the *Temperance Advocate*, both weekly and published in Columbia, S. C., had the largest number of subscribers. A few persons received the tri-weekly *Charleston Courier* and *Charleston Mercury*. Copies of four or five different religious papers were received; also three copies of the *New York Herald* and one or two copies each of the *Greenville Mountaineer* and *Edgefield Advertiser*, which were at that time probably the only county newspapers in the State. The demand for light literature was supplied chiefly by the *New York Mirror*, (weekly,) *The Philadelphia, Saturday Courier*, (weekly,) which was very popular,

Godey's Ladies Book (monthly,) and *Graham's Magazine*,* (monthly,) the last two published in Philadelphia and *The Southern Literary Messenger*, (monthly,) published in Richmond, Va.

I have in my possession a list of all the papers and magazines received at the Post-Office in 1840. They number altogether 352, and may be classified as follows : Political and general news, 114 ; literary, 73 ; temperance, 63 ; agricultural, 20 ; sporting, 4 ; religious, 78 ; viz.: Associate, Reformed and Presbyterian, 17 ; Lutheran, 5 ; Baptist, 17 ; Methodist, 19 ; Catholic, 4 ; Universalist, 16.

My brother, Z. W. Carwile, was the partner of Mr. Pitts in his mercantile business. He had a taste for good literature, and during the time I was employed in the Post-Office, gave me to read Dickens' first novel, *Nicholas Nickleby*. ("The Pickwick Papers" appeared before Nickleby, but can not properly be called a novel.)

Dickens was then writing over the signature " Boz." His real name was unknown, at least to American readers. I remember seeing afterwards in the *Gentleman's Magazine*, published in New York and edited by William E. Burton —a celebrated comedian of that day—a portrait of Dickens, accompanied by a sketch of his early life. His real name

---

*The following item recently appeared in several prominent daily newspapers: (March 1887.)

There lies in a New York hospital an aged and almost friendless invalid whose name was once famous in the world of letters. George R. Graham was for many years the leading publisher of Philadelphia. For *Graham's Magazine* Edgar Allan Poe wrote much of his best work. Graham was at one time part owner of the Philadelphia *North American*. He was, thirty-five or forty years ago, a power in the literary world, but would now be in the poorhouse were it not for the kindness of a philanthropic Philadelphian.

had just been revealed. The sketch contained something like the following lines:

> " Who the dickens, Boz could be,
> Puzzled many a learned elf,
> Till time unveiled the mystery
> And Boz appeared as Dickens self."

I had never heard of "Boz" before. I had previously read such books as were usually placed in the hands of lads of my age, including the Arabian Nights, Scottish Chiefs Robinson Crusoe, and that immortal allegory, The Pilgrim's Progress. But here the doors of a new and enchanted literary palace were thrown wide open before me; and as I passed the threshold I felt in every part of my spiritual nature the touch of the magician's wand.

What a revelation Nicholas Nickleby was to me! With what infinite zest I devoured its pages. How rapidly the long winter nights sped away as I read. How my blood boiled over the account of the inhuman treatment of poor Smike, by Squeers the schoolmaster, and the villainy of old Ralph Nickleby. How I admired the manly courage of Nicholas, and the sweet patience of his sister Kate. How my tears came as I contemplated the impending fate of the lovely Madeline Bray, and my heart rejoiced over her deliverance. And then what delightful humor came out in the minor characters.

I have read since that time, nearly every thing that Dickens wrote, and there are some of his books which I admire much more now; but none of them ever did me such service as Nicholas Nickleby.

Horse-racing was one of the sports engaged in by some of the early inhabitants of Newberry. An organized Jockey Club existed in the town for a number of years. The first race-course I remember was in a field which embraced the present homestead of John C. Wilson. The second was on the east side of the highway leading from the village, by Springfield, the residence of Judge O'Neall, and near the present residence of Thomas M. Neel. The last one was on the east side of the highway, leading from the town to Bouknight's Ferry, about a mile-and-a-half from the Court House.

A training stable of race-horses was kept open several seasons in Newberry, by Col. Simeon Fair and Governor Pierce M. Butler. It was under the management of "George," a very intelligent negro, who belonged to Gov. Butler. Each horse had a negro groom and a rider. George was a complete autocrat, he required both grooms and riders to obey his orders implicitly and without hesitation. Yet neither grooms nor riders ever made attempts to escape from his tyranny. They were so fascinated and elated with their employment that they were willing to submit to any amount of rough treatment from the trainer, rather than be remanded to their ordinary work.

The training stable had an irresistible attraction for school boys. It broke in upon the monotony of their lives, and gave them something new to talk about. "We boys" paid visits to the stable nearly every afternoon, after school hours, and spent many hours there on Saturdays, when we were not engaged in fishing or rabbit hunting. George petted us, and talked very learnedly to us about horses. We became thoroughly educated in stable lore. We knew just what the horses in the stable were fed upon, at what hour they went out for their morning exercise upon the highway, and when they would go the race-course for a gallop. We had many heated discussions about the relative merits of different horses. Indeed, I fear that for the time, we knew more about George's curriculum, than that of our institution of learning.

So my dear reader you see that boys were boys then as they are now, but I think you should be a little lenient in your judgment of the boys of that time. Remember that they were more than fifty miles, and twenty years in point of time, distant from a railway, and that the arrival of a single stranger in the town was an event of importance then.

Besides the two gentlemen just mentioned, the principal owners of racing studs, who brought their horses to Newberry to contend in the races, were: Col John D. Williams, Wm. R. Smith, and Col. James H. Irby, of Laurens District; and Maj. Wm. Eddins, of Abbeville District. Mr. James Fernandis, who was one of the original owners of the Newberry Hotel, was also a patron of the turf, and had a stable of race horses about two miles west of the village.

My father never attended the races himself, and did not, as a rule, permit his boys to attend them. On one occasion, however, with his consent, I went during race week to the second course, which I have mentioned. When I arrived I found a large crowd of people already assembled. Every available foot of space in the grand stand was occupied. A good many boys and some men had climbed into trees, in a wood which skirted the quarter-stretch, in order to get a good view of the course. Finding it difficult to secure an eligible position from which to view the races, I climbed—with a younger brother and other boys—upon the roof of a long one story frame building, which stood some distance in rear of the judge's stand.

I remember that all the jockey's were negro boys, dressed in fanciful costumes, each of a different color, and that one of the horses which ran in the principal race, was a beautiful gray, owned by Maj. Eddins, and called by the euphoneous name of "Hualpa." I can remember no other incident connected with the races.

I have a vivid recollection, however, of another scene which I witnessed that day. I did not know what use was made of the building upon the roof of which I had mounted, and while sitting there waiting for the horses to start could hear men, talking in loud, excited tones below me. Presently I discovered an opening in the roof, which gave me a view of nearly the whole of the room below. I shuddered and held my breath when I looked down; for there, just beneath me, I saw for the first and last time in my life, the interior of a "Gambling Hell." On tables covered with green cloth, were spread out the paraphernalia of different games of chance. On one side of these tables there stood several men with calm, cold, relentless looking faces. On the other side an excited, turbulent crowd, some looking pale and haggard from disappointment, others elated and flushed over their winnings; some went out at the door, after losing all they had, with misery and despair pictured on their faces; others, heated with drink, cursed their ill luck, and defiantly charged the dealers with villainy. A man whom I knew came out crazed with his success, waving a handfull of bank bills over his head and proclaimed aloud the amount he had won. Altogether, the scene filled me with astonishment, horror and disgust, and remains firmly fixed in my memory.

CHAPTER V.

THE OLD LOCUST—DOCTOR BURR JOHNSTON—REMOVES TO ALABAMA—AFFECTING SCENE ON THE DAY OF HIS DEPARTURE FROM NEWBERRY—MEMORIES OF THE OLD LOCUST—PAUL JOHNSTONE—HOWARD CALDWELL—SONNET BY MR. CALDWELL—DOCTOR WILLIAM H. HARRINGTON—MAJOR C. H. SUBER—THOMAS PRATT—HIS JOURNEY TO PHILADELPHIA, ON HORSEBACK, IN 1813 TO PURCHASE GOODS—PRIESTLY PRATT—JOHN W. STEWART, RICHARD C. CARWILE, JOHN C. HIGGINS AND PRIESTLY PRATT VOLUNTEER FOR THE MEXICAN WAR—THE LAST FAREWELL—ONLY HIGGINS LIVES TO RETURN—GEORGE GUZMAN—HIS NOBLE CONDUCT AND DEATH IN MEXICO.

> "Come back! ye friends whose lives are ended,
> Come back, with all that light attended,
> Which seemed to darken and decay
> When ye arose and went away."
> LONGFELLOW.—*The Golden Legend.*

ON the north side of Court House Square, near the intersection of Boyce and Caldwell streets, there stood for many years a locust tree of enormous size. Its spreading branches extended far out over the square on one side and on the other, overshadowed a small building occupied by Dr. Burr Johnston as an office. This tree was cut down in 1853 to make room for a new range of buildings. It was a melancholy sight to see the old tree, around which clustered so many happy memories, bow its stately head, before the axe, and fall prostrate upon the ground. But it had to be. The peaceful valleys around the once quiet village had already echoed the shrill whistle of the locomotive, and everything that stood in the way of the inexorable demands of commerce had to go down.

In a volume of poems, written by Howard H. Caldwell, and published in 1855, there is a short poem, with the title, "Memories of the Old Locust," in which the old tree is made to soliloquize as follows:

> "All my companions gone! and soon I may
> Be borne away by the tide now bearing all;
> A palace stand where I was wont to be,
> And commerce hurry with her busy call,
> And yet how oft beneath my spreading shade
> The young, the light of heart and free of soul,
> Have sat, as slow the day began to fade
> Nor marked how fast time's fleeting moments roll.
> Oh! may they think when I am fading fast,
> Of the dark hour when life's new roseate bloom
> Must fade in Night that knows no dawn at last,
> The voiceless silence of the waiting tomb."

Dr. Burr Johnston, who occupied the office under the locust, was born in Fairfield District. He was graduated from the South Carolina College in 1811, studied medicine with Dr. Joseph Waldo, in Newberry in 1812-13, and was graduated in medicine from a college in Philadelphia in 1814. Immediately after his graduation as a physician he opened an office in Newberry. He rose rapidly in his profession and became the leading practitioner of the town. He was firm but gentle with a patient, and not easily excited or confused. He was scrupulously neat in his dress, methodical in his habits, and deliberate in all his movements.

No one ever saw him in a hurry. No matter how urgent the case might be, he never walked rapidly, nor urged his horse, (if on horseback) beyond a moderate pace. yet I never heard that any one complained of his tardiness or inattention; on the contrary, his patients were devoted to him He was a type of the old-time, high-spirited, honorable, professional gentlemen.

One of the most familiar objects to be seen on Court House Square, during the latter years of Dr. Johnston's stay in Newberry, was his milk-white horse standing before his office, under the old locust tree. I learned from my father's colored hostler and man of all work—from whom I derived most of my knowledge on such subjects—that Hayes, the Doctor's hostler, spent most of his time in washing off and grooming that white horse, and had received strict orders from his master not to a'low a speck of dirt to be seen on him, from the point of his nose to the end of his tail, whenever he was brought out for the Doctor to mount.

The "emigration fever," which carried away so many of the best and most thrifty people of South Carolina to the vaunted rich lands of the Southwest, seized Dr. Johnston, and caused him to remove to Alabama in 1840. His removal was universally regretted In my father's family and many others, in which he had practiced for many years, his departure was regarded as a calamity.

As there was no railway communication then between the two States, Dr Johnston made the journey overland, his negroes in wagons and on foot, and his family in carriages. On the morning of his departure, his relatives and many of his friends assembled to take leave of his family and himself. It was an affecting scene, many tears were shed even by gray-headed men.

In the midst of the leave-taking and the weeping, one of

those ludicrous incidents which sometimes obtrude themselves upon such solemn occasions, occurred.

Two trunks had been strapped, one above the other, behind one of the carriages. Upon the top of these some one had mounted a little negro maid. When the Doctor saw her he was naturally greatly surprised, and under a sudden impulse exclaimed: "Good heavens! is that little 'nigger' to go to Alabama mounted on top of those trunks?" This caused a commingling of smiles and tears in a good many faces. It was too much for S. J., one of the Doctor's nephews and myself; we had to stuff our handkerchiefs, which we had been freely using to wipe our eyes with, into our mouths, and retreat behind a corner of the house until we had regained our composure.

Dr. Johnston made only one visit to Newberry after he removed to Alabama. He died in 1858.

"'Tis ever wrong to say a good man dies."

The office which Dr. Johnston vacated when he left Newberry was removed in 1853. Silas Johnstone and C. H. Suber, as Attorneys at Law, were its last occupants. During its occupancy by Johnstone & Suber, many pleasant summer evening re-unions were held beneath the old locust by a company of young men, which included the two last mentioned gentlemen, and in which I had the honor and the pleasure to be numbered. Some of that happy company went down to early graves, others having passed the meridian of life, were called away before the twilight of its evening began to approach; while only two or three are left behind. I ardently hope, that those who still remain are prepared to adopt the sentiment of the following beautiful lines, by Paul Hayne, who has himself but recently crossed over the river.

" We have passed the noonday summit,
    We have left the noonday heat,
    And down the hill side slowly
    Descend our wearied feet.
    Yet the evening airs are balmy,
    And the evening shadows sweet.

" Our summer's latest roses
    Lay withered long ago;
    And even the flowers of autumn
    Scarce keep their mellow glow.
    Yet a peaceful season woos us,
    'Ere the time of storms and snow.

" Like the tender twilight weather,
    When the toil of day is done,
    And we feel the bliss of quiet,
    Our constant hearts have won,—
    When the vesper planet blushes,
    Kissed by the dying sun,

" So falls the tranquil season,
    Dew like on soul and sight,
    Faith's silvery stars rise blended,
    With memory's sunset light,
    Wherein life pauses softly,
    Along the verge of night."

Ah! how quickly do we realize the rapid flight of time, whenever we pause to look into the past. It seems but yesterday, that two of our number,—Paul Johnstone and Howard Caldwell—were parted from us. Yet both of them have been for many years quietly sleeping in their graves:

"Time in advance, behind him hides his wings,
    And seems to creep decrepid with his age;
    Behold him when passed by: what then is seen,
    But his broad pinions, swifter than the wind."

Paul Johnstone was the eldest son of Chancellor Job Johnstone. He was endowed by nature with a strong and active intellect, which he had sedulously cultivated. He was a diligent student and a sound thinker. He read law, but his feeble health prevented him from entering upon the practice of his chosen profession. He wrote and published "The *Electoral Question Discussed*," a tract which received high encomiums from some of the ablest statesmen and jurists of the country. His mind had a natural bent for mathematics. I never knew him to fail in the solution of any mathematical problem, however difficult, which may have been submitted to him.

Notwithstanding, his bodily sufferings, arising from wasting disease, he was always patient and cheerful. Being cut off to a considerable extent from out-door pursuits and enjoyments, he had invented some ingenious and amusing ways of relieving the tedium of his confinement. One of them was to convert into other languages,—paying more attention to the sound than the spelling—the names of people of his acquaintance. This process sometimes compelled him to combine two foreign words into one.

There was a Presbyterian minister living in Newberry named Hyde. Seeing him pass by one day while we were engaged in conversation, he said to me : " There goes the Rev. Mr. Pellis." A very respectable colored barber, who had a shop in Newberry, and whose name was Seymour, he addressed as " Vide-Plus." And so with many others.

He was keen-witted, but not harsh or cruel ; humorous, but never coarse or rude. He was quick at repartee, and could parry the thrusts of the most wary antagonist in an intellectual encounter. Yet he was conscientiously considerate of the feelings of others In his character there was a striking combination of childlike simplicity and manly courage.

He was an exalted type of the Christian gentleman. He died on the 15th of August, 1859, in the 40th year of his age. He was at the time of his death, and had been for many years previous, a member of Aveleigh Presbyterian Church at Newberry.

Howard Hayne Caldwell was born in Newberry, on the 20th of September, 1831. He was the son of Chancellor Jas. J. Caldwell and Nancy (McMorries) Caldwell. His parents having removed to Columbia, S. C., during his childhood, he was educated chiefly in that city, graduating from the South Carolina College in 1851 Shortly after his graduation he returned to his native place and remained several years, during which time he read law, and was admitted to the Bar. In January, 1857 he was married to Miss Agnes Montague, of Columbia, and from that time until his death, with the exception of about one year spent in Mobile, Alabama, he resided in Columbia.

He devoted most of his time to literary pursuits. Very early in life he began to develop a genius for poetry. While yet a school boy, he wrote some verses, and published them in a newspaper at Columbia, without the knowledge of his parents. His mother, who, as well as his father, had excellent literary taste read the verses when the paper was brought in, and was so much pleased with their spirit that she spoke in high praise of them that evening in the family circle. Noticing that young Howard was much confused and blushing deeply, she interrogated him as to the cause, when, to her great surprise and joy, he confessed that he was the author of the verses.

He published in 1855, "Oliata, and other Poems," and in 1858 another volume, under the simple title, ' Poems." He also published many prose articles in the newspapers and magazines of the day. In his last published volume there are two short poems. "The Night when last we met," and "A Sonnet on the death of J. B. Anderson," which are especially good; and the whole book exhibits a very decided advance both in conception and style. His books attracted considerable attention, but met the fate of those of all Southern authors.

A critic of excellent literary taste and judgment, in a recent notice of the writings of John Esten Cooke, of Virginia, writes thus: "If John Esten Cooke had been a New Englander, and had written as many attractive works upon the history of New England as he has given us upon Virginia history, he would have been known and honored throughout the United States. There is as much local pride in Virginia as in New England, but, unfortunately, it does not to the same extent take the form of pride in literature." This judgment will apply with equal force to South Carolina. The works of William Gilmore Sims, one of the best of American novelists, receive far less attention from the people of South Carolina, his native State, than they do from the people of the Northern States, while the works of Cooper are to be found in almost every library in the land. And who in South Carolina that loves good literature and feels a pride in the success of our own writers, does not grieve over the hard struggles and sad fate of Henry Timrod and Paul Hayne.

It is probable that Mr. Caldwell was somewhat hasty in publishing his books. Some of his judicious friends were of that opinion. Still if his literary efforts had received from his own people the fostering attention which they deserved and his life had been spared, his success as a writer would doubtless have been secured.

Mr. Caldwell read extensively, especially of history and the works of great authors, both in his own and other tongues, in the realm of poetry and light literature. As a conversationist, he was unusually attractive and entertaining. His manners were polished and graceful, hence he was a welcome guest in all polite social circles. His taste in all things relating to belles-lettres and the fine arts was refined and discriminating. His wit was keen, sometimes cutting, but never malicious. He was humorous, but his humour was free from slang and buffoonery.

I remember when he returned to Newberry after his graduation, and joined our self-constituted " Locust Club," how pleased we all were to find him so affable and agreeable in manner and so free from the pedantry often displayed by young collegians. Our meetings under the locust were never more enjoyable than when he and Paul Johnstone met in a friendly tilt. They regaled us with animated discussions on all sorts of subjects, interspersed with brilliant sallies of wit and irresistible humour.

Among other accomplishments Mr. Caldwell played well on the piano-forte, the organ and the guitar. He possessed that rarest of all musical gifts, a good tenor voice. I look back with infinite pleasure to many happy evenings spent with him in his chamber, listening to his highly entertaining talk and his songs, and now and then, in a feeble way, supporting his clear and mellow tenor with an inferior barytone:

> " Sweet memory wafted by thy gentle gale
> Oft up the stream of Time, I turn my sail,
> To view the fairy haunts of long lost hours,
> Blest with far greener shades, far fresher flowers."

We were both young and full of life and hope then. O the inspiring hope of youth—of young manhood ! who that has once experienced it can ever forget it ? The future seemed all bright before us, but alas! for human hopes, my brilliant and gifted friend was cut down ere the dewy freshness of his youth, had fully given place to the maturer ripeness of manhood. He died in the twenty-eighth year of his age. His body is sleeping in the cemetery of St. Peter's Catholic Church, Columbia, S. C.

I close this feeble tribute to the memory of my beloved friend, by introducing the following short poem of his, to which I have already referred:

SONNET

On the death of J. B. Anderson, who having directed his servant to leave him alone at his prayers, was discovered, a short time afterwards, dead upon his knees:

> A warrior, dying with his armor on,
> A prophet, in his singing robes at death,
> A lover, yielding in fond vows his breath,
> A king, deceasing on his regal throne,
> A priest, expiring at the altar-stone:
> All these are types of thee, beloved friend!
> Blest was thy life, and more than blest thy end,
> For in that end life's highest glory shone.
> Green be the turf above thy guileless breast,
> Calm be thy sleep and be thy memory blest!
> Thy ruling passion strong in death, we see
> An angel-instinct from some holier sphere
> Bend o'er thy head to place life's crown on thee.
> *That* life, like sweet perfume, breathed out in prayer!

Our assemblings under the locust were often cheered by the presence of Dr. William H. Harrington, who died on the 16th of February, 1889, in Mississippi. The following well merited tribute to him appeared in the *Newberry Observer*, a few days after his death:

"Dr. William Henry Harrington died at his home in Crawfordville, Miss., on the 16th instant. He was born at Newberry on the 19th of November, 1816, and was the son of Young John and Nancy (Calmes) Harrington. After receiving a good literary education, he entered the medical profession, having been graduated from the Medical College of Charleston, S. C.

He was married on the 18th of November, 1841, to Miss Sarah Strother O'Neall, the only surviving child of Chief Justice John Belton O'Neall. She died in August, 1857. He was again married in 1858, to Mrs. Hollingsworth, of Edgefield, S. C., who survives him.

Dr. Harrington lived in Newberry from his birth until 1865, when he removed to Mississippi. During his residence in Newberry he represented Newberry District in the House of Representatives of South Carolina for two years. In order to devote himself to his planting interests, he gave up the practice of his chosen profession some time before he left South Carolina, but resumed it after he removed to Mississippi, where he pursued it with much success.

Dr. Harrington inherited his father's abilities and graceful manners, and the gentleness and amiability of his mother. By inheritance and by marriage he came into possession of wealth, which he employed not in making senseless displays, but in adorning and rendering attractive a happy home, in acts of beneficence, and in dispensing a generous hospitality. Having leisure—especially before the disasters of the recent war—to devote to books, he read extensively and to good purpose. Few men excelled him as a conversationist, and by his attractive manners and unfailing courtesy he threw a charm about every social circle into which he entered. The habitual expression of his countenance was serene and pleasant, indicating a heart free from guile and malice. As a mere man, he was impressive; his erect, handsome figure, manly deportment and intelligent face harmonizing with the refinement and dignity of his character. He seemed to have been born to bless the world with his unselfish disposition, his unvarying cheerfulness and his exemplary piety. It was well said of him by a gentleman, on the streets of Newberry, when he heard of his fatal illness: 'He is one of Nature's Noblemen.' He is to be remembered among the men whose lives have shed honor and renown upon the County of Newberry."

I shall always count it among the happiest experiences of my life, that I enjoyed for so long a time the society and the friendship of Dr. Harrington. Like the Chevalier Bayard, he was "simple, modest, a sterling friend, and tender lover, pious, humane and magnanimous." And like the Chevalier, he possessed that "Kingliest of virtues, *justice*." It was delightful to sit at his hospitable board, or stroll with him about his grounds, and listen to his talk; erudite, pathetic, humorous;—always animated and entertaining—ranging over the wide fields of science, art, history, theology and belles-lettres. How the fragrance of those pleasant hours lingers in the memory!

His mind had an esthetic and scientific tendency. He indulged a good deal in meditation, and, to some extent, in speculation especially as to the probable progress and results of scientific investigation. These features of his character caused some persons to look upon him as a visionary man, and one lacking in practical knowledge. It is true that he did not make the accumulation of wealth a special object of his life, but he was prudent in the management of his financial affairs, as well as some private trusts committed to his hands. And he had a clear comprehension of "business matters" when they were presented to him. I think that in his life we have an illustration of the fact, that the cultivation of the intellect and the taste and the pursuit of scientific knowledge, are not incompatible with a due regard to the practical duties and obligations of life.

Dr. Harrington, united with the Newberry Baptist Church, on the 27th of October, 1832, and was for a good many years preceding his removal from the State a deacon of that church. At the time of his death, he was a member and a deacon of the Baptist Church at Crawfordville, Mississippi.

Alas! alas! the circle narrows rapidly. Major Christian Henry Suber, another of the few remaining members of the Locust Club, died at his home, in Newberry, on the 12th of March, 1890, in the sixty-second year of his age.

Major Suber was born in Newberry County, near Pomaria. He received his school education chiefly at Lexington, and at Laurens, S. C.; was graduated from the South Carolina College in 1848, and came at once to Newberry to read law. He was admitted to the Bar in 1851, and practiced his profession at Newberry nearly forty years. He was, at one time, the law partner of Silas Johnstone, Esq. After Mr. Johnstone was elected Commissioner in Equity, for Newberry, he was associated in the practice of his profession with Gen. A. C. Garlington; and after Gen. Garlington left Newberry for Atlanta, he became associated with J. F. J. Caldwell, Esq., with whom he continued to practice law until his death. He represented the County of Newberry for several terms, in the Legislature of South Carolina, and was a member of some important political conventions. He was gifted with unusual elocutionary powers, but did not often make speeches either at the Bar or before the people. In the practice of law he was most distinguished as a wise and judicious counsellor. He had good literary taste, and was especially devoted to the study of Shakespeare, whom he often quoted, both in his speeches and conversation. He was a sagacious and successful man of affairs. He entered the quartermaster's department of the Confederate army early in the recent war, as Captain, and was afterwards promoted to the rank of Major. He was never married.

Major Suber's life, though rather uneventful, was, in some respects very remarkable. He was, in his youth, in the maturity of his manhood and with the silvery traces of the winter of life resting upon his brow, a strikingly handsome and distinguished looking man. Those who saw him for the first time would always desire to know who he was. He was known all over the United States, and even beyond its limits. He had probably a larger number of acquaintances and personal friends than any other man in South Carolina. And numbered among his friends people of every class, from presidents of the United States down to the humblest citizens. Yet he never sought the notice of people by fawning or sycophancy; on the contrary, he was modest and unpretending, and at times even diffident. But there was about him an indescribable charm which attracted and held the friendship and confidence of all who came in contact with him. A person who ever knew him once never forgot him. His humor—often so closely allied to pathos, as to cause smiles and tears to mingle with each other—and his wonderful knowledge of events and of the personal history of so many people in all parts of the country made him a most engaging and interesting conversationist and an admirable story-teller.

The most beautiful feature of his character was his love for the young. He was never so happy as when engaged in conversation with a group of young people, or in a romp with some little children. Nor was his notice confined to any class. The children of the wealthy and refined and the children of the lowly and destitute, were alike the recipients of his loving and thoughtful attention. And as with the children, so with the grown-up people; he was kind and gentle to all.

Thomas Pratt, whose place of business on the south side of Court House Square, has already been referred to, came to Newberry in 1806. He was married in 1816 to Miss Dorothy Brooks Nance, the eldest daughter of Major Nance of Newberry. Mr. Pratt was, at the time of his death, which occurred in 1837, the leading merchant of the village. He was highly esteemed for his integrity and uprightness of character. During the war between the United States and England in 1813-14, in company with Kerr Boyce, (who afterwards became a prominent merchant and probably the wealthiest man in Charleston) he made several trips to Philadelphia on horseback, purchased goods and had them transported in wagons from that city to Newberry. He sold all sorts of goods, ranging from a blacksmith's anvil to a cambric needle.

I remember a little incident which will serve to illustrate something of the difference in values then and now, as well as Mr. Pratt's ideas of economy: While quite a small boy I was often at Mr. Pratt's house exchanging visits with one of his sons, who was about my age. One day we made a visit to the store and while there the son asked the father to give him a lead pencil. "Well, my son," said Mr. Pratt, "Those pencils which you see in the showcase are too expensive for little boys, but I will make one each for you and your friend." He took a bar of lead, such as was used for moulding into rifle balls, hammered it thin upon an anvil, and after cutting it into small strips and pointing the end with his pocket knife, gave us one each, for pencils. I have never forgotten Mr. Pratt's pencil, nor the affectionate and wholesome advice which he gave—pausing occasionally to bend his head and look at us over the rims of his spectacles as he fashioned them. I have used a great many pencils of various kinds since that time, but never one that lasted as long as Mr. Pratt's; in fact, I think, it never did wear out.

The friendship which existed from childhood between the the lad who shared in the gift of the pencils and myself was interrupted only by his death.

Priestly Pratt, or "Priest," as "we boys" always called him, was a bright, happy boy, full of life and humor. He had wonderful powers of imitation. He could imitate, with remarkable exactness, the songs and cries of birds. A most curious and highly amusing exhibition of this he gave by selecting the names of two Irish tailors, O'Connor and Shay, who lived in the village, and Philip Gelder, (always called Phil. Gelder,) who resided near by, and constructing out of them an imitation of the cries of the jay bird. He would begin by crying out, (moderato,) O'Connor, O'Connor, O'Connor ; then (allegro crescendo, in a higher key). Shay ! Shay ! Shay ! then (diminuendo,) Phil. Gelder, Phil. Gelder, Phil. Gelder. Any one who has closely observed the blue jay will understand how these names, when given the proper musical pitch, can be made to imitate his notes. Priest generally mounted aloft in some convenient tree to go through with this performance.

Priestly Pratt grew up to be a strikingly handsome young fellow. He was six feet in height, and stood perfectly erect. His head was well formed, and richly ornamented with dark, brown hair, his features were of Grecian caste, his chest was broad, and his limbs full and symmetrically shaped. He would have been pronounced by that accomplished scholar and master of the English tongue, Sir Edward Bulwer Lytton, a beautiful man.

When war was declared between the United States and Mexico, Young Pratt. John W. Stewart, Richard C. Carwile and John C. Higgins, all former schoolmates and companions of my youth, offered their services, and were accepted, as members of Capt. James H. Williams's company of the famous Palmetto Regiment. These young men entered the army with the dew of youth still upon them, glowing with anticipations of stirring adventure and visions of military glory :

"How beautiful is youth, how bright it gleams,
With its illusions, aspirations, dreams!
Book of Beginnings, Story without End,
Each maid a heroine and each man a friend!
Aladdin's Lamp and Fortunatus Purse,
That holds the treasures of the Universe!
All possibilities are in its hands,
No danger daunts and no foe withstands;
In its sublime audacity of faith,
Be thou removed it to the mountain saith,
And with ambitious feet secure and proud,
Ascends the ladder leaning on the cloud."

Alas! how little did they know of the dark future just ahead of them.

Capt. William's company, on the day before it left Newberry, was encamped at the old Ebenezer Camping-ground. It marched thence to Hamburg, S. C., where it joined its regiment. On the morning of its departure I accompanied my young friends as far as the highway leading to Bouknight's Ferry. Here the company was halted and the soldiers given a few minutes in which to take leave of their friends. After farewells had been exchanged, I remounted my horse, and, with a sad heart, watched the receding forms of my youthful companions until a turn in the road hid them from my view It was the last time I ever looked into the faces of Pratt, Stewart and Carwile. They all died of disease in Mexico. Only Higgins lived to return.

Ah! how well do I remember that parting scene! I remember even the appearance of the lane in which we stood, and surrounding objects, as we often remember that upon which the eye rests almost unconsciously in a supreme moment of our lives; and the memory of the faces and forms of those dead boys, and of all the happy years we spent together, exploring the streams and forests, and roaming over the fields around Newberry in the long past, is deeply graven on my heart and can never be effaced.

The body of Stewart was brought back to Newberry, and now sleeps in Rosemont Cemetery. The bodies of Pratt and Carwile are sleeping beneath the inhospitable soil of Mexico. Diligent efforts were made to recover them, but without success.

Just before the Mexican war, one George Guzman, a German music teacher, came to Newberry. He was very poor, but had evidently known better days. I do not know that he ever gave any account of his previous history. He played with skill and taste. There are some persons still living in Newberry who will remember his exquisite playing of "Home, Sweet Home," in two parts on one violin. He very soon organized a small orchestra from his pupils, and gave to the people of Newberry, who had not been so fortunate as to visit larger places, their first enjoyment of orchestral music. He was quite skilful in arranging music and always had before him, when drilling his orchestra or playing in public, a large book, which he called his "Partitura," in which was written all the parts of each piece on the same page, so that he could detect at once a mistake made by any of the performers.

With that spirit of adventure which probably brought him to Newberry, Guzman joined Capt. Williams's company when it was being organized for the Mexican war.

As the war progressed there were many anxious hearts in Newberry, awaiting the slow progress of the mails to bring them news of their friends, but very few, if any, thought of Guzman. When the army began its toilsome march from Vera Cruz to the city of Mexico, fighting as it advanced, letters began to be received, telling of the sickness of one and the death of another. Then it was that the nobleness of Guzman's character was brought to light. These letters contained stories of his unselfish devotion to the sick, weary and dying young men of his company, which brought tears to the eyes of strong men, and caused mothers, while they earnestly prayed for the preservation of the lives of their sons, to remember also, in their prayers, the poor, homeless wanderer who, sometimes in disregard of his own comfort and safety, carried their boys on his back rather than leave them behind.

Guzman gave up his life a sacrifice to his adopted country, and sleeps with hundreds more of the gallant Palmetto Regiment, under Mexican soil.

CHAPTER VI.

THE OLD COURT HOUSE—A DAY COURT—GEN. H H. KINARD SHERIFF—JUDGE O'NEALL ON THE BENCH—Y. J. HARRINGTON CLERK—JAMES J. CALDWELL SOLICITOR—RAPID DISPATCH OF BUSINESS—FLEXIBILITY OF THE OLD JUDICIARY SYSTEM—L. J. JONES, HIS REMARKABLE CAREER OF FIFTY YEARS AS A LAWYER—JOHN CALDWELL, MEMBER OF THE LEGISLATURE, CASHIER OF THE BANK OF THE STATE, HIS ELOQUENCE AT THE BAR AND BEFORE THE PEOPLE—P. C. CALDWELL, MEMBER OF THE BAR, OF THE LEGISLATURE, OF CONGRESS, OF STATE SENATE—SILAS L. HILLER, LAWYER, MEMBER OF THE LEGISLATURE, TEACHER—HENRY SUMMER, ATTORNEY, MEMBER OF THE LEGISLATURE, ELECTED TO SOUTHERN CONGRESS IN 1851, MEMBER OF STATE CONVENTION IN 1865, ENTHUSIASTIC LOVER AND COLLECTOR OF BOOKS—GRAPHIC ACCOUNT OF THE PERILS AND SUFFERINGS OF THE FAMILY DURING SHERMAN'S MARCH (1865), NARRATED BY HIS WIFE, MRS. FRANCES SUMMER—ADAM G. SUMMER, HIS SHORT CAREER AT THE BAR, DEVOTES HIMSELF TO AGRICULTURE AND LITERATURE, HIS SAD DEATH—GEORGE EPPS, HIS PROMISING PROFESSIONAL LIFE CUT SHORT BY HIS EARLY DEATH.

Fabian.— I will prove it legitimate, sir, upon the oaths of judgment and reason.
Sir Toby.—And they have been grand jury-men since before Noah was a sailor.   *Twelfth Night.*

THE old Court House, (which was removed in 1850), though not so commodious, was far more attractive to the eye than the present one. It had evidently been designed by an architect of more than ordinary skill and taste.

Before the main entrance, which was in the eastern end of the edifice, there was a portico, extending about two-thirds of the way across the front of the building. The entablature of the portico was supported by four large Tuscan columns, resting upon a brick floor, beneath this there was a vestibule. Through this vestibule you entered an arched hall-way, upon which the offices of the court officers opened. The floor of the portico was reached by semi-circular flights of granite steps on each side. From the portico you passed through a spacious doorway, into a hall, on both sides of which were stairways leading to the spectators' gallery above. At the opposite end of this hall you passed through a high arch-way into the court-room, the ceiling of which was very high and vaulted; the points of the arches supported in part by two tall Tuscan columns standing equi-distant between the centre and the side-walls of the room. The seats and tables provided for the Bar were on a platform in the middle of the room, elevated some distance above the floor; the seats for the juries were arranged in tiers diagonally across the corners of the court room, on the right and left of the Judge's seat, which was at the end of the room, opposite the entrance.

Let us in imagination go back nearly half a century; pass through the front door, with its massive shutters thrown wide open—fit emblem of a Court of Justice—and look upon the scene within.

It is the first day of the term. The Sheriff, Gen. H. H. Kinard, standing at the railing of the portico, has just made, in a clear ringing voice, the following announcement:

"Oyez! Oyez! All manner of persons having business in this Court of Common Pleas and General Sessions, for Newberry District, are required to give attendance, for this

Honorable Court now sits."* Judge O'Neall, in the vigor of his manhood, and arrayed in a flowing black silk robe is seated on the bench, his eyes glancing rapidly over the assembly. At a desk in front of, and just beneath the Judge's seat stands the clerk, Y. J. Harrington, and by his side sits his life-long friend, busily engaged in writing ; the assistant clerk, John S. Carwile. At a table opposite the clerk's desk, we see the tall and spare, but very erect figure of the solicitor, James J. Caldwell, who is administering oaths to witnesses in order to send them before the grand jury. The calm repose of his clear-cut features, and compressed lips plainly disclose the unflinching resolve of the faithful public officer, yet in his eyes there is an expression of gentleness approaching to sadness, arising from his well-known compassion not only for the accused, but also for the innocent and helpless ones, upon whom the punishment and disgrace of a guilty criminal so often falls with their most crushing effect.

The grand jury having been organized and furnished by the Solicitor with a number of indictments for investigation, Judge O'Neall proceeds at once to deliver his charge. He speaks in a clear, sonorous voice, which can be distinctly heard out upon the Public Square. The moment he begins to speak there is a rush by the crowd outside to gain admittance into the Court-room. This produces a temporary disturbance, which is quickly repressed by the imperious voice of the sheriff. The Judge proceeds and the people listen in profound silence and with unflagging attention, as he points out to the jury the far-reaching

---

*In the days of which I am here writing, and for many years afterwards, the announcement of the opening and adjournment of the Court was made by the sheriff himself and not by a constable, as at the present time.

power and authority with which they are clothed, and boldly and earnestly adjures them to be diligent and fearless in the discharge of their duties.

The grand jury having retired; the petit juries are speedily organized. Now while the solicitor is still engaged in swearing witnesses to go before the grand jury, in order that other bills may be given to them, Judge O'Neall at once takes up the business of the Common Pleas, by passing orders, and by rapidly disposing of cases on the Summary Process and Enquiry Docket.*

Here we see the flexibility of an admirable judiciary system, which enables a judge to turn at any time from one side of the Court to the other, as the business may demand.* The Court proceeds with the utmost dispatch. No tedious delays are allowed ; and woe-betide the lawyer, officer of Court or witness who is not promptly in his place.

Among the Attorneys at the Bar, we see John Caldwell,

---

*Cases on the Summary Process Docket, were heard at the first term after suit was brought, and decided by the Judge; except in rare instances where a jury was demanded by one of the parties to the suit. The Summary Process Docket embraced all cases in which the sum involved was not less than $20 nor more than about $85. The Enquiry Docket embraced all cases, above the Summary Process jurisdiction, in which no defence had been put in. When, however, leave was obtained during the session to put in a defence the case was transferred to the Issue Docket. If there was no defence the case was referred to the c'erk, who assessed the damages and wrote a decree for the amount on the Declaration, now called the Complaint.

* Equity cases were heard in a separate Court, called the "Court of Equity," over which Chancellors presided. The writer is not a lawyer and cannot therefore claim to be a very competent critic ; and he is aware that some of his honored legal friends are of a different opinion ; yet he believes that it was a sad day for South Carolina, when her venerable Courts were uprooted to make way for the present judiciary system.

Patrick C. Caldwell, Simeon Fair, Henry Summer, Thomas H. Pope, Adam Summer, Lambert J. Jones, Silas L. Heller, and George Epps, of Newberry; James H. Irby, C. P. Sullivan and Henry C Young, of Laurens; and Z. P. Herndon, Wallace Thompson and Davis Goudelock, of Union.

Of all this goodly company, Lambert J. Jones is the only survivor.

Mr. Jones, who is a native of Newberry County, is still actively engaged in the pursuit of his profession. After his admission to the bar, he began the practice of law at Newberry in 1839, and since that time has not been absent from a single session of the Courts at that place. His remarkable career of fifty years as a lawyer has been filled with unflagging professional labor and attention to the interests of his clients, and exceeds, in point of time, that of any other lawyer who has ever practiced at Newberry.

Of James J. Caldwell, Simeon Fair and Thomas H. Pope, I shall write hereafter.

John Caldwell was born in Newberry District, near Mill Creek, on the 9th of September, 1785. He was the eldest son of William Caldwell,*whose remarkable career as a soldier of the Revolution is recorded in Judge O'Neall's "Annals of Newberry." Having received a good academical education, he entered the South Carolina College, and completed the course in 1807, being a member of the second class, graduated from that institution. He was married in

---

* This distinguished family, once so numerous in Newberry, has not now a male representative of the name in the County. The only representatives of the family in the County are, Mrs. Elizabeth Higgins, her children, grand-children and great-grand-children. Mrs. Higgins still owns her share of her father's real estate, which has been in the family one hundred and seventeen years."—" *The Caldwells of Mill Creek*." *Newberry Observer*, April 28, 1887.

1808 to Miss Elizabeth Hunter, of Laurens District. In 1809 he was admitted to the bar, and entered upon the practice of law at Newberry.

"In October, 1812, Mr. Caldwell was elected to the House of Representatives, in the General Assembly of South Carolina. In December of that year, originated the Bank of the State of South Carolina. Mr. Caldwell was one of its most active supporters, and was elected a director, and to his astonishment, at the extra session of 1813, found he had vacated his seat in the House, by accepting a directorship in the Bank. He was elected Cashier of the Branch of that Bank in Columbia, and removed there in the spring of 1814. In May, 1814, Judge O'Neall, who had studied law with him, was admitted to the bar, and settled at Newberry, as the partner of Mr. Caldwell, and together they did a large and profitable business. * * * In January, 1816, Mrs. Caldwell died. * * * This unfortunate event determined Mr. Caldwell to remove from Columbia. He resigned his cashiership, which was far, very far from profitable to him; indeed he sustained a heavy loss in settling his accounts. * * * * He returned to the town of Newberry, and on the 17th of October, 1816, he was married to Abigail, eldest daughter of Hugh O'Neall, and sister of Judge O'Neall.

"The partnership between him and Judge O'Neall closed about the period of his first wife's death. * * * From 1818, Mr. Caldwell resumed business, as a lawyer, at Newberry and Lexington. In 1824–'26 and '28, he was returned as a member of the House of Representatives of South Carolina."*

About the year 1835 Mr. Caldwell was paralyzed both in his limbs and tongue, having previously received a serious

---

* "*O'Neall's Bench and Bar of South Carolina.*"

injury by a fall. Notwithstanding these misfortunes he continued for some time to attend the sessions of the Courts at Newberry, but his career as a lawyer may be said to have ended when his great afflictions fell upon him.

Mr. Caldwell died on the 15th of January, 1856, in the 71st year of his age.

In the sketch from which I have already quoted, Judge O'Neall says : " John Caldwell, when young, was possessed of more physical powers than usually fall to the lot of man.
* * * * * * * * *
Intellectually, he was no common man. If he had had industry, he ought to have compared very well with his great kinsman, John C. Calhoun.* He was an excellent accountant and surveyor. As a lawyer, he did not pretend to learning ; as an advocate, in the management of a case, he possessed unrivalled talents. His quick, clear perception of everything made him ready for any turn of his case. Before a jury his power as an advocate very often gave him success. Indeed, at Lexington he had unrivalled sway."

Mr. Caldwell does not seem to have been a very diligent student, or a pains-taking practitioner. He appears to have relied too much upon his powers as a speaker, and this, together with his convivial disposition, interfered to prevent the achievement of that full measure of success, which should have crowned his life.

His eloquent tongue was restrained by the hand of Providence before I was old enough to appreciate his gifts as an orator, but I have often heard my father and others—contemporaries of Mr. Caldwell—speak in unqualified praise of

---

*Martha Caldwell, the daughter of William Caldwell, (the grandfather of John Caldwell,) married Patrick Calhoun, and from this marriage sprang South Carolina's greatest statesman, John Caldwell Calhoun.

his admirable speeches. He was an ardent supporter of "Nullification," and his greatest oratorical efforts were probably made during the exciting discussions of that question. From all the accounts which tradition has brought down to us, there can be no doubt that he was one of the most brilliant and eloquent orators that Newberry has ever produced.

The last time I saw Mr. Caldwell, he was sitting by his fireside, dressed in a long, red flannel dressing gown which he commonly wore, his body sadly bent from the effects of rheumatism and paralysis. But he was bright and cheerful, (indeed, I never saw him depressed,) and one could see in his expressive face, illuminated, as it was, by his bright, piercing eyes, something of the power by which, in former days, he could so wonderfully sway the feelings of a multitude.

Patrick Calhoun Caldwell was born in Newberry District on the 10th of March, 1801. He was the son of William Caldwell, and the brother of John Caldwell, whose life has just been sketched. He was graduated from the South Carolina College in 1820, and admitted to the Bar in 1822. On the 13th of December, 1827, he was married to Frances E. Nance, (the daughter of Major Frederick and Elizabeth Rutherford Nance,) who died on the 3rd of March, 1832. He was elected a member of the House of Representatives in the Legislature of South Carolina from Newberry in 1836, and re-elected to the same position in 1838. In 1840 he was elected a member of the House of Representatives in the Congress of the United States from the Congressional District of South Carolina, then composed of the Districts of Laurens, Newberry, Fairfield and Lexington.

In the canvass which preceded his election to Congress, Mr. Caldwell is said to have displayed unusual ability and effectiveness as a "stump-speaker." His opponents were Col. James H. Irby, of Laurens, and Mr. Samuel Barclay, of Fairfield. I can recall only one scene in that canvass. In company with some other boys I walked out one summer day to "Teague's Old Field," about three miles west of the village, to witness a review of the 38th Regiment of Militia, by Gen. James J. Caldwell, (who was afterwards made a Chancellor.) At the close of the review the General, sitting on his tall, clean-limbed, sorrel horse, "Snipe," delivered a stirring speech to the Regiment. After the parade was over the crowd repaired to a grove near by, to hear speeches by Col. Irby and Mr. Caldwell. (Mr. Barclay was not present.)

I remember nothing about the questions discussed. I have, however, a distinct recollection of the personal appearance of both the speakers, and of many others who were present; among them the erect, portly figure and handsome face of General John K. Griffin, who had previously represented the Congressional District for many years; but had at this time declined to be a candidate again. I also remember that "we boys" remained silent during the applause which followed Col. Irby's speech, but when Mr. Caldwell had finished his speech, with characteristic home pride—we "just hollered" and threw into the air our straw hats, already badly damaged, from frequent use in attacking "yellow jackets'" nests and scooping minnows from the branches, and that we left the "muster ground" thoroughly convinced that Col. Irby had been completely demolished by Mr. Caldwell, who we believed could "beat anybody."

In 1848, Mr. Caldwell was elected to the Senate of South Carolina, from Newberry District.

I have not been able to find any records that throw much light upon the public career of Mr. Caldwell, and as I was quite a young man when he was compelled from bodily affliction to retire from the active duties of life. I am not so well informed as to the extent of his legal learning and abilities as I could wish to be. He must have been, however, a successful lawyer; he left at his death, a handsome estate, much of which I suppose he accumulated from the income of his practice. He was for a number of years the law partner of Chancellor James J. Caldwell. His career as a Representative and Senator in the State Legislature, and as a Representative in the Congress of the United States, through not marked by any special distinction, appears to have been very successful, and to have given entire satisfaction to his constituents.

Of all the men of the past in Newberry, whom I knew, I think he enjoyed the most uniform popularity. He was cheerfulness personified. His very appearance and manner were suggestive of good humor and pleasantry, he was short of stature, of rotund figure, walked with quick short steps; and there was always a merry twinkle in his eyes; and a pleasant smile on his face. He was cordially greeted by the people wherever he went. He died on the 22d of November, 1855, from the effects of a stroke of paralysis which fell upon him three years before.

Silas L. Heller, was a native of Newberry District. From the most reliable information, I have obtained, I infer that he was born, about the year 1803. He was graduated from the South Carolina College in 1826. In 1831, he was married to Miss Mary Lorick, of Newberry District. He was elected a member of the House of Representatives of South Carolina from Newberry, in 1832. About the year, 1848, he removed to Texas. During his residence in South Carolina, he was at different times engaged in school teaching, at Prosperity, at Newberry, and at Cokesbury, S. C. As a teacher he was very successful in imparting knowledge to his pupils.

Mr. Heller's early life gave promise of great usefulness and success. He was a thorough Greek and Latin scholar, master of the English tongue, and a gifted and fluent speaker. But he appears to have been deficient in energy, and attention to the practical details of business; and he early fell into habits of intemperance so that his professional career cannot be said to have been a successful one.

It has now been many years since he went down into the valley of death, and I gladly turn from the mention of his frailties, to speak of his virtues and drop a tear to his memory. He was a man of undoubted integrity, kind hearted and inoffensive. I shall never forget his patient kindness, and painstaking attention as my teacher at school, and as my private tutor afterwards.

After the death of his wife, which occurred in Texas, Mr. Heller came back (about the year 1872), to Newberry; and died shortly af er his return, at the home of his brother, Joel B. Heller.

Henry Summer was descended from German ancestors. He was the son of Captain John Summer, and was born at Pomaria, Lexington District, S. C., on the 11th of April, 1809. His paternal great-grandfather, Colonel John Adam Summer, emigrated from Pennsylvania to South Carolina before the American Revolution. He was the pioneer settler and founder of the German colony which settled in that portion of the Districts of Newberry and Lexington between the Broad and Saluda Rivers, still known as the "Dutch Fork."

Both his paternal great-grandfather and his grandfather, (Nicholas Summer), were soldiers in the American army during the Revolution. The grandfather was accidentally killed at Granby, near Columbia, S. C., during the war.

The wife of Captain John Summer (and mother of Henry Summer) was the daughter of William Frederick Houseal, of Lexington District, S. C.

Mr. Summer was graduated from the South Carolina College in 1832. After his graduation he read law, and was admitted to the Bar in 1833. "He began the practice of law at Lexington, S. C., where he remained one year, and then removed to Talladega, Alabama, where he continued to practice law until the death of his brother Nicholas, who was killed in the Florida war. His brother left his law library to him on condition that he should return to South Carolina and practice law at Newberry C. H., which he did."*

On the 22d of December, 1846, he was married to Miss Frances Mayer, the daughter of Major Adam Mayer, of Lexington, and the sister of Dr. O. B. Mayer, Sen., of Newberry.

He was elected a member of the House of Representatives of South Carolina in 1846, and was re-elected to the same position in 1848.

In 1851 Mr. Summer and Dr. J. J. Wardlaw, of Abbeville were elected to represent the Districts of Edgefield, Abbeville, Newberry and Lexington, (composing the —— Congressional District of South Carolina) in a Southern Congress, to be assembled to consider the attitude of the Federal Government towards the slaveholding States, and recommend some course to be pursued.† There were two parties in the State at the time; one in favor of separate State action, if the co-operation of other States could not be se-

* Biographical sketch, *Newberry News*, October 18, 1878.
† Act of Legislature, passed December 1850.

cured; and the other in favor of action, only, with the co-operation of other States. Mr. Summer and Dr. Wardlaw were the candidates of the Co-operation party, which triumphed in a majority of the Districts of the State. The proposed Convention, however, never assembled. In September, 1855, he was elected a member of the Convention which convened in Columbia on the 13th of that month, under the proclamation of B. F. Perry, Provisional Governor of South Carolina, " for the purpose of altering and amending the present Constitution of South Carolina, or remodeling and making a new one, which will conform to great changes which have taken place in the State."

Mr. Summer was from its organization an ardent friend of Newberry College, and was for many years the Secretary of its Board of Trustees.

As a lawyer, he occupied a highly respectable position. He was methodical in his habits, and prompt in his attention to business. Indeed, so absorbed would he become in any business which he might have in hand that some persons who approached him at such times and who did not understand his peculiar temperament, were disposed to think that he was too stern and unbending. But he did not intend to be so; his disposition was amiable and kind. One of the most prominent traits of his character was his truthfulness. As a speaker, he was not especially gifted, yet I have heard him on some occasions when he was truly eloquent. In the social circle, he was very agreeable and entertaining. He was a great lover of books; the enthusiasm he displayed in collecting the best editions of the works of celebrated authors amounted almost to bibliolatry. He devoted much time to miscellaneous reading; and his taste for other literature often led him away from the severer study of the law.

In the latter part of the year 1864,—the Courts having been virtually suspended—Mr. Summer removed from Newberry to his farm in Lexington District. During Sherman's memorable march through the State in 1865, Kilpatrick's command—as it swept over that portion of the country which lies along the western bank of Broad River, between Columbia and Alston—destroyed Mr. Summer's houses and other property; and some of the soldiers went so far as to prepare for the hanging of Mr. Summer himself.

I am sure that my readers will not find in all these pages any thing more interesting than the following letter addressed to me by Mr. Summer's very intelligent and estimable widow, which gives a most faithful narrative of the sufferings of the family at that time, and of the inhuman treatment to which they were subjected. It deserves to be handed down to posterity, as a striking and graphic picture of the horrors of that march, in which hundreds of families in South Carolina became the victims of the incendiary's torch and the insults of brutal soldiers:

POMARIA, January 18th, 1888.

My Dear Sir: I received your letter a few days since, and will endeavor to comply with your request as well as I can. After the lapse of twenty-three years, with their accompanying trials and sorrows, many things have passed from my mind.

Saturday morning, 19th of February, 1865, we apprehended no immediate danger, as Wheeler's men had been passing all day Friday, and two Confederate soldiers lodged with us that night; and early Saturday morning, two men, professing to be friends, assured us that none of the enemy were near, although we knew that there had been fighting around Lexington the day before.

It was not long before we saw columns of smoke arising below us, and gradually nearing us. While looking with much fear on all this, we were greatly alarmed at seeing a body of ferocious-looking men charging up the Lexington road that crossed the Prosperity road in front of our house. They surrounded and entered the house, and the work of plunder began. We realized that we were helpless, with no friend near us, and at the mercy of thousands of lawless men, under no restraint. My husband had hoped that his age and feeble health would shield him from abuse and violence; but the events of the day proved his mistake. He had on a light suit of jeans,—as the weather was mild, but kept his large shawl near, to throw around him when he needed it; that they seized for the first thing and all his clothing followed, but what he had on. By this time they came swarming in from every direction, until the yard and surrounding grounds were filled with armed men charging about, and even attempting to ride into the house; and the work of destruction went on. Every door, trunk, and bureau was broken open with hatchets, if the lock did not yield immediately, and the contents carried off, or scattered over the floor, to be trampled under their feet, or picked up by others, who crowded in after them. As one party passed out, loaded with what they fancied, another came in; so that the house was packed with the vile wretches all day. I cannot now remember or repeat all their abusive and insulting language. My husband's pockets were searched many times and every thing taken, but a pocket calendar; the last man seized that, thinking it was a silver coin, but another man, standing by, ordered him to restore it, which he did. About one o'clock the large barn and other buildings in the lot were burned.

We were told by some of the better men, that all this

plunder and destruction was done by stragglers, who went ahead of the army, under no control, but when the regular army came up, disciplined and controlled by officers, we would be respected and protected ; but that was not so, for in the midst of this confusion Kilpatrick came up, looked on with indifference, and saw his men carrying out every moveable thing to the roadside, to await their wagon train. He commanded the left wing of Sherman's army, eight thousand strong, mostly cavalry, but he must have had a large force of infantry, for while he was at the house they marched by; and both roads fronting the house, as far as the eye could see, were so densely packed with men that no one could have passed between them; while around the gate, over which a large United States flag was floating, cavalry and infantry seemed to trample upon each other.

As soon as I learned that Kilpatrick was at the front steps, (he did not enter the house, but his staff and others crowded into my room where I and my children were,) I made my way, unaided, to him. My husband was standing in front of him, civilly answering such questions as he asked, such as the route to Hughey's Ferry, to Alston and Ravenscroft. I caught him by the arm to attract his attention, and begged, as only one in my extremity could, for protection. He impatiently answered: "I am busy, go to the Provost Marshal." I found him standing by the front door, inside the house, who, in answer to the same request, said: "That nothing could be done." But that was another falsehood ; for, while Kilpatrick was talking with my husband, a large column of infantry was marching down the road to Hughey's Ferry—he quietly said to some one standing by: "Halt that column!" and in a few minutes they had turned into the Alston road ; showing how well disciplined they were, and how quick to obey orders.

After Kilpatrick had all the information he wanted, he rode off, leaving us to our fate, not caring what it would be. When the sun went down, the men were all ordered within the picket lines, and we were left to ourselves. Then the horrors of the night began. We could not sleep, or let the light go out, fearing that the house would be burned over our heads. Only the younger children lay down to sleep, while the rest of us sat up during the long night, and kept a bright light. It was during that fearful watch that my husband told, for the first time, the trying ordeal through which he had passed that morning. Three or four of the savages forced him to go with them to the barn, and while they were putting a rope around his neck, demanded his gold and silver. He told them he had no gold, no money at all, for all had been already taken from him. They then made him stand on a sill, or something raised from the floor, and again demanded gold, declaring that they would hang him if he did not give it up. They then threw the rope over a peg high up the wall, and made the same demand with the same threat. My husband, believing that death was very near, closed his eyes, and offered up an audible prayer for himself and also for the men who were about to murder him.* That prayer, or something, seemed to touch one of the num-

---

*In a letter written in 1857, to a friend, Mr. Summer, describing the scene in the barn, writes thus: "The only help I had was in that God in whom I have always trusted; and to Him I offered a prayer for protection, as I had told the truth, and commended myself to His power.

In the same letter he relates the following colloquy between the leader of the party at the barn and himself, which ensued after his release. "I asked him, just as he was about mounting his horse, what his name was, and where he was from? 'Green, and from Ohio,' was the reply. I looked him direct in the face, and asked him if he ever prayed. He said: 'Sometimes, when he was at home.' I said to him: 'Will, you pray for me.' He said: 'He would when he got home.' I then replied, with earnestness and emphasis: '*I can pray for you.*' He then mounted his horse and rode off."

ber, as he called the others aside, and after consultation, returned and told him to come down, but they still believed that he had the gold.

Sunday morning dawned, and with the light our troubles began, and the whole day we were harassed by foraging parties of eight or ten who would gallop around the house like madmen, tramp through the house, look into the room where we were sitting, make some taunting or insulting remark, and then go out to make way for others.

I must not omit here to say, that after early breakfast Saturday morning we had nothing to eat—everything was taken from us. After night one of the servants went into the storeroom, and, by sweeping and dusting the hominy barrel, got enough to make a scanty meal, by boiling husk and all. That we ate as well as we could, without spoons or knives. Sunday morning we found still some rice left, and that was all we had to eat until we came away.

Sunday, about 2 o'clock, as we were sitting in our room, dejected and miserable, not knowing what the next hour would bring to us, two men rushed hastily into the room; one of them seized a match and said : 'Give me one hundred dollars, or I will burn your house." With that he rushed up stairs, where everything combustible was scattered over the floor. My husband said to his companion : "Surely you will not allow that man to burn my house." He replied, indifferently, he did not think he would do it. By this time the wretch had applied the match to papers and cotton at the head of the stairs, and in five minutes everything was blazing. There was no water at hand, and we made no attempt to put out the fire, for the servant women, as well as ourselves, were too much exhausted to do anything but gather up a few things that were lying about on the floor, and make our escape to the orchard. Two of their men galloped up in this time, and did everything in their power to save everything from the burning building. They managed to take out the bed in my room and the children's beds.* While we were sitting by the little pile of things saved, we were still annoyed by the savages, for parties of them would ride around us, shoot their carbines, dismount and turn over whatever was lying around us, to rob us still further, if they saw anything to suit them. Some of them told the negroes that if we went into their house, which was the only one left, they would come back that night and set it on fire. We therefore remained in the orchard until dark, and each one was thoroughly chilled. Hoping, then, that the last one had gone within the lines, we ventured to go into the negro house, where we passed another miserable night.

When Monday morning came, we could not see ten steps from the door; we were girdled by fire, the woods having caught from the burning houses. The smoke was so dense that when the sun arose it looked like a ball of fire. The desolation was indescribable. Our nearest neighbor, who had been hiding out, now came up, and told us that the whole army had gone.

Monday evening, about 4 o'clock, a message came from brother William Summer for us to try and get to his house, as they had a little bread and a shelter left. So we started and walked the distance of four miles, the youngest child being only seven years old. Our children behaved admirably during that trying time; John was thirteen and Kate seven. Although frightened, they were calm and quiet, and never once asked for anything to eat, which would

---

*Mr. Summer had carried about eight hundred volumes (a part of his valuable library) from his home in Newberry to his farm in Lexington. All these were destroyed with his house.

have added much to my distress, for I did not have it to give them.

The crowning evil and injury caused by the events just related was yet to follow. I shall always believe that my husband's death was hastened by exposure with insufficient clothing to the inclement weather that followed shortly after, and anxiety about the condition of his family, and his great losses. True he was an invalid, but the great care that he took of himself would have prolonged his life many years perhaps.

Very respectfully, your friend,

FRANCES SUMMER.

After the destruction of his property, Mr. Summer returned to Newberry, where he remained until his death, which took place on the 3d of January, 1869.

Adam Geiselhardt Summer, who was the son of Captain John Summer, and the brother of Henry Summer, was born at Pomaria, on the 22d of August, 1818. He received a good academic education, chiefly at Lexington, S. C. He was not a graduate of any college. He was admitted to the bar in 1840, and entered upon the practice of law at Newberry.

Mr. Summer was a man of unusual mental power—he seemed to absorb knowledge as a sponge takes up water. He readily acquired a knowledge of the theory of the law, but had no taste nor aptitude for the dry and practical details of its practice. He was most successful as an advocate, especially in cases where there were opportunities offered for appealing to the humanity of juries, or for the display of wit and satirical humor. He early gave up the practice of law, and removed to Columbia, S. C., where he published and edited for several years the *South Carolinian*, a weekly newspaper. Having disposed of his interest in the *Caro-*

linian, he subsequently removed to "Ravenscroft," a farm in Lexington District, and devoted himself chiefly to agriculture. In 1850 he was elected a member of the House of Representatives of South Carolina from Saxe-Gotha (Lexington) District. In 1857 he purchased land in Florida and removed to that State.

"In the time of the Confederate war he adhered to his principles, volunteered and went to Virginia, and was made Brigade Judge Advocate under General Magruder, and afterwards commissioned as a commissary and a command put under his charge to go to Florida and forward supplies to the army. In this latter position he remained until the end of the war."*

On the 22d of September, 1865, he was married to Miss Margaret J. Starke, the daughter of Maj. Thomas Starke, of Kershaw District, S. C.

While on a visit to Charleston, in 1866, he became quite ill, and, contrary to the wishes of his friends, started to join his wife (in accordance with a previous promise made to her), who was then with her grandmother, Mrs Starke, in Kershaw. But after leaving the railway train at Ridgeway he became so exhausted that he had to stop, within eight miles of Mrs. Starke's, at Col. John Peay's, and died there on the 6th of July of that year.

The picture of Mr. Summer dying in the prime of life, within a few miles of his beloved wife, upon whose face his eyes were never to look again, nor to be gladdened by the sight of his only child (a daughter), born a few days after his death, would be inexpressibly sad and sombre, if unrelieved by his entire submission to the will of God. His life-long friend, Dr. O. B. Mayer, Sen., who

---

* Biographical Sketch.—*Newberry News*, 1878.

was with him at the time, relates: "That just before he died he attempted to sit up, under a sense of suffocation. He was too weak to rise, and recognizing the true nature of his distress, he gave me a look of deep tenderness and said, joining his hands in a feeble clasp, 'Well, I place all my affairs in the hands of God.'" These were his last words, and in a few moments after he passed away.

Mr. Summer was a somewhat erratic and visionary man, yet many of the schemes which his enthusiastic nature led him to adopt—though they yielded very little profit to himself—were productive of much benefit to the country. He introduced new methods of farming, new agricultural implements and machinery, and improved breeds of live stock into the country. He was a member and active supporter of the Newberry Agricultural Society for many years, and wrote many articles for agricultural journals. He had a refined and cultivated literary taste. His genial manners and fine conversational powers secured for him a hearty welcome into the most cultivated and intelligent circles. He devoted much time to literature, and numbered among his friends many of the most prominent literary people of the day. He wrote articles for the *Southern Quarterly Review*, the *Southern Literary Messenger*, and other Southern periodicals. He also wrote humorous character sketches and and stories for the *New York Spirit of the Times*, which attracted considerable attention. "The Last Quaker Meeting," a sketch republished in Judge O'Neall's Annals of Newberry, was written by Mr. Summer, and originally published in the *Newberry Sentinel.**

My heart always grows warm when I think of Adam

---

*The Newberry Sentinel, the first newspaper ever published in Newberry, was established by James H. Giles, in 1847. Mr. Giles died at Graniteville, S. C., Sept. 12th, 1885, aged 72 years.

Summer, the friend of my youth. He was distinguished for his disinterested kindness and generosity. Wherever he found young persons striving to acquire knowledge, or exhibiting a love and taste for music, or other branches of the fine arts, he encouraged them by the loan of books, and in every way within his power. And while the inspiration they derived from him may not have always led to practical results, it certainly served to refine, elevate, and make their lives brighter and happier.

In his excellent library I saw, soon after its publication, the only copy of Audubon's magnificent work, "The Birds of America," ever brought to Newberry. Never can I forget the impression made upon my youthful mind by its life-like and beautiful illustrations. If a purse of gold and the book had been presented together, I would have scorned the gold and gladly accepted the book.

Measured by the commonly received opinion that the accumulation of wealth is the test of a man's success, Mr. Summer's life might be considered a failure. But how can that life be considered a failure which was filled with deeds of kindness, and carried sunshine and happiness to so many hearts.

George F. Epps, who was the son of Daniel Epps, was born in that section of Newberry County known as "Mollohon." He was graduated from Randolph Macon College, Virginia, was admitted to the Bar in 1841, and entered upon the practice of law at Newberry.

I do not remember any young man who began his professional career under more favorable conditions than Mr. Epps. He was not wealthy, yet he was free from the restraints of poverty, and the privations which often beset the path of a young professional man. He was well informed, of studious habits, and withal a thorough man of affairs, who gave attention to the practical side of life. He was affable and courteous in manner, buoyant and hopeful in disposition.

His professional career of five years was too short to have fully developed his capacity as a lawyer, but he may be said to have been very successful for one who had been for so brief a period at the Bar.

It was my good fortune to be numbered among Mr. Epps' intimate friends and associates. In the latter part of the summer of 1846, accompanied by George Parks,* a young man highly esteemed by both of us, he came to Greenville, S. C., (where I was loitering on my return from a summer tour into the mountains of western North Carolina) to spend a week with me. We (Epps, Parks and myself) occupied during the visit a large airy apartment in the famous old Long Hotel. We gave ourselves up to that free and unalloyed mirth and enjoyment, which only those who are bound together by the most intimate and cordial ties of friendship and congeniality can know. The happy week passed away all too soon. My regret at parting with my friends was mitigated however by the confident expectation of rejoining them in a short time at home.

---

*George Parks was a native of one of the New England States He came to Newberry about the year 1835, to take charge of the Male Academy, over which he presided successfully for several years, and then removed to Charleston, S. C., where he died. He was graduated, I think, from Brown University, Rhode Island. He very soon convinced the people of Newberry that New Englanders were not all cold and distant in manner and disposition, as they had been disposed to think of them. He was a jovial, whole-souled, generous fellow, full of vivacity and good nature and not without the more solid attractions of a well cultivated intellect, and a wholesome Christian example. He made many friends in Newberry, and his departure was universally regretted.

But I was never permitted to greet Mr. Epps again. He died (on the 19th of September, 1846) only a few days after his return to Newberry.

Mr. Epps had been for many years previous to his death a devoted member of the Methodist Church.

" His death-bed impressed deeply and indelibly upon the minds of his friends who saw it, the purity and sincerity of his past life and profession.   *   *   *   *   *   *

Bright were his prospects in this life, but still brighter, on a deathbed were his prospects for eternity. He dropped into the grave like ripe fruit, fully matured. Like the descending snowflake which noiselessly sinks into the bosom of that maternal ocean which first exhaled its virgin vapors, his pure and spotless spirit softly and silently sunk back to repose into the bosom of the Divine mercy from which it sprang, and to which it had long been tending."*

---

*Obituary published October, 1846.

CHAPTER VII.

GREAT RELIGIOUS AWAKENING—ORGANIZATION AND HISTORY OF THE BAPTIST CHURCH—PICTURE OF A CHURCH EDIFICE FIFTY YEARS AGO—REV. J. M. BARNES—REV. N. W. HODGES—REV. DANIEL MANGUM —REV. THOMAS FREAN—REV. SAM'L. GIBSON—REV. JNO. G. LANDRUM—REV. M. C. BARNETT—REV. RICHARD FURMAN, D. D.

WHEN I was brought by my parents to Newberry in 1828, there was no Church organization, or House of worship in the place. There were but few church members, probably not more than fifteen or twenty altogether, then living in the village. The Rev. Samuel P. Pressly, of the Associate Reformed Presbyterian Church, was the only minister of the Gospel residing in the place. He was engaged during the week in teaching school, and his sabbaths were employed in preaching to four churches in the surrounding country. He preached occasionally to the people of the village in the Court House.

The house of worship, of the Newberry Baptist Church, was the first church edifice erected in the village. In giving some account of the early history of this Church and of the great religious awakening, out of which it sprang, I shall quote freely from a "Memorial Discourse" delivered on the 1st day of January, 1882, by the Rev. Luther Broadus, (now deceased), who was then pastor of the Church.

It is a fact that has been commented upon, but has never been satisfactorily explained, that great political movements are often attended or followed by great religious movements.

In January 1830, during the firm and independent administration of that man of iron will, Andrew Jackson, occurred the celebrated debate between Hayne and Webster, with reference to States rights and Federal relations, and in November, 1832, the Ordinance of Nullification was passed in South Carolina. For several years the most intense political excitement prevailed throughout the country, culminating in this State, and threatening to precipitate the dreadful conflict which was destined to come thirty years later, and deluge the country in blood.

In the midst of this political fermentation, the most remarkable religious awakening of this century, if not in the history of this country, took place. A great tidal wave of religious interest swept over the Atlantic States, depositing its precious treasures in almost every village and hamlet and home in the country. As the political excitement before referred to reached its highest point in this State, so this religious interest was perhaps more intense and widespread here than anywhere else. From the mountains to the seaboard, the people were thoroughly aroused, and gathered in multitudes wherever preaching could be heard. In this movement a large number of the strongest and most influential Churches in South Carolina had their origin.

In the summer of 1831 at the house of John S. Carwile, then a deacon of Bush River Church; in a circle of three or four friends, reference was made to a great meeting in progress at Edgefield Court House under the direction and preaching of some young men, students of the Furman Theological Institution, (then located at High Hills of

Santee, S. C.), and a desire being expressed that such a meeting might be held here, Mr. Carwile at once agreed to take the matter in hand, and after correspondence with the young ministers at Edgefield secured their promise to come to Newberry.

Sometime during the month of September, 1831, four young ministers, Nicholas W. Hodges, James M. Chiles, Josiah Furman, and John M. Barnes, came to Newberry and began preaching at a stand, such as is now, sometimes used for political speakers, in a large grove some distance in the rear of where the residence of A. M. Bowers now stands.

The novelty of the proceeding, and the fame of similar meetings elsewhere, soon attracted a crowd which continued to grow until people from all parts of Newberry and neighboring Districts, came in great numbers to hear the Word. Every class of people was reached, from the humble and obscure, including the lowly slave, to the most intellectual, honored and refined. A remarkable feature of the meeting was the absence of violent exhibitions of excitement. A profound stillness fell upon the people when they assembled, and they listened with solemn and eager attention to the preaching.

It was not long before visible results followed. The neighboring churches of all evangelical denominations received of the fruits of the meeting in increased numbers and quickened spiritual life.

As one of the results, the Newberry Baptist Church was organized on the 30th day of September, 1831, with forty-four members. Two of this number—John S. Carwile and James Divver—presented letters of dismissal from the Church at Bush River. The remaining forty-two were principally, if not altogether, persons who had been baptized during the progress of the meeting. It is worthy of note that of those who united in the organization of the church, nine were negro slaves and two free persons of color.

The Council which constituted the church was composed of the following ministers: Nicholas W. Hodges, Jonathan Davis, S— Worthington and Daniel Mangum. The exercises consisted of a prayer by Mr. Mangum, the adoption of a Constitution and Declaration of Principles by the Church, an address by Mr Davis on Church Organization and Church Government, and the reading of a part of the third chapter of First Timothy, with remarks on the qualifications of Deacons by Mr. Hodges.

The Church then proceeded to elect John S. Carwile Deacon and Rev. John M. Barnes Pastor, and the Council at once ordained them. On the 5th of November following, Y. J. Harrington and Thomas Pratt were elected Deacons.

The following is a copy of the Constitution and Declaration of Principles adopted by the Church:

"1. We agree to meet statedly from time to time, for the maintenance of discipline, religious exercises and mutual edification.

"2. When assembled for Church business, due and proper order and decorum shall be observed. All the male members shall be allowed to speak—one, however, at a time—and express their sentiments on all matters that may come before the Church. A decision shall be finally made by submitting the question to vote, and when unanimity cannot be obtained it shall be the duty of the minority to submit. The majority, however, shall feel themselves bound to exercise towards the minority, in all cases where their consciences would be aggrieved, all Christian forbearance and meekness.

"3. We agree to take the Scriptures of the Old and New

Testaments as our only guide, and rule of faith and practice, and from them deduce the following principles of belief, viz.:

"1st. We believe in one Eternal God, Father Son and Holy Spirit, and each of these Three, exercising distinct offices in the great work of man's redemption ; it being the province of the Father to forgive sins, of the Son to atone for sin and intercede with the Father, of the Holy Spirit to apply this atonement to the heart of the sinner so as to regenerate and sanctify him.

"2d. We believe in a future judgment, the resurrection of the bodies, both of the righteous and wicked, and eternal rewards and punishments.

"3rd. We believe there are two ordinances in the Church of Christ designed for perpetual observance, viz. : Immersion and the Lord's Supper, and that believers are the only fit subjects.

4th. "As a Church, we believe that we are an independent body, and acknowledge no head but Christ, no rule of discipline but His Word. We feel bound, however, to pay all due respect to the advice and opinions of Associations, and more particularly to obey those who may have the rule over us, who may have spoken unto us the Word of God, considering the end of their conversation : Jesus Christ, the same yesterday, to-day and forever."

The following is a list of the names of the persons who united in the organization of the Church : Y. J. Harrington, Nancy Harrington, William Wilson, Eliza Stewart, M. T. Mendenhall, Phœbe Mendenhall, John S. Carwile, Mary Carwile, Elvira Henderson, James Divver, Sophia Divver, Thomas T. Sheppard, Temperance Sheppard, Mary Shell, Charles G. Gary, Caroline Gary, John Tillery, William Bridges, Nancy Bridges, James

H. Wilson, Elizabeth Johns, Esther Moore, Mary McConnell, Euclidus Longshore, Lura Burton, Lucinda Glenn. John Moore, Reuben Pitts, John S. Clark, Wm. Croker, Mary Croker, Mary Coate, John Ramage, Lucinda, (slave of Wm. Calmes,) Amy, (slave of Judge O'Neall,) Lucy, (slave of Major F. Nance,) Lucy, (slave of Rev. S. P. Pressly,) Peggy, (slave of Y. J. Harrington,) Sarah, (slave of Chancellor Johnstone,) Sam and Jerry, (slaves of John Caldwell, Esq.,) Andrew, (slave of Jacob H. Hunt,) Sally Jackson and Hannah, (free persons of color.)

Among those who united with the Church shortly after its organization are the following, whose names will be familiar to many of the present citizens of Newberry : Mrs. Elizabeth Wilson, (the wife of James H. Wilson,) Mrs. Lucy Ramage, Jacob H. Hunt, Mrs. Hannah G. Hunt, Mary Harrington, Wm. H. Harrington, John C. Harrington Thomas Pratt, Mrs. Dorothy B. Pratt, Mrs. Catherine Holman. (the wife of John Holman,) Robert Maxwell, Benjamin Lake, Mrs. Anna Lake, Francis B Higg'ns, Mrs. Elizabeth A. Higgins, Drayton Nance, Mrs. Lucy W. Nance, Mrs. Elizabeth Carwile, Sarah C. Carwile, Caroline Farnandis Sarah Farnandis, Isabella Moore, Robert R. Nance, John Belton O'Neall, Mrs. Helen O'Neall, Sarah O'Neall, Rebecca O'Neall, Mrs Nancy Caldwell, (the wife of Chancellor Caldwell,) Mrs. Teresa Gillam, (the wife of Wm. Gillam,) Polly Goulding, Dorothy Coate, Susan Pope, Wm. P. Butler, Bathsheba Pope, Mrs. Abigail Caldwell, (the wife of John Caldwell, Esq.)

The church edifice was erected in 1832. The lot of land upon which the Church and the parsonage stand was the joint gift of Y. J. Harrington and John T. Young. The bell, (which is still in use,) was presented by the Hon. Kerr Boyce, of Charleston, S. C. The church edifice when first erected, did not have an open porch in front, as at present You entered at once from the outside into the audience room, which was furnished with benches, with backs consisting of two narrow boards far apart The old pulpit was a square-paneled structure, elevated about five feet from the floor, resting on small pillars, with a semi-circular projection, midway in front, in which the preacher stood. It had doors on each side with flights of steps leading up to them. When the preacher entered it and took his seat after closing the door behind him, he disappeared from view like a "Jack in a box." Just above the preacher's desk a remarkable contrivance called a sound-board was suspended from the ceiling by an iron rod. The architect must have modeled it after the pyramids of Egypt. This wonderful piece of architecture was intended to arrest the sound of the preacher's voice in its upward ascent and propel it forward. When a little boy, and sitting in the church, I would sometimes tremble as I contemplated the possibility of its falling on the preacher's head. The interior of the church, except the pulpit, was unpainted. At night it was lighted by candles, in tin sconces, hung upon nails driven into the walls and into the columns supporting the gallery, and two candles in tall brass candlesticks on the pulpit. Now and then as the light of the candles grew dim, the sexton, with a pair of snuffers in his hand, would go around and take careful sight on each candle, and then suddenly snuff it, parting the wick afterwards with the pointed end of the snuffers, to increase the light. The preacher was furnished with an extra pair of snuffers, which he could use "*ad libitum.*"

For several years after the erection of the church edifice no provision was made for heating it ; and the doors—even in winter—were seldom, if ever, closed during service. I suppose the good people of that time thought that it would be unfortunate to have the doors of the church closed in the face of any unregenerate wayfarer who might chance to come along and would otherwise come in. After a long service on a cold Sunday, the usual winter salutation of the inhabitants of St. Petersburg, "How is your nose" might have been appropriately used by the assembly. Let it not be supposed, however, that in the midst of what now appears to be circumstances of so much discomfort the people were indifferent. On the contrary they listened with reverence and attention to the message of the Gospel, and did not regard the inclemency of the weather so great a hindrance to their attendance at church as people do now.

The following is a list of the names of all the pastors who have served the church from its organization to the present time:

Rev. John M. Barnes, from September to December, 1831; Rev. N. W. Hodges, 1832-34 and in 1837 and part of 1838; Rev. Daniel Mangum, assisted by Rev. Elbert Lindsey, 1835-36; Rev. Thomas Frean, 1839-42, (in 1840 Rev. A. J. Chaplain was assistant pastor,) Rev. Samuel Gibson, 1843-45; Rev. John G. Landrum, 1846-47; Rev. M. C. Barnett, 1848-49; Rev. John J. Brantley, D. D., 1850-66; Rev. J. T. Zealy, 1867-68. Rev. Richard Furman, D. D, 1869; Rev. John Stout, 1870-73; Rev. F. W. Eason, from July 1874 to November, 1877; Rev. Luther Broadus from January, 1878 to October 26th, 1885. Of these only Dr. Brantley, J. T. Zealy, John Stout and F. W. Eason are known to be living. The present pastor, Rev. C. P. Scott, came to the church in January, 1886.

Rev. John M. Barnes, the first pastor, is described as a young man of attractive pulpit gifts, and an impressive preacher. Little is known of him after his short pastorate of the church. It is said that he removed to the West and became identified with another denomination.

Rev. Nicholas W. Hodges, was a native of Abbeville County, and at the time he became pastor of the church was quite a young man. He had received the best education the times afforded, was a graduate of the South Carolina College and of the Furman Theological Institution and was an instructive and effective preacher. He was greatly beloved and honored by all who knew him. He died at Greenwood, S. C., in 1842, and was buried at Mount Moriah Church, in Abbeville County. A monument over his grave was erected by the Mount Moriah and Newberry Churches.

In resolutions passed, just after his death by the Board of Trustees of Furman University, and adopted by the Baptist State Convention of South Carolina, he is referred to as a "conscientious, laborious, self-denying minister of Jesus Christ, exemplary for his singular devotedness to the interests of religion, and crowned by the providence of God with an uncommon measure of usefulness, he has gone down to the grave amidst the deep regrets of many who loved him for his work's sake."

Rev. Daniel Mangum, was a tall robust man of great physical endurance and a powerful voice, who preached with impassioned earnestness and zeal. By industrious application he improved a limited education, and became a successful preacher, sometimes rising to the heights of real eloquence.

His delivery was peculiar, when he became thoroughly aroused, he would suddenly fall into a style of speaking which somewhat resembled intoning. Perhaps it will be better described as a sort of ecclesiastical recitative. (For the benefit of my readers who may not understand musical terms, I will explain that recitative, is defined as "a species of singing approaching towards ordinary speaking."

These outbursts could not fail to astonish persons, not accustomed to them. But, to the people of his charges it would have seemed unnatural if he had left them out of his sermons. He was a man of excellent character, and great usefulness both as preacher and citizen He died in 1858, at the age of sixty-five, and was buried in the cemetery at Bush River Church, of which church he had been pastor for about thirty years.

Rev. Thomas Frean, was born in Tipperary County, Ireland, in 1793. He received a good education in his native country. In his youth he came to Charleston, S. C., on a visit to some of his relatives. During his sojourn in that city, the war between the United States and England, known as the "War of 1812," began; and he, with other British subjects was sent into the interior of the State to remain during hostilities. The result was that he did not return to Ireland.

In 1814, he was married to Miss Hannah Elmore, of Newberry District. After his marriage, he led for some years, a roving and rather unprofitable life—residing for a time in Charleston, then in Newberry, going from Newberry to Spartanburg; where he remained until (probably) about 1825, when he came back to Newberry. Shortly after his return to Newberry from Spartanburg, he united with the Methodist Church, and became a "local preacher."

In 1835, his religious views having undergone a change, he united with the Baptist Church, at Newberry, and was soon after licensed to preach; and subsequently, (1837), ordained to the full work of the ministry.

Mr. Frean, like many of his countrymen, was full of impulse and enthusiasm. He had an imaginative turn of mind and a poetic fancy. He made occasional contributions of poetry to the newspapers. His sermons evinced considerable study and culture. Owing to an excitable temperament and a very perceptible brogue, his delivery was rather hurried and at times somewhat indistinct.

Having resigned his pastorate at Newberry, in 1842, he retired from active ministerial work, and removed to Columbia, S. C., where he filled at different times, the offices of Surveyor General, and Deputy Treasurer of the State. He died April 7th, 1860, and was buried in the "Quaker Cemetery" near Langford's Mill in Newberry County.

Rev. Samuel Gibson was born in England. In 1815, having determined to seek his fortune in America, he landed, with his family, in Charleston, S. C., friendless and almost penniless; his means having been well-nigh exhausted by the expense of the voyage.

The day after he landed, being Sunday, he repaired to a Baptist Church in the City. When the minister had read a hymn the leader of the music failed to pitch the tune, though he made several attempts. The minister also, it seems, was unable to sing the hymn, and things were getting in an embarrassing condition, when Gibson pitched the tune and, with the aid of his wife and sister-in-law, sang the hymn through without the help of another voice.

This circumstance introduced him at once to the notice of his brethren, who learning that he was a blacksmith, employed him to make some repairs about the church bell, for which they paid him ten dollars, though he insisted on not taking more than two. After a short stay in Charleston he determined to seek a home in the up-country, and settled in a rather wild, thinly populated region in Greenville County, where the Gospel had seldom been heard. The

Sabbath was generally disregarded, and the vices incident to society in a rude state went unrebuked.

This condition of things first made a deep impression on his wife. "The harvest," she said, "is ready and there is no one to reap it," and Gibson began to preach, moved, as he always declared, by her entreaties.

Through the influence of his wife he applied himself assiduously to study, and, having been endowed by nature with a strong intellect, he became one of the most effective and powerful preachers of his day.

The following extract is from Griffith's *Life of John G. Landrum*, a book which I have freely used, in the preparation of this and some other sketches: "Well does the author remember, when a little boy, to have gazed with childish wonder, mingled with awe, upon a little red-faced old man, with white hair, scrupulously neat in his dress and peculiarly solemn in his appearance, seated in a sulky and driving a snow-white horse rapidly toward a neighboring church; and well does he remember how that wonder increased and that awe deepened, when he noted the death-like stillness that reigned in the congregation as he ascended the pulpit, and saw the trembling of strong men and gay women under the power of his soul-stirring words."

The foregoing pen-picture of Mr. Gibson—even to the sulky and horse—is a very life-like and familiar one to the present writer, who still remembers with gratitude and pleasure his earnest preaching and his entertaining and instructive conversation, in the family circle, especially when he told the story of his early struggles, both in England and in this country.

During his three years service in Newberry, Mr. Gibson, only visited the Church once a month, riding from his home in Greenville County—a distance of more than sixty miles—to meet his appointments. He died several years ago, at an advanced age, and was buried at Milford Baptist Church, (Greenville County,) within a few feet of the pulpit which he had so often occupied.

Rev. John G. Landrum, like his predecessor, (Mr. Gibson,) rode once a month from his home in Spartanburg County, to fill his appointments for preaching. He, as well as Mr. Gibson, preached both on Saturday and Sunday during each visit.

Mr. Landrum was born in Tennessee on the 22d of October, 1810. With a view to the improvement of his health, he came in 1828 to Union County, S. C., intending to remain one year. He did not return to Tennessee, and his intended visit of one year, was converted into a residence of more than half a century in South Carolina.

He was licensed to preach in 1829, and ordained to the full work of the ministry in 1831.

His earliest ministerial work was probably done in Union County, but his life work may be said to have done in Spartanburg County.

He was the first pastor of the Baptist Church in the village (now city) of Spartanburg, and was the pastor of Mount Zion, and probably one other Church in Spartanburg County, for fifty years.

He was married in 1836 to Miss Elizabeth Montgomery of Spartanburg, who died in 1857. He was again married in 1859 to Miss Nancy Miller Earle, also of Spartanburg, who died in 1863. Mr. Landrum died in 1882. He had risen to a high position of honor and usefulness, both as minister and citizen.

"The fact that the announcement of his preaching would draw a large congregation anywhere; the fact that he preached to large congregations at the same places through a long course of years; the fact that, during his ministry he baptized five thousand converts, and the further fact that his Churches would not have surrendered him as leader for any other man, bear witness that your deceased pastor was a 'Prince and a great man.' It would have been impossible for him to have gained and maintained such a hold upon the minds of others in the absence of superior intellectual powers. These he manifestly possessed. * * * * He was a hard student and a great searcher for truth. * * * Yet intellect and studiousness are not the only elements of a minister's acceptableness. Quite as important is the loving heart. * * * How his great heart yearned for the good of others! Compassion for the guilty and the perishing, and tender regard for the image of Christ, even when seen amid the evidence of weakness and error, gave its hue to his ministrations, and this serious and earnest tone of his spirit enabled him to steer clear of levity and acrimony. * * * For myself I can say, that not the least charming feature in John G. Landrum was his spirit of deep devotion. His prayers were in no sort what have been called preaching prayers, and yet had he done nothing but pray in public, he would have have done more good than many preachers."*

The few remaining members of Mr. Landrum's congregation at Newberry still warmly cherish the memory of his faithful and affectionate ministrations among them.

Rev. M. C. Barnett also came from Spartanburg County. He was the first pastor for many years, who had no other charge, and who preached to this Church every Sunday. But as he resided four or five miles from the town, and taught school near his residence, he had very little time for

---

* From Memorial Discourse, by Rev. J. C. Furman, D. D.

pastoral visiting. His sermons were illustrated and enforced, to a great extent, by appropriate quotations from the Scriptures, which his remarkable memory enabled him to repeat with minute accuracy. His delivery, though somewhat hurried, was animated and attractive.

"He was no revivalist, no exhorter, and hardly ever attempted to take the lead in a protracted meeting. He preached the Gospel truth as he understood it, in the most pointed and eloquent language he could command, and then took his seat, having said more in thirty minutes than most men can say in an hour."*

He was modest and diffident, and greatly underrated his own powers. He was a good preacher, a lover of books, and an interesting conversationist. His character was irreproachable and singularly free from angularities. He died in Spartanburg County in 1872.

Rev. Richard Furman, D. D., was born on the 9th of November, 1816, at Gillisonville, Beaufort County, S. C. He was the son of Rev. Samuel Furman, D. D., and Eliza Ann (Scrimzeour) Furman, and the grandson of Rev. Richard Furman, D. D., of Charleston, S C., who was distinguished for his eloquence and patriotism during the American Revolution.

He received his literary education from his father, and studied theology in the Furman Theological Institution, then located at High Hills, of Santee, S. C.

He was married on the 21st of April, 1840, to Miss Mary Marshall McIver, the daughter of Dr. John K. McIver, of Society Hill, S. C., and died at Fort Worth, Texas, on the 1st of October, 1886.

Dr. Furman began to preach before he reached his majority. His first pastorate, upon which he entered at the

---

* Griffith's Life of Landrum.

close of 1838 or early in 1839, was at Cheraw, S. C. He was afterwards pastor at New Berne, N. C., Society Hill, Greenville, Sumter, Newberry and Ridge Spring, S. C. His pastorate at Newberry was cut short by his shattered health. But notwithstanding his short stay, his presence and his preaching proved a rich and lasting blessing to the Church and the community.

Rev. W. M. Grier, D D., President of Erskine College, Due West, S. C., wrote as follows in the *Associate Reformed Presbyterian*, of which he is editor, shortly after Dr. F.'s death: " Although he (Dr. Furman) was practically relieved from the ministry on account of failing health, for twenty years before his death, yet we remember him well as a preacher, though we never heard him preach but one sermon.

"In August, 1860, he preached the Baccalaureate Sermon before the graduating class of Erskine College. The writer was a member of that class. So striking and impressive was the discourse, and presented with such unwonted force and unction, that it burned into our very hearts. To-day we can, not only recall the text, but can repeat parts of that sermon *verbatim*. * * * *. * * * *

" We are not surprised at the appreciative notices which we find in our Baptist exchanges. This man of God, an eloquent Apollos, was worthy of them all. We beg the privilege of this humble tribute to his memory."

The following brief but judicious notice of Dr. Furman is from the pen of the Rev. John A. Broadus, D D. :

" Dr. Furman showed how talent and devoted labor can achieve marked usefulness, notwithstanding feeble health and personal disadvantages. He was a deeply earnest Christian, a model of unselfishness and delicate consideration for others, and supreme desire to do good. When his feeble frame was racked with pain, or perhaps his sensitive spirit stung by some unkindness, he could keep it all to himself, and his very suffering would kindle his soul into more ardent zeal in preaching the Gospel he loved, and trying to honor the Saviour on whom he relied. While scarcely remarkable for originality of thought, he made the familiar truths of the Gospel attractive by his deep personal experience and profound reflection, and by his singular clearness and beauty of style. The poetical gifts which produced a volume of pleasing verse,* showed themselves also in his harmonious prose. Lifelong cultivation of style, with refined taste, and then clear thinking, and the passionate feeling which instinctively strives after harmonious expression, enabled him to produce sentences that were quite inelaborate, but thoroughly symmetrical, and melodious in every movement. When he was pastor in Greenville, S. C., we used sometimes to notice that his extemporized addresses might have been printed, paragraph after paragraph, without needing the alteration of a word. Yet he was in no sense a phrasemonger, nor did he ever seem to be thinking about his language—he was thinking of the Gospel, the soul, the Saviour."

---

*" The Pleasures of Piety, and Other Poems," published in 1859.

NOTE—A Biographical Sketch of Rev. Luther Broadus, will be found in Chapter XVII.

CHAPTER VIII.

METHODIST EPISCOPAL CHURCH—ORGANIZATION AND HISTORY—REV. ANGUS M'PHERSON—REV. GEORGE W. MOORE—REV. SAMUEL DUNWOODY—REV. CHARLES S. WALKER—REV. SAMUEL TOWNSEND—REV. JOHN R. PICKETT—REV. W. A. M'SWAIN—REV. A. W. WALKER—REV. CORNELIUS M'LEOD—REV. BOND ENGLISH.

THE Newberry Methodist Episcopal Church was organized soon after the Baptist Church (probably in 1833.) The Church edifice was erected within a short time after the organization. When first built, it was very similar in its construction and appointments to the Baptist Church edifice. The pulpit was not elevated quite so high, and it had an altar, surrounded by a balustrade in front of it.

I regret that I have not been able, after diligent inquiry, to find the early records of this Church. Nor have I been so fortunate as to find any one who can furnish accurate information as to the precise date of its organization, or the names, in full, of its original members. There seems to be no doubt that among those who united in the organization were : Philip Schoppert and his wife, Mrs Polly Schoppert, Mrs. Schoppert, the mother of Philip Schoppert ; Martha Turner, Mrs. Sarah Lorick, (now Mrs. Sarah Pope,) Mrs. Precious Shell, (and probably Mrs. Sarah Cheshire,) Josiah Bishop and his wife, Thomas Pratt, Jr., and Daniel Boozer. Besides these none others can be remembered. It is generally understood that there were but few members at first, but there is abundant evidence of their energy and pious devotion, in the fact that they so soon erected a house of worship. The membership increased rapidly, and the Church soon occupied, and has continued to occupy, a prominent place among her sister Churches.

For more than twenty years after its organization the Church was embraced in the Newberry Circuit, and was visited semi-monthly by the ministers who rode that Circuit. From January, 1854, it was set apart as a "Station," and from that time has enjoyed the entire services of its different pastors.

I acknowledge my indebtedness to Dr. Shipp's "*History of Methodism in South Carolina,*" for most of the material used in the following sketches of some of the faithful and laborious men who preached to the Church during the first twenty years of its existence:

Rev. Angus McPherson was born in Cumberland County, N. C., May 10th, 1802, and entered the ministry in 1826. He rode the Newberry Circuit in 1836. His deportment was serious, his manners modest and retiring. He made it a matter of conscience never to disappoint a congregation, and his last sermon was preached while in the custody of the King of terrors. He was quite useful as a minister, and everywhere he labored was much esteemed by the people. He died at the house of Dr. James Kilgore, near Newberry, on the 4th of November, 1836, with the words "sweet heaven" on his lips.

Rev. George W. Moore was born in Charleston, S. C., on the 27th of September, 1799. He entered the ministry in 1825, and preached in Newberry in 1840-41. He was a faithful, efficient and successful preacher, never shunning to declare the counsel of God, nor to assert his uncompromising opposition to sin in whatever form developed, or in whatever circle practiced. He was one of the first to enter the mission field among the colored people, and his last days were spent in special attention to that class at Spartanburg. The reward of faithfully preaching the Gospel to the poor is his. I cannot ascertain the day of his death, which took place some time after 1863, at a camp-ground in Anderson County. He died in the pulpit, at the close of his first prayer, in the afternoon service, on Sunday, with the Bible and Hymn-Book for his pillow. His last words were words of prayer. His last act an act of worship.

Rev. Samuel Dunwoody was born in Chester County, Pennsylvania, on the 3d of August, 1780. He entered the ministry in 1806, and preached at Newberry in 1844-45. He was placed upon the superannuated list in 1846, after a term of nearly forty years' service as a minister of the gospel.

As a preacher he was original, both as to matter and manner, and his sermons were masterpieces of their kind ; as a student he was eminently a man of one book—the Bible ; as a Christian his life and example were irreproachable. He died July the 8th, 1854. He was a man of very peculiar and eccentric manners and habits. He would often appear to be unconscious of everything going on around him, so absorbed was he in his own thoughts.

One Sunday afternoon he came riding on horseback along the street which passed by my father's house. My father and myself were sitting facing each other, each with an arm resting on the front balustrade of the piazza which stood immediately on the street. A shower of rain had recently fallen and a considerable pool of water had collected near the entrance of the piazza. Mr. Dunwoody had his eyes cast down upon the pommel of the saddle, and held the reins loosely in his hands. His horse, which must have been quite thirsty, came to the pool of water and began to drink from it. While the horse was drinking I could without rising from my seat, have caught Mr D by the arm or lifted his hat from his head with my hand, yet he evidently did not see me, or my father, or the house.

One Sabbath evening after he had preached his sermon in the Church at Newberry, he began to read one of Charles Wesley's hymns, of which the following is the concluding stanza:

    Come back! this is the way!
      Come back! and walk herein!
    O may I hearken and obey,
    And shun the paths of sin!

After reading the first stanza of the hymn his voice descended into a low monotone which was not varied, until he reached the last stanza, where he paused, and appeared for a few moments to be lost in thought. Just at this time a gentleman in the congregation arose from his seat to leave the Church, and had proceeded a short distance towards the door, when Mr. Dunwoody suddenly looked up, and exclaimed: "Come back!" and then paused again. The gentleman supposing that Mr. D. had addressed him turned round and in great astonishment waited to hear what was to come next. Presently Mr. D., in a low, quiet tone continued the reading of the stanza: " this is the way! come back! and walk herein, &c;" whereupon the gentleman walked out.

An almost endless number of stories have been told about the odd things he did and said. Many of these stories originated before he was born, and many more doubtless have very little foundation in fact. It is the common lot, however, of all eccentric people to have many things charged against them of which they are innocent.

Rev. Charles S. Walker was born in Charleston, S. C., on

the 22d of January, 1815, entered the ministry in 1834, and rode the Newberry Circuit in 1853. He was a man of stern integrity, sound judgment and high moral courage, and to these qualities may be added great simplicity and purity of character. He died at Spartanburg, S. C., on the 18th of January, 1857.

Rev. Samuel Townsend was born in Marlboro district, S. C., on the 29th of October, 1814, entered the ministry in 1836 and rode the Newberry Circuit in 1854. He was an earnest, sound and practical preacher. In his regular itinerant work he acquired a ruling desire for the circulation of books, and while acting as agent for the Tract Society, he laid the foundation of what afterwards became an extensive book store in Columbia, S C. He was on his way from the North, where he had been on business, when he was arrested by disease, and died in Philadelphia July 31st, 1865.

The following is believed to be (nearly, if not altogether), a complete list of the names of the ministers—though not in regular order of succession—who have served the Church since 1854: John R. Pickett, W. A. McSwain, A. W. Walker, Cornelius McLeod, Marcus McKibben, Bond English, Emory Watson, Thos. J. Clyde, Jno. W. Humbert, Samuel W. Black, O A. Darby, Jno. A. Mood, R. P. Franks, Manning Brown, C. H. Pritchard, A. M. Chreitzberg, Jno. B. Campbell, R. D. Smart, A J. Clifton, H. F. Chreitzberg, J. L. Stokes, and at this time (1880) W. S. Wightman. Of these, John R. Pickett, W. A. McSwain, Cornelius McLeod, A W. Walker, and Bond English, are dead.

In giving some account of these deceased pastors, I am again indebted to Dr. Shipp's History, for valuable information concerning them.

Rev. Jno. R. Picket was born in Fairfield District. S. C., on the 2d of April, 1814. He entered the ministry in 1835 and was pastor of Newberry in 1854. He had quick perceptive and analytic powers of mind, was not wanting in imagination, and aspired after a high degree of scholarship. In the early part of his ministry he carried about with him a huge Polyglot Bible, in a tin case, and made it his daily companion. He was a great reader, especially of periodical literature, and "knew something about everything, and a great deal about some things." His manner in the pulpit was self-possessed and deliberate, but as he proceeded in his sermon he generally warmed with his subject, and his voice assumed a depth and fullness of volume which was wonderful. He was one of the sweetest singers of his day, and often used this talent most efficiently in his ministry. Following a custom which for a long time prevailed among Methodist ministers, he would frequently introduce the services by singing a solo. He had the simplicity of a child, and was remarkable for a large-hearted charity. He died in 1870.

Rev. William A. McSwain was born in Montgomery (now Stanley) County, N. C., November the 5th, 1814. He was licensed to preach May 21st, 1836, and was pastor in Newberry in 1855-56. He was a man of studious habits, a diligent reader, and a pious, eloquent and able minister. He was respected and beloved by all denominations of Christians and all classes of people. He was amiable and pleasant in disposition, and polite and courteous in manner He died in Laurens, S. C., probably in 1866, from injuries received by leaping from his buggy to escape from a frightened and unruly horse.

Rev. Alexander W. Walker was born in Charleston, S. C., on the 22d of January, 1815, and was admitted with his twin-brother, Charles S., into the South Carolina Conference in February, 1834, and appointed to Laurensville Circuit. He was pastor at Newberry in 1857, and died in 1870. He was distinguished for the purity, truthfulness and sincerity of his character, and for the kindness and generosity of his heart. He was modest in the expression of his opinions, but was courageous in the support of his convictions of duty. Of an affectionate and loving disposition, he won the hearts of all who knew him, and dying left behind him a name which "is as ointment poured forth."

Rev. Cornelius McLeod, was a native of North Carolina, and entered the South Carolina Conference in 1837. He spent the year 1858, at Newberry. In 1866, he was placed upon the superannuated list, and died probably in that year, in Richland County, S. C.

He was a diligent student, and without the assistance of an instructor, learned several of the ancient and modern languages. Devoted to books and having a retentive memory he acquired a large fund of knowledge. He was a successful preacher, and being remarkably amiable in disposition, won without effort the affections of those with whom he associated.

Rev. Bond English, was born in Kershaw District, S. C., January 31, 1797. He was for forty-six years an earnest, successful and honored minister of the Gospel. His talents commanded for him the highest regard of his brethren, who intrusted him with many positions of responsibility. He was pastor at Newberry during the troublous period of the recent war, (probably in 1863-64). He was an ardent patriot, and believed firmly in the justice of the cause of the Southern Confederacy. The simplicity and directness of some expressions he used in his prayers, such as : "That our enemies might be taught to let us alone and go about their own business," will be remembered by many who attended the Wednesday afternoon union prayer-meeting of all denominations held in Newberry during those stormy days. He died at his residence near Sumter, S. C., March the 4th, 1868.

CHAPTER IX.

AVELEIGH (PRESBYTERIAN) CHURCH – INTERESTING LETTER OF CHANCELLOR JOHNSTONE'S—ORGANIZATION AND HISTORY OF THE CHURCH—REV. R. C. KETCHUM—REV. JOHN M'KITTRICK—REV. E. F. HYDE—REV. A. D. MONTGOMERY—REV. E. H. BUIST.

FOR many years I supposed that the Baptist, was the first Church organized in the town of Newberry. I find, however, from a letter written by Chancellor Job Johnstone, and published in "*Howe's History of the Presbyterian Church in South Carolina*," that he (the Chancellor) speaks of a Presbyterian Church organization which existed in Newberry previous to that of the Baptist Church; but which had—as he expresses it, probably fallen through.

The following extract from the Chancellor's letter gives, not only an account of the Presbyterian Church organization just referred to, but also an account of the first movements toward the organization of Aveleigh Church.

"My former wife informed me that there was formerly, as far back perhaps as 1822, a Presbyterian Church organized in this village. I remember there was a meeting of Presbytery held at that time in the old Male Academy then taught by the Rev. Joseph Y. Alexander, and that he received ordination at its hands. And I find by a memorial in my family Bible that he baptized my son, Silas, at my wife's request, on the 18th of June, 1822, at my house, being the first baptism by that minister. Yet so stupid was I that I never for a moment suspected, until years afterwards that there had been a Presbyterian organization at Newberry.

"Mrs. Johnstone when she gave me the information stated that her sister, Mrs. Harrington, and her sister-in-law, Mrs. Dr Johnston, had all been members, and that Mr. Thomas Boyd, of Bush River, had been an elder. All that I had noticed was that there was regular preaching in the Courthouse, and that there was less of shooting and kite flying in the streets on Sabbath than formerly.

"On the removal of that excellent man, Mr. Alexander, to Georgia, I suppose the Church fell through; for on the 15th of July, 1832 I find that my wife had three of our children baptized at Head Spring (Seceder) Church, by the late Samuel P. Pressley, subsequently a Professor in Athens College, Georgia, but at that time pastor of Cannon Creek, Prosperity, Indian Creek and Head Spring Churches. By the three children being baptized at the same time, I suppose that was the day, she herself joined Mr. Pressley's Church. In 1833 or '34, Mr. Pressley went to Georgia, by which his Churches were for a time left vacant. He was a very liberal man, and under his administration his churches relaxed the rigor of close Communion. All the Presbyterians in the neighborhood united with him, and in the course of the few years he was minister here, his Churches had more than doubled the number of their communicants. On the 14th of September, 1834, I united with the Church at Cannon Creek, at a Communion administered by the Rev. Mr. Boyce of Fairfield, acting as temporary supply. I stated at the time, that on the first convenient opportunity I should unite with the Presbyterian Church and that I should exercise the privilege of open Communion.

"On the 30th of November, 1834, Mr. Pressley, in a farewell visit to his Churches, administered the sacrament of the Lord's Supper at Head Spring I remember there was an eclipse of the sun during the Communion. Mr. P. spent a night at my house during the meeting. He was then about to transfer his connexion to the Presbyterian Church, and we had a consultation about the prospects of a Presbyterian Church here. On Monday after the Communion at Head Spring, being December the 1st, 1834, and sale day, I drew a subscription paper for the building of the Church subsequently called 'Aveleigh.' The necessary amount was soon subscribed. Mr. Robert Boyce conveyed five acres of land as a lot for the Church to be built on, at Hunt's Cross Roads, one mile and a half from the village of Newberry."

Aveleigh Church was organized May the 30th, 1835, with thirty-one members, by the Rev. Moses Waddell, D. D., and Rev. Samuel B. Lewers. The Church edifice was completed very soon afterwards.

The following is a copy of the congregational covenant entered into by the Church on the day it was organized, and the names of thirty-one persons who sighed the same:

"Believing that the true God is justly entitled to the reverential and social worship of all intelligent creatures, and that their social homage is conducive in the highest degree both to the present comfort and future happiness of mankind, we, the undersigned, inhabitants of Newberry District, S. C., residing near the Court House, have felt a strong desire to associate and unite ourselves together in the capacity and relation of a religious society for the purpose of improving ourselves in the knowledge and practice of our duty to God and man, and of exciting ourselves to love and to good works, and believing that the doctrine and discipline approved and adopted by the General Assembly of the Presbyterian Church in the United States of America, as set forth in their Confession of Faith, conforms most nearly to the system of faith and order taught in the Gospel, we profess our desire and design to unite with and place ourselves under the pastoral care and direction of that ecclesiastical body, so long as they adhere to that Confession. In testimony of which we have voluntarily attached our names to the above, this 30th day of May, 1835.

(Signed) "John Garmany, Jr., David Griffith, Andrew Spence, Sen., Joseph Y. Hunter, David Clary, Matilda W. Saxon, Eliza M. Johnston, Sarah Boozer, Margarett Piester, Sarah B. Caldwell, Mary Welch, Rachel Keller, Sarah Glasgow, Sarah K. Foote, Elizabeth Clary, Mary Garmany, Maria Garmany, Isabella Foote, Elizabeth Gillam, Catharine Johnston, Isabella H. Chambers, Sarah Belton, Mary Marrs, Barbara Boozer, Williams Welch, Isaac Keller, Mary Griffith, Job Johnston, Alexander Chambers, Thomas J. Brown, Mary Sligh."

The Church received into its membership on the day it was organized "John Garmany, Sen., and on the next day John Senn, Sen., Mary Senn, and Harriet Coppeck on examination."

Isaac Keller and Alexander Chambers were elected Ruling Elders on the day the Church was organized, and ordained on the day following. Chancellor Job Johnstone and Dr. Geo. W. Glenn were ordained Elders on the second Sabbath in March, 1839.

I quote again from Dr. Howe's history: " At length it became apparent, says Chancellor Johnstone, that one grand obstacle that stood in the way of the prosperity of this Church, was its location. Being situated a mile-and-a-half from town, it was but seldom that any of the town people found it convenient to attend ; and yet, inasmuch as it was located there with a view to secure their attendance, the country people regarded it as a town Church, and therefore, did not care to attend it. This is not the only instance in which a Church has been located with the hope of securing the attendance of both the town and the country people, and the result has been that it failed to secure the attendance of either. It was determined, therefore, that an effort should be made to secure, by subscription, an amount sufficient to erect a new Church edifice in the town of Newberry.

"That object was at length attained. The old house and the lot were sold; and a new house, small but neat and commodious, was erected on a lot generously given for that purpose, by Mr. E. Y. McMorries, in the town of Newberry. The new Church edifice was dedicated to the worship of God on the 17th day of December, in the year 1852. The Church still retained the name of Aveleigh. After its removal, some of the country members found it more convenient to attend worship at Gilder's Creek, and Mt. Bethel Churches. The Church then numbered only about twenty members.

"Signs of greater prosperity were soon apparent. * * * * * * At almost every Communion meeting there were additions, more or less, to the Church."

During the year 1835, services were held occasionally by Dr. Waddell, Mr. Lewers, and Rev. E. Holt, Agent Board of Foreign Missions, Rev. Joseph Johnson supplied the Church, once a month, during part of the year 1836. In the latter part of that year and during 1837, Rev. Isaac Waddell, James Lewers and Richard C. Ketchum occasionally preached to the congregation.

On Saturday, before the 4th Sabbath in January, 1838, Rev. R. C. Ketchum was installed pastor. Mr. Ketchum resigned in the latter part of 1839.

The following is a list of the names of ministers who have officiated as pastors, (with the date of the installation of each,) since the resignation of Mr. Ketchum : Rev. John McKitterick, August 29th, 1840 ; Rev. E. F. Hyde, October 26th, 1845 ; Rev. W. B. Telfourd, June 8th, 1850 ; Rev A. D. Montgomery, June 29th, 1856 ; Rev. E. H. Buist, June 6th, 1862 ; Rev. R. A. Mickle, November 30th, 1866 ; Rev. R. A Fair, October, 1874. Of these, only Rev. W. B. Telfourd, Rev. R. A. Mickle and Rev. R. A. Fair are now living.

The present pastor, Rev. J. S. Cozby, took charge of the Church in 1886.

The Rev. R. C. Ketchum, was born in Augusta, Ga., in 1833, and died in the 63d year of his age. " Having graduated in the University of Georgia in 1833, he entered the Theological Seminary, in Columbia, S. C., in the same year, and finished his course there in 1836 His ministerial life was spent in Newberry and Hamburg, S. C., and Atlanta, Ga. His naturally good mind had received careful and continued culture 'till he had attained an accuracy of scholarship that but few reach. Added to his fondness for, and proficiency in the natural sciences, he had so mastered the Greek language as to read it with almost the familiarity of his native tongue. But excellent as were his intellectual attainments, they were excelled by the goodness of his heart, * * * * * * * Perhaps the most marked and admirable trait of his character was his unaffected humility.

* * * * * * * *

"He was prompt and punctual in the discharge of all his ministerial duties, however onerous they may have been As a preacher he was sound in doctrine, judicious in the interpretation of the Word, clear and instructive in his presentation of the truth. He lived a life of calm abiding trust in God; and his death was in perfect harmony with his life."*

As my father's family was connected with another Christian denomination, I did not often hear Mr Ketchum preach, but I retain most pleasant recollections of the man. His manners and social qualities were very attractive. He was very much interested in young people, and entered heartily with them into all their innocent and rational amusements and recreations. He was brim-full of animation and good nature, and carried sunshine with him wherever he went. And while some staid and undemonstrative people would sometimes give their heads an ominous shake when they saw him in his more gleeful moods, the truth was that he never sacrificed the dignity of his character as a minister of the Gospel. He never failed to reprove any young man who might swear an oath or be guilty of any other misconduct in his presence; and this he did in such a judicious, gentle and kindly manner as to secure the respect of the person reproved.

I should here present some notice of Rev. John McKitterick, but regret that I am unable to do so. My personal knowledge of him was quite limited, and I have failed, after diligent inquiry, to procure any records of his life.

"Rev. Ezekiel Foster Hyde was born near Sincoe, Province of Ontario, Dominion of Canada, on the 1st day of May, 1814. His father, Sherman Hyde, was born in the State of Connecticut, a descendant of an English family that settled in Connecticut in Colonial times. * * * *
E F. Hyde, who was the third son, went to the State of New York in the fall of 1832, and continued to reside there until 1841, when he came to South Carolina. During his

---

* Memorial Volume of the Semi-Centennial of the Theological Seminary, at Columbia, S. C., 1884.

residence in the State of New York he became a member of the Presbyterian Church : his religious training had been in the Church of England, or the Episcopal Church of Canada. When about twenty-one years of age, he became impressed with a sense of duty to prepare for entrance upon the work of preaching the Gospel.

"His education had only been that of the primary schools of Canada. He prosecuted the studies preparatory to admission into College, under the training of one Capt. Richard Ashley, who was a graduate of the West Point Military Academy. He graduated at Union College in the class of 1841. In October, 1841, he entered the Theological Seminary at Columbia, S. C., and completed the course of studies in that institution in the class of 1844. He was licensed to preach the Gospel by the Charleston Presbytery at the Spring session of 1844 at Columbia S. C. In the fall of 1844 he was called to be pastor of Aveleigh, Smyrna and Gilder's Creek Churches, in Newberry County. His connection as licentiate having been transferred to the South Carolina Presbytery, he was ordained at the Spring (1845) session of the Presbytery at Gilder's Creek Church, '*sine titulo*,' and was installed pastor of the above Churches by action of Presbytery, Fall session of 1845."*

Mr. Hyde remained in Newberry about four years, and went from Newberry to Laurens County. In 1852 he removed to Mississippi where he remained four years and then returned to South Carolina. He died on the 22d of October, 1884. He was married in 1845 to Miss C. A. Hammond (a sister of Governor Hammond of S.C.) who died about three years afterwards. In 1850 he was married to Miss N.

---

*Unfinished Autobiographical Sketch found among Mr. Hyde's papers after his death.

A. Hunter of Laurens, who survives him. "For more than fifty years he was a professor of the religion of Jesus Christ, and for more than forty years a preacher of the Gospel, and yet never was there a blight on his Christian character. He was modest, gentle and unassuming in society and among his brethren. He was an earnest and instructive preacher, and in conversation was especially entertaining. His faith was strong and his end was peace."*

When Mr. Hyde came to Newberry, I was a young man just entering upon the battle of life. I early made his acquaintance and found in him a warm, sympathizing friend. I met him at Newberry only a few months before his death. It had been many years since I had seen him before. Notwithstanding the enfeebled state of his health, which could be plainly discerned by his wasted figure, he uttered no complaint, and exhibited only his old time cheerfulness and cordiality.

Rev. Archibald D. Montgomery, was born in Caswell County, N. C., on the 22d of May 1791, and died at Lexington, N. C., on the 21st of April, 1870.

He was the son of James and Rebecca Montgomery. His mother whose maiden name was Rebecca Davis, was a Virginia lady of unusual personal attractions and mental gifts. His father who was a farmer, was a useful citizen, and an exemplary Christian.

Mr. Montgomery entered the ministry in 1820. He was married on the 11th of December, 1822, to Miss Eliza Lewis, (eldest daughter of John and Lucy (Macklin) Lewis of Mecklenburg, Va.,) who was eminently qualified by her intelligence, energy, piety and amiable disposition for a ministers' wife.

---

* Minutes South Carolina Presbytery, 1885.

His ministerial life was spent chiefly in North Carolina, until 1852, when he removed to Abbeville, S. C., and became the pastor of the Long Cane Church near that town. After remaining there four years, he received a call from Aveleigh Church, Newberry, and was installed as its pastor on the 29th of January, 1856. He continued in this office until September, 1861. After resigning his charge at Newberry, he preached from time to time during the remaining years of the recent war, to the Church at Washington, Ga., and in May, 1868, being then in the seventy-second year of his age, he was invited to become pastor of that church, but his age and feeble health forbade his acceptance of the call.

I have gathered the foregoing facts in the life of Mr. Montgomery, from a memorial notice of him published in the *North Carolina Presbyterian* shortly after his death, which concludes as follows: "The few remaining years of his life were spent with his children, mostly in North Carolina. His wife died January the 14th, 1869. He survived her only a little more than one year. His means which were never limited to his salaries, enabled him to dispense a generous hospitality, heightened by those graces of head and heart which adorned the character of his pious companion. And he especially delighted to entertain his brethren of the ministry. While the social circle could boast of no more genial companion, he testified in behalf of the cause of his Master, by a fearless denunciation of sin in high places and the fashionable amusements of the day.

"In all the relations of life he was warmly demonstrative, and though candid and outspoken, he never failed to gather around him a circle of devoted friends.

"His preaching, says a worthy and intelligent elder *of* one of his churches, 'was always evangelical, faithful and affectionate, but his best efforts were those delivered upon the spur of the occasion, when he seemed to be inspired with love of immortal souls, and the weight of his own responsibility as a messenger of salvation.'"

Rev. Edward Henry Buist was born in Charleston, S. C., on the 5th of October, 1837. He was the son of Rev. Arthur Buist, and the grandson of Rev. George Buist, D. D., the first pastor of the Scotch Church in Charleston, S. C., and a minister of much celebrity in the Presbyterian Church.

Mr. Buist was graduated from the South Carolina College in 1858, taking the first honor in a large and talented class, and studied Theology in the Presbyterian Theological Seminary at Columbia, S. C.

Aveleigh Church was his first charge. While still a licentiate he began to supply the pulpit in 1861, and was ordained at Newberry in June, 1862.

He was married in 1864 to Miss Carrie Sebring of Charleston, S. C., (formerly of Tarrytown, N. Y.) He left Newberry in the summer of 1865, and went to Tarrytown where he remained for sometime. He became the pastor of the church at Cheraw, S. C., in 1869. His pastorate at Cheraw continued until his death which occurred on the 11th of September, 1882.

By reason of his talents, his scholarly attainments and his social qualities, Mr. Buist should be ranked among the foremost preachers who have filled the different pulpits in Newberry in the past. I prefer that those who were more intimately associated with him than myself should speak of his virtues, and it affords me pleasure to be permitted to present the following extract from a memorial adopted by the Session and read before the congregation of Aveleigh Church, on the 8th of October, 1882 :

" Rev. Edward Henry Buist was taken from us so suddenly, that it is hard for us as yet to appreciate the void his death has occasioned. It is proper that Aveleigh Church should offer some testimonial to his memory, as it was here that his ministerial life began. This was his first charge. While still a licentiate, he supplied this pulpit, beginning June, 1861, and it was not until June, 1862 that he was ordained pastor. It shows his great conscientiousness that he hesitated twelve months before he could be induced to accept the pastorate. This relation though practically severed the year previous—was not formally dissolved until the 15th of February, 1866—so great was the desire of this congregation to retain his services. His life during these years of civil strife is closely interwoven with that of the Church.

"Although young, his character even then had been sufficiently developed to enable us to give a proper estimate of it, and to judge from the fruits of his efforts at that time, what influence he must exert when his faculties were fully matured. He was scholarly in his manner, and in all his ways—as a pulpit orator and as a debator. He was a fine linguist, especially proficient in the ancient languages; learned in ecclesiastical history; a master of logic and a profound student of metaphysics. His natural talent for the last science and his love of it, tinctured his whole line of thought and mode of expression. He greatly resembled in this respect his beloved teacher, Thornwell, with whom he had also in common that thorough earnestness which carries conviction to the mind of the hearer.

"As to his moral qualities, what mainly distinguished him was his conscientiousness, his charity both in opinion and action, and his exceeding cheerfulness which so thoroughly imbued him, that he imparted it to all with whom he came in contact; it divested his religion of all gloom—although he was orthodox—invested it with a warmth to which may be ascribed a great share of his success.

"In the wider sphere of the Presbyterian Church as in the pulpit, he was distinguished by his clearness of thought and logical statement, which caused his opinions to be treated with great consideration. His loss will be felt, his memory cherished throughout our entire Church."

CHAPTER X.

ST. LUKE'S (EPISCOPAL) CHURCH—SERVICE IN THE COURT HOUSE AND FEMALE ACADEMY IN 1836 BY REV. CRANMORE WALLACE—IN 1845 BY REV. R. S. SEELY, FOLLOWED BY REV. E. T. WALKER—CONSECRATION OF CHURCH EDIFICE IN 1855—REV C. R. HAYNES—REV. LUCIEN LANCE — REV. MAXWELL PRINGLE — REV. E. R MILES — REV. P. F. STEVENS — REV. JOHN KERSHAW--REV. S. H. S. GALLAUDET—REV. FRANK HALLAM — REV W. F. DICKINSON — REV. W. H. HANCKEL.

THE early records of St. Luke's, are supposed to have been burnt in the great fire which occurred in Newberry, in 1866

The following sketch has been prepared almost entirely, from information furnished by Mrs. Stiles Hurd, of Stratford, Connecticut, (formerly a resident of Newberry,) and Miss Ella M. Blake, of Charleston, to both of whom I gratefully acknowledge my indebtedness.

From an old record it is ascertained that as early as 1836, the Rev. Cranmore Wallace, having been appointed "Missionary to destitute parishes," held services occasionally at Newberry, in the Court House.

In 1845, Rev. R. S Seely was sent to Newberry by Bishop Gadsden. Mr. Seely remained about two years, and held service in the Court House.

Among the earliest Episcopalians in Newberry were, the

families of Stiles Hurd, Wm. C. Johnson and William B. D'Oyley, Miss Susan McCammon, (afterwards Mrs. Wm. F. Anderson), Norman Brownson and A. C. Garlington Esq. All or nearly all of these were living in Newberry when Mr. Seely came.

The Church organization bears date from 1846, in which year it was admitted into union with the Diocesan Convention of South Carolina.

In 1848, and for some time after, Rev. Clement Johnson was Missionary to Newberry and Laurens, and during at least part of the time, resided in Newberry.

About 1850, the membership of the Church was increased by the addition of the families of Edward S Bailey, R. H Greneker and H. T. Peake, C. H. Kingsmore and others whose names cannot be remembered. Mr. Hurd and Mr. Bailey were the Episcopalians most active in trying to establish the Church, permanently, while Col Simeon Fair and others not Episcopalians showed a willingness to act as vestrymen, or to aid in any way in their power.

In 1853, Rev E. T. Walker, of Beaufort, S. C., became Rector, holding services in the Female Academy, and occasionally in the Baptist Church, by invitation of Rev. Dr. Brantly, the pastor. During the rectorship of Mr. Walker, efforts were made to raise funds with which to build a Church edifice. This was accomplished and the present Church was consecrated in the summer of 1855, by the Right Rev. Bishop Davis, D. D. The clergymen present were Rev Edmund Bellinger, Rev. Benjamin Johnson and Rev. E. T Walker. The wardens at the time were Stiles Hurd and Edward S. Bailey and the vestrymen Wm C. Johnson and Wm. B. D'Oyley. At the same time seven persons were confirmed, among them was the venerable Wm. C. Johnson, who died a few years ago, respected by all who knew him, for his integrity and uprightness of character   He was subsequently elected a warden and continued in that office until his death.

At the consecration of the Church, Miss Carrie Hurd, (now Mrs. E. E. Jackson, of Columbia,) presided at the Organ, which was the gift of Edward S. Bailey.

The Church edifice, when first erected, was the handsomest and most Church-like House of Worship in the town. It had a very symmetrical tower standing at the northeast corner, which, unfortunately, (owing to defective work) had to be taken down within a few years after its erection

In the winter of 1856, Mr. Walker gave up his pastorate in Newberry, and was succeeded by Rev. Benj. Johnson, of Abbeville, who officiated two Sabbaths in each month Mr. Johnson was succeeded by Rev. C. R. Haynes, who officiated until 1862, when he resigned to accept a call to a parish in Virginia.

Rev. Lucien Lance, one of St. Luke's best beloved pastors came next. Fitted by inclination, education and association for his high calling, Mr. Lance won the sincere affection of his flock, and in the darkest hours of the recent war, his gentleness, sympathy and unwavering faith, were as sunbeams, entering and brightening many an overshadowed home, and sustaining the drooping hopes of many, who, driven from their homes near the sea, had sought refuge in Newberry.

The following brief obituary notice of Mr. Lance, appeared in the "*Sunday Magazine*," (April, 1883).

"The Rev L. C. Lance, S. T. D., Chaplain of Kemper Hall, Kenosha, (Wisconsin), died on Friday, January 12th, (1883), after a short illness. He had lived ten years at Kenosha. Mr. Lance was born at the Murat homestead on the Deleware River, near Bordentown, N. J., on the 7th day of

September, 1832. He came of an illustrious family, being the nephew of the Princess Lucien Murat, and related to the DeMonchy family; his father William Lance, was a prominent lawyer of Charleston, S. C. He was graduated at the early age of seventeen at Charleston College, in the Class of 1849; other members of the class were Paul Hayne, the poet; Ch. Richardson Miles, at present a leading lawyer of Charleston; Robert Hume, and the late John McCrady, Professor of Geology and Zoology, at Harvard. Mr. Lance entered the General Theological Seminary in New York, in 1851, graduating three years later. Mr. Lance was ordained to the Diaconate by the late Bishop Davis, of South Carolina, in 1854, and admitted to the Priesthood, two years later. His first position was that of assistant minister of All Saints' Parish, Waccamaw, S. C., where he remained five years, when he married Miss Georgianna Hasell, the daughter of a prominent physician. From there he went to Charleston to assume the Rectorship of Calvary Church, for the colored people. This was in 1860. In 1869, he became Rector of the Church of the Ascension, Frankfort, Ky., succeeding the Rev. Jno. Norton, D. D. In 1872, he resigned this Parish to accept the Rectorship of St Matthew's Church, Kenosha, which parish he retained five years, during which the fine stone Church building of the parish was erected. For the last five years he has been Professor and Chaplain of Kemper Hall."

During the latter years of the recent war, and for sometime afterwards the Church edifice was in such a dilapidated and comfortless condition that services were held in the Hotel parlor and the Lutheran Church, which had been kindly offered for that purpose. But through the indefatigable efforts of the members, assisted by the former Rector, Rev. E. T. Walker, who enlisted the sympathy of some wealthy Episcopalians in Charleston and elsewhere, the Church was soon repaired and made comfortable again.

From 1867 to 1868, Rev. Maxwell Pringle, officiated once a month. Upon his resignation the Church was again without a pastor, but occasional services were held by Rev. E. T. Walker, and others.

In 1870, Rev. Edward R. Miles, lately ordained, was installed as the regular pastor of St. Luke's, and the parishes of Anderson and Laurens. Mr. Miles was beloved by his flock, and admired and respected by all who came in contact with him. He was a graduate of the College of Charleston. His family, are all talented. He was himself, " a gentleman of the old school," highly cultivated and fitted to adorn almost any sphere in life. Yet he was contented and happy in the limited one in which he moved; refusing tempting calls to wider fields; believing that he was most needed in that part of the Master's vineyard in which he was laboring. Entering the ministry late in life, Mr. Miles seemed anxious to work while it was day, feeling that the sunset of life was not far distant for him. His feeble health was a constant reminder of the limited period allotted for his labors, and his heart and hands were ever busy in his work. When in 1885, he was called " up higher," the only regret he expressed was that he had not been able to do more for his Master's service.

When Mr. Miles resigned, in 1873, the parish was without regular service for one year. But lay reading, by Capt. N. B. Mazyck, was kept up during that time.

In 1874, Rev. P. F. Stevens, Rector of Grace Church, Anderson, and Professor in the Male and Female Collegiate Institute of that place was placed in charge, in connexion with the parish of Anderson. Mr. Stevens was a graduate of the Citadel Academy, of Charleston, of which he afterwards became the Superintendent. He studied for the ministry while he was in charge of the Citadel. Having resigned the position of Superintendent of the Military Academy, he was ordained Deacon, in Charleston, by Bishop Davis, in the summer or fall of 1861, and took charge as missionary of Trinity, Black Oak. He was afterwards ordained Priest, but the date of the ordination has not been ascertained.

In the winter of 1861 Governor Pickens appointed him Colonel, and offered him the opportunity to form the Holcombe Legion, which he did. He was ordered to Virginia in Gen. Evans' Brigade in the summer of 1862, and was at the second battle of Manassas as Brigade Commander, was slightly wounded, and was mentioned by Gen. Longstreet for special gallantry. He resigned and resumed his parish (St. John's) in the winter of 1863.

"In 1875, becoming dissatisfied with the discipline of the *Old* Church, he resigned and united himself with the *New*, the 'Reformed Episcopal.' He has since been made a Bishop, is very zealous, especially among the negroes, who have joined (in considerable numbers) the schismatic movement inaugurated by Bishop Cummings, of New York."

In June, 1876, Rev. John Kershaw, of Abbeville Church, was called to the charge of St. Luke's, officiating one Sunday in each month, until April, 1879, when he resigned.

Mr. Kershaw is a talented and thoroughly educated man. After practicing law for several years, he became convinced that it was his duty to enter the ministry, and having relinquished the legal profession, he has ever since been actively and zealously engaged in his sacred calling.

His resignation was deeply regretted by his people at Newberry.

The two parishes, Abbeville and Newberry, again united

in a call to a Rector. The Rev. S H. S. Gallaudet, of Maryland, responded, and in September 1879 officiated for the first time. In 1880 he removed to Spartanburg, having been invited to take charge of the Church at that place.

Rev. Frank Hallam, who was highly respected and esteemed, succeeded Mr. Gallaudet in the charge of the two parishes. After remaining one year, he became convinced that St. Luke's should have a resident pastor, and through his efforts—aided by the Bishop—the services of the Rev W. F. Dickinson, of Grace Church, Long Island, were secured, and in January, 1882, he entered upon his duties. As he was a highly cultivated gentleman, an eloquent preacher and possessed of engaging social qualities, his resignation (tendered in December, 1882,) was accepted with regret. He went from Newberry to Spartanburg, to take charge of the Church of the Advent, at that place. Since then no effort has been made to secure a resident minister, the congregation being to small to support one.

In January, 1883, Rev. William H. Hanckel, of Pendleton became Rector, in connexion with the parish of Abbeville. Mr. Hanckel has continued to fill the office of Rector of the two parishes most acceptably since that time.

CHAPTER XI.

LUTHER CHAPEL (EVANGELICAL LUTHERAN CHURCH)—
ORGANIZATION AND HISTORY—REV. T. S. BOINEST—
REV. WILLIAM BERLY—REV. THEOPHILUS STORK,
D. D—REV. J. P. SMELTZER.

FROM the records of Luther Chapel, I have been permitted to make the following extract: " The flourishing town of Newberry, surrounded by a considerable Lutheran population, and presenting inducements to men of business to locate there was by many regarded as a desirable place for the erection of an Evangelical Lutheran Church and the organization of a congregation. The importance of such an enterprise was greatly increased during the year 1852, by the removal to this place of several prominent and influential members and families of our Communion, when with commendable liberality, Nathan A. Hunter proposed, if the enterprise were taken hold of, to donate an eligible lot of land on which to erect the Church.

"Subscriptions were immediately opened for the purpose of securing funds for the completion of a House of Worship, and the Rev. T. S. Boinest began, occasionally, as opportunity was offered him, to preach in the town. He appointed from among the contributors the following trustees and building committee: Trustees—Henry Summer, Esq., B. J. Ramage, Esq., Thomas W. Holloway, Geo. G. DeWatt, Esq., E. P. Lake, C. H. Suber, Esq., and Jacob Kibler. Building Committee—Maj. J. P. Kinard, Maj. A. C. Garlington, Dr. O. B. Mayer, E. Y. McMorris, and N. A. Hunter.

"To the Trustees Mr. Hunter executed a title for the lot, and they at their first meeting authorized the building Committee to erect the Church on the same."

On Sabbath July the 10th, 1853, Rev. T. S. Boinest preached in the Court House, and after service the congregation was organized by the enrollment of the following names, who were in regular communion with some one of the neighboring Churches, but to whom this place was most convenient: Mathias Barre, Mrs. Jane C. Barre, W. W. Houseal, Mrs. Eliza Houseal, David Werts, Mrs. Sarah Werts, J. L. Morgan, Mrs. Harriet Morgan, J. L. Aull, J. K. Schumpert, John J. Schumpert, Mrs. Susan Kinard, Mrs. Louisa C. Hunter, Mrs. Herselia F. Cline, Mrs. Harriet Schumpert, Miss Elizabeth Morgan, Miss Mary Ann Barre, Miss Elizabeth Whitman, Miss Eliza Jane Gauntt, Miss Amanda C. Stockman, Miss Minerva E. Schumpert.

" Immediately after the organization of the congregation, John L. Morgan and W. W. Houseal were elected Elders.

" On Wednesday August the 10th, 1853, the corner-stone of the Church was laid with appropriate ceremonies, and the Rev. Dr. Bachman of Charleston delivered the sermon in the Court House which was filled to overflowing."

The Church was completed on the first day of December, 1854, and dedicated on Sabbath, December 10th, 1854. The dedication sermon was preached by the Rev. John Bachman, D. D., of Charleston.

The following list of pastors who have served the Church was handed to me by Mr. W. W. Houseal:—Rev. T. S. Boinest, 1853-54, Rev. William Berly, 1857-58, Rev. Theophilus Stork, D. D., 1859-60, Rev. J. P. Smeltzer, D. D., 1861-68, Rev, Jacob Hawkins, D. D., 1871, Rev. H. W. Kuhns, D. D., 1873-78, Rev. S. P. Hughes, 1879-81, Rev. Jacob Steck, D. D., 1882-84, Rev. A. B. McMakin, 1885-86; of these, Rev. T. S.

Boinest, Rev. William Berly, Rev. Dr. Stork and Rev. J. P. Smeltzer are dead.

The present pastor, Rev. W. C. Schaeffer, came to the Church in November, 1887.

In the preparation of the following notices of Rev. Mr. Boinest and Rev. Mr. Berly, I am, to a great extent indebted —for information concerning them—to "Memorials" of each published in the Minutes of the Sessions of the Evangelical Lutheran Synod of S. C. That of Mr. Boinest in 1871, and of Mr. Berly in 1873.

Rev. Thaddeus Street Boinest was born in the City of Charleston, S. C., on the 17th of December, 1827.

He received the rudiments of an education at the school of the German Friendly Society of that city, and afterwards served an apprenticeship as an engineer under Mr. Thomas Dotterer. At an early age he was confirmed in St. John's Church, by his pastor, Rev. Dr. Bachman, who was always his firm friend and spiritual father.

Impressed with the duty of preaching the Gospel, he resolved, contrary to the wishes and advice of some of his friends, to devote himself to a preparation for that work.

Prof. W. J. Rivers, (afterwards of the South Carolina College,) consented to aid him by giving him lessons at night while he still plied his trade by day. In this way he advanced rapidly. On the 6th of September, 1847, he entered the Classical and Theological Seminary at Lexington, S. C., under the tutorship of Rev. William Berly and Rev. E. L. Hazelius. Having graduated with honor, he was licensed to preach the Gospel at a Synod held at Ebenezer, Ga., in November, 1851.

He was aided in his support while at Lexington by that noble band of ladies, whose praise is in all the Churches. "The Society for the promotion of Religion," of St. John's,

Charleston. He accepted a call to St. Luke's Colony, and St. Matthew's Churches, in Newberry County, and preached his first sermon at St. Luke's, December 14th, 1851. The next December he resigned at St. Matthew's, and in January following took charge of Bethlehem. He was in due time ordained to the holy ministry.

On the 10th of July, 1853, he organized a Lutheran congregation at Newberry, and became their pastor. This pastorate, however, he soon resigned, that he might serve Bethlehem and other Churches then under his care, and thus, as also by his happy marriage in the neighborhood of Bethlehem, he early identified himself with the temporal and spiritual welfare of the good people among whom he died.

He was, from his entrance upon the ministry, one of the most progressive and useful members of the Synod of South Carolina. He was for many years an active member of the Boards of the Seminary and Newberry College, and was for four years President of the Synod of South Carolina.

He died on the 4th day of September. 18—, aged 43 years.

Rev. William Berly was born in Newberry County, S. C., on the 25th of December, 1810, and died at his residence, in Lexington village, April the 18th, 1873.

Having received a thorough English education in the classical school connected with the Theological Seminary of the Synod of South Carolina, located at Lexington C. H., he pursued a full course of theology under the Rev. Dr. Hazelius, and graduated on the 11th of November, 1836, being a member of the first class that entered that institution. He entered upon his pastoral duties as licentiate of the Evangelical Lutheran Synod of South Carolina, in which capacity he labored until November, 1837, when he was ordained to the Gospel ministry at St. John's (Calk's Road) Church, Lexington County, S. C. From that time until his death he labored diligently and faithfully in the cause of his Master.

Immediately after his licensure he became pastor of several congregations in Newberry County, which he served with eminent ability and success. By his untiring devotion to the work of the ministry, and the faithful discharge of his duties as pastor, he not only added largely to the membership of his charge, but being deeply imbued with a true missionary spirit, he visited and preached in destitute neighborhoods, and to his efficient labors and zealous efforts several of the most flourishing Lutheran Churches in Newberry County owe their origin.

In addition to his arduous labors in the ministry, he was employed for thirty years as an instructor of youth. He was for several years the efficient principal of a Female Academy in the town of Newberry, and served for several terms as principal in the Literary and Classical Institute connected with the Theological Seminary at Lexington. After the removal of this institution to Newberry, he established a Female Academy in the immediate vicinity of Lexington village, of which he remained principal up to a short time previous to his death, filling at the same time, with great satisfaction, the Lexington pastorate.

The Rev. Theophilus Stork, D. D., was born near Salisbury, N. C., in August, 1814. He was the son of the Rev. Carl Augustus Gottlieb Storch, (which was the original German family name.) His mother's name was Christiana Beard.

His youthful morals were of the strictest character, for his father's discipline was of the good old German Lutheran type; but Theophilus was a boy of a naturally gentle disposition, who easily yielded to paternal control. He thus grew up to be a blameless man, whose fair name was never sullied by the breath of suspicion. He graduated from the Gettysburg College in 1835. Then studied in the Seminary at that place two years, which at that day was the prescribed time. In 1837 he began his first pastorate at Winchester, Va. In 1841 he became pastor of St. Matthew's Church, Philadelphia, and afterwards of St Mark's, in the same city. In the autumn of 1858 he resigned the latter pastorate to accept the Presidency of Newberry College.

Just before he came to Newberry, his health began to be seriously impaired, which induced him to believe that a residence in the South would be beneficial.

In a letter addressed to his son Charles (dated November 5th, 1858,) while he was considering the question of removal to the South he writes :

" I am happy to find you so responsive to my suggestions in relation to the South. I feel a longing for some position in which I could prosecute my studies, and at the same time be devoted to the Church and the glory of God. Such a position is now offered to me, and I feel disposed to accept it. * * * * * I expect to go South next week to view the place and property, and after my return will decide the matter. Let us pray, Charles, that God may guide us in this important decision."

In a postcript to the foregoing letter, (among other things) he writes : " I have been South. I am delighted with almost every thing. The town of Newberry is a very pleasant place. It has the best society in South Carolina, and that is saying a good deal."

Hee ntered upon his duties as President of the College in February, 1859, and was very soon thereafter elected pastor of Luther Chapel. After residing in Newberry about two years, he concluded that the state of his health, which had not been improved, would not permit him to remain longer, and resigned both the Presidency of the College and the Pastorate of the Church. I have not ascertained the precise dates of these resignations.

The following extract is from the "*Stork Family in the Lutheran Church,*" by the Rev. John G. Morris, D. D., an interesting book, to which I am indebted for most of the material of this sketch :

"During the second year in the Seminary, and especially in vacation time, he (Dr. Stork) occasionally preached. His method at that time was to write his sermons with much care, and then so familiarize his mind with the discourse as to deliver it without much use of the manuscript. His delivery had all the force and freedom of extemporaneous speaking. Nor did he confine himself to the written sermon. Under the influence of excitement he sometimes burst forth into impromptu eloquence of great power.

" Dr. Stork possessed a heart in an unusual degree free from guile. * * * * His talents and taste peculiarly fitted him for the pulpit. By nature and grace he was richly endowed to preach salvation to perishing sinners. * * * He disliked all shams in religion and worship He was deeply in earnest while dealing with divine things. Though not of a strictly theological cast of mind, he delighted in the great doctrines of grace, and presented them with great unction and power. There was a fervor and a glow at times that filled the heart. He was emphatically a heart preacher. His style was clear and elegant, highly finished, and always lively and vigorous."

Dr. Stork was the author of nine publications in bookform. A volume of his sermons edited by his sons was published after his death. His writings are chiefly on Biblical subjects. He was also employed a good deal in editing and writing for various religious newspapers and magazines. It is said that in his writings : "He reveals his devout and loving heart, a wide range of reading and fine æsthetic talent."

I have not had the pleasure of reading his books, and cannot therefore speak of their merits. But my recollection of the man leads me to confirm all that has been said in the preceding extract of his preaching and his Christian character.

After he left Newberry he was engaged in preaching—as his health would permit—in Baltimore and Philadelphia. He was twice married. His first wife, was Miss Mary Jane Lynch, of Jefferson, Md., who died in 1846. Two years after, he married Miss Emma Baker, of Philadelphia, who survived him. He died in Philadelphia on the 28th of March, 1874.

Rev. J. P. Smeltzer, D. D., died October 31st, 1887. The following brief, but comprehensive sketch of his life appeared in the Charleston *News and Courier*, newspaper, November 1st, 1887 :

"The Rev. J. P. Smeltzer, D. D,, died at the residence of his son, in this city, yesterday morning. He was one of the oldest, as he was likewise one of the ablest and best ministers of the Lutheran Church in South Carolina.

"Dr. Smeltzer was born in Frederick County, Maryland, September 10, 1819. He received a liberal education, and about the time he reached manhood was ordained a minister of the Lutheran Church. He was for several years principal of a well-known and popular educational institution at Harper's Ferry, Virginia, and was at different times pastor of the Churches at Shepherdstown and Salem, Virginia. In 1861, so great had become his reputation as an instructor, that he was elected President of Newberry

College in this State. He removed to South Carolina and conducted the affairs of this institution with signal ability. when the College was located at Newberry, and after its removal to Walhalla, until 1879, when the College was again taken back to Newberry. In that year he resigned the Presidency of the institution, and established at his mountain home the Walhalla Female College, of which he was the head until 1885. During his labors as a teacher Dr. Smeltzer did not discontinue his work in the pulpit, and was Pastor of the Spring Hill Lutheran Church, in Lexington County. Last spring, his health having given way under the ceaseless toil of many years, Dr. Smeltzer came to Charleston, where he spent the last few months of his life.

"Dr. Smeltzer was a very forcible preacher. He was possessed of profound powers of analysis, and preached with great effectiveness. For his theological learning the degree of Doctor of Divinity was conferred upon him by Erskine College. His attainments were solid. He did not indulge in oratorical pyrotechnics in the pulpit, but preserved at all times a proper respect for the work of his exalted mission. He was highly esteemed by all who knew him, for his eminent piety, his transparent truthfulness, and for the solid oak of which his life was built. His death will be sincerely deplored by the Lutherans of the State and by none more sincerely than by the Lutherans of Charleston."

CHAPTER XII.

THOMPSON STREET (ASSOCIATED REFORMED PRESBYTERIAN) CHURCH—HISTORY—REV. E. P. M'CLINTOCK—REV. H. L. MURPHY.

THE early records of the Thompson Street Church are supposed to have been destroyed by fire. In the summer of 1875, a committee was appointed by the Church to collect any facts in its history that could be obtained, and record them in some permanent form. From the report of that committee (which I have been kindly permitted to examine,) the following historical facts have chiefly been gathered : In 1853 steps were first taken to establish an Associate Reformed Presbyterian Church at Newberry, and in that year and the year following the Rev. D. F. Haddon, and other Associate Reformed Presbyterian ministers, preached occasionally in Newberry.

In the year 1854, Dr. Thomas W. Thompson, of Newberry, conveyed to Joseph S. Reid and Robert C. Wright, Trustees, a lot of land, as a donation to the Church, to be used for the purpose of erecting a house of worship thereof.

The church edifice was completed in 1855. The building committee consisted of Dr. Thomas W. Thompson, Col. James M. Crosson, William Steele and Robert C. Wright.

The Second Associate Reformed Presbytery furnished the congregation with supplies of preaching during the building of the house. Among the ministers who preached during this period; the following names are recollected : Rev. R. C. Grier, D. D., Rev. W. R. Hemphill, Rev. D F. Haddon, Rev. H. T. Sloan, Rev. H. L. Murphy and Rev. J. N. Young. During the year 1855 the congregation united with that of King's Creek in extending a call to Rev. H. L. Murphy to become their pastor. This call was accepted by Mr. Murphy, who was soon after ordained and installed pastor of the two congregations. The installation services were held in the Presbyterian Church at Newberry, most of the members of the second Associate Reformed Presbytery being present and participating in the exercises. The Rev. E. E. Pressly, D. D., presided as Moderator, and the Rev. H. T. Sloan preached the ordination sermon. (The date of Mr. Murphy's ordination is not given in the report.)

The Rev. Mr. Murphy preached in the Court House from the time of his ordination until the house of worship was ready for use.

Soon after the building was completed a protracted meeting was held, during which the house was dedicated to the only Living and True God. In the organization of the Church, Dr. Thomas W. Thompson and Col. James Crosson were elected Ruling Elders, and Dr. D. W. Reid and J. Sims Brown, Deacons.

The committee, in concluding their report, say : " For a considerable period this congregation enjoyed as much prosperity as could reasonably be expected. With preaching on every alternate Sabbath, a prayer-meeting during the week and Sabbath-School exercises every Sabbath, there seemed to be good promise of a large and growing congregation. In the course of a few years, however, the congregation began to suffer by removals, and at length entered, while yet in its youth, into the sore experience to which the Southern Churches were subjected in the war between the States.

"At the close of the war the congregation found itself

little more than a skeleton. Among the office bearers Dr. Thompson had died, Col. Crosson had removed to another State, William Hood, elected some years after the organization, had been elected Treasurer of the State and had removed to Columbia ; William McMorries alone remained of the Elders. The Deacons had both removed to other congregations. The membership was reduced to a handful, and many of them stripped of their wealth by the war. The pastor, Rev. Mr. Murphy, was discouraged, both with the state of his congregations and the condition of the country. This discouragement on the part of the pastor became so great that, in the latter part of 1866, he abandoned the congregations and removed to another State.

" From this time for a number of years these Churches remained vacant. The second Presbytery furnished occasional supplies. Among those supplying the pulpit with occasional services were, Rev. R C. Grier, D. D , Rev. W. R. Hemphill, Rev. J. N. Young, Rev. J. P. Pressly, Rev. W. F. Pressly, Rev. J. F. Hemphill, and Rev. D. F. Haddon.

"Rev. W. M. Grier was sent to this Church and that of King's Creek, as stated supply for one year. After remaining this time, he was sent to some other field."

Then follows : "A list of names remembered as office-bearers and members during the pastorate of Rev. H. L. Murphy. Ruling Elders : Thomas W. Thompson, James M. Crosson, William Hood, and William McMorries. Deacons—D W. Reid and J. C. S. Brown. Members—Mrs. Thomas Thompson, Mrs. James Crosson, Mrs. D. W. Reid, Mrs. Lavinia Brown, Charles Jones, Jane Jones, James Crawford, ——— Crawford, Eliza Montgomery, William Steele and wife, Thomas Chapman and wife, Mrs. Mary Graham, Mrs. Rosa Harriss, R. C. Wright and wife, William Martin and wife, Mrs. Jane McMorries, Miss Nannie McMorries, Miss Erin

McMorries, Miss Ann Montgomery, Miss Rosa Wright, Mr. —— Robinson, Samuel Warnock, William Osbourn. Colored Members —Mary Reid, Elizabeth ———."

The Rev. E. P. McClintock (then a licentiate) preached part of the time during the years 1869 and 1870, to the Thompson Street Congregation.

In July, 1871, he was invited to become the pastor of King's Creek and Thompson Street Churches. This invitation he accepted, and on the 12th of August following—at a meeting of the Second Presbytery, held at King's Creek Church, was ordained, and installed pastor of the two congregations. In October, 1884, he resigned the charge of the King's Creek Church, and gave his whole time to the Thompson Street Congregation, of which he is still the pastor.

It will be observed that Mr. McClintock has been the pastor of Thompson Street Church since 1871. Under his faithful and judicious oversight the Church has steadily increased in numbers and efficiency. He enjoys the confidence and affection of his own people, as well as the esteem and respect of the entire community.

There does not appear to be any reason why his pastorate —already the longest in the history of Newberry, may not continue until the close of his life.

The Rev. Henry Leland Murphy, the first pastor of Thompson Street Church, was born near Due West, in Abbeville County, S. C., on the 9th of September, 1823.

The progress of his education was interrupted by the death of his father, which occurred in Tennessee, to which State he had removed.

Being a hopeful and persevering youth, Mr. Murphy did not in the face of the difficulties of his situation abandon his cherished hope of securing a liberal education. Fortunately for him two kind maiden aunts, living in the vicinity of Due West, S. C., came to his relief, and generously offered him a home, and the means with which to go through Erskine College.

After completing the literary course at Due West, he very soon after began the study of Theology in the Seminary, at that place, then under the superintendance of Rev. E. E. Pressly, D. D. In March, 1850, he was licensed to preach by the Second Presbytery of S. C., at Head Springs, in Laurens County. He, then, spent about two years in Missionary labor, partly in the West.

Returning to South Carolina, in 1851, he was happily married to Miss M. A. Hurst, of Abbeville County, who is still living, and was ever a faithful wife and self-sacrificing help meet to her husband in his laborious calling. The first year after his marriage was spent spent in teaching school, and preaching in Tennessee. In 1855, he became the pastor of King's Creek, and Thompson Street Churches, in Newberry, in which office he remained until after the close of the recent war, when he accepted a call from Churches in Tennessee and removed to that State, where he died on the 24th of November, 1878.

The Rev. J. H. Strong of Tennessee, in an obituary of Mr. Murphy published soon after his death, and which I have freely used in the preparation of this sketch, writes thus: "Mr. Murphy occupied a high place among his brethren as a preacher; he was a good scholar and an attractive and impressive speaker. * * * * * He had an inquisitive and speculative mind, and occasionally manifested these traits in his sermons. It was my privilege to hear him often in the pulpit, and I found him truly powerful and happy when he told the 'simple tale of Calvary', and entreated sinners to come to Christ for help and salvation."

CHAPTER XIII.

SOME LIVING MINISTERS WHO WERE FORMERLY PASTORS IN NEWBERRY.—REV. J. J. BRANTLY, D. D., REV. H. W. KUHNS, D. D , REV. R. A. FAIR.

REV. J. J. BRANTLY, D. D.

REV. JOHN JOINER BRANTLY, D. D., who is now Professor of Belle Lettres and Modern Languages in Mercer University, Macon, Ga., was pastor of the Newberry Baptist Church from 1850 to 1867. His pastorate extended over a period of nearly seventeen years, being at the time of his resignation the longest in the history of the town. It embraced the four years of the War of Secession and two years immediately following, and during its continuance many of the oldest and most prominent members of his charge passed away.

Dr. Brantly was born on the 29th of December, 1821, at Augusta, Ga. He is the son of Rev. William T. Brantly, Senior, D. D. His mother's maiden name was Margaretta Joiner. His father was a native of Chatham County, N. C. and his mother a native of Beaufort, S. C. When he was about five years old his father moved to Philadelphia, where he lived until 1837. Here he (John J.) received his school education. He was graduated from the Charleston, (S. C.) College (of which his father was then President), in 1840.

After his graduation, he taught school at different times in Pittsboro and Fayetteville, N. C. and Augusta, Ga. He was licensed to preach by the First Baptist Church of

Charleston, S. C. in 1844. His father then prostrated by paralysis, signed his license as pastor of the Church, which was the very last official act of his life.

In 1845, he was married to Miss Della Smith of Fayetteville, N. C. In 1846, he was ordained to the full work of the Gospel Ministry at Fayetteville, and remained there teaching and filling the position of pastor of the Baptist Church at that place until 1850, when he removed to Newberry.

Dr. Brantly's sermons preached in Newberry, were always sound, intellectual and instructive, and accomplished a quiet but effective and permanent work. He was calm and dignified in the pulpit and spoke with deliberation. While he never elevated his voice to a high pitch, he could be distinctly heard in every part of the Church. He did not attempt oratorical displays, but he had, without seeming to be aware of it himself, unusual power over the feelings of his hearers. By the beauty and pathos of a single sentence, he would often send a thrill through the hearts of his listeners, and bring silent tears into many eyes. His illustrations and descriptions were striking and graphic.

During the latter years of his residence in Newberry, he taught a Female School with much success. The character of his preaching and his labors in the school-room, made a profound and lasting impression in the mental as well as the moral development of the young of the community. Being an accomplished linguist, his language in preaching, in teaching and in the social circle was chaste, appropriate, and free from slang and vulgarisms.

Dr. Brantly is every inch a student and a man of varied attainments. Before he left Newberry, he had accumulated a large library of valuable books in many languages. In addition to Latin, Greek and Hebrew, he had mastered the German, French, Italian and Spanish. He takes particular delight in linguistic studies, and his knowledge of languages, is both copious and exact; qualities not apt to be found together. Having naturally good powers of acquisition and good ability to digest and assimilate thought so as to make it his own, it may well be supposed that his mind is stored with the best thoughts contained in human literature. His mind has an æsthetic tendency, and a poetic vein runs through his mental habitudes.

His native diffidence and studious habits incline him to retirement. The late Dr. H. H. Tucker, who was President of Mercer University when Dr. B went there, and for several years after, once said of him: "His home and his heaven are in his study, and his books are his angels." While he resided in Newberry he did not mingle very freely with the people, yet his amiable disposition and blameless life won for him the respect and confidence of every class of the community.

His removal from Newberry was deeply regretted by the people of his charge, and it may be mentioned that the Presbyterian, Methodist and Lutheran Churches of the town testified their appreciation of his character by suspending their services on the day he was to take leave of his people, in order that their respective congregations might go to the Baptist Church and hear his farewell sermon, the Presbyterian Church having previously sent to Dr. Brantley and his Church, copies of the following preamble and resolutions, which had been adopted by them:

"17TH DECEMBER, 1866.

"The Session of the Aveleigh Church having heard of the contemplated removal from this community of the Rev. John J. Brantly, D. D., and consequently the dissolution of his pastoral relation with the Newberry Baptist Church, deem it not improper to adopt the following resolutions :

"*Resolved*, That we deeply sympathize with our brethren of the Baptist Church in their anticipated loss of the services of their beloved Pastor, Rev. J. J. Brantly, whose purity of character, rare attainments and Christian excellence have endeared him to us all—recommending them to Him who, having removed Elijah, in his stead gave Elisha.

"*Resolved*, That we, though members of another denomination, yet witnesses of his faithfulness to his people and our community, tender to Dr. Brantly assurances of our affectionate regard and brotherly love, and also of our high esteem for him as a minister of the Gospel, praying our Heavenly Father to direct him and strengthen him in his new field of labor, and that he may be comforted with the knowledge that the good seed which he has sown in this community continues to yield rich harvests to the honor and glory of God.

"*Resolved*, That copies of these proceedings be furnished to the Newberry Baptist Church, and to the Rev. Jno. J. Brantly, D. D.

"R. A. MICKLE, *Moderator*."
"SILAS JOHNSTONE, *Secretary*.
"G. D. SMITH.
"JAMES M. BAXTER.
"W. J. DUFFIE.
"SAML. P. BOOZER.
"ISAAC KELLER.

REV. H. W. KUHNS, D. D.

Rev. Henry Welty Kuhns was born on the 23d of August, 1829, in Greensburg, Pa. He was the son of John and Susan (Welty) Kuhns. His maternal ancestors came from

Wirtemberg, Germany, and his paternal ancestors from Strasburg on the Rhine. He received his school education in his native town. A determination to become a preacher of the gospel was formed in his boyhood, and never relinquished, though for a time held in abeyance. His health, during his youth, was delicate, and through the advice of the family physician his father induced him to learn a trade, with the hope that his health might be thereby improved. He accordingly served an apprenticeship of three years at carriage making, and afterwards worked one year as a journeyman. He had become a rapid and expert workman, and commanded good wages, so that he managed to save a considerable sum of money.

During the years of his apprenticeship and the year following he devoted some time at night to his books, and in this way kept up with his studies. The four years of labor greatly improved his health, and, with the desire to become a preacher still stirring within him, he determined to go to college.

He entered Gettysburg College in April, 1851, and graduated from the literary department in 1856 and from the theological department in 1858. His college expenses were defrayed by money he had saved while working at carriage making and with some assistance from his father.

In September, 1858, under the auspices of the Alleghany Synod of Pennsylvania, he undertook what was known as the Nebraska Mission. He was the first Lutheran minister to enter that Territory, which was then being rapidly filled with white settlers. His headquarters were at Omaha, but he visited all parts of the Territory and was successful in establishing churches and in inducing other ministers of his denomination to come and take charge of them.

During his residence in Nebraska he was Chaplain to the

Legislature for three terms and was elected to the chair of Natural Science in the University of Nebraska, but declined the position.

His health having failed again he visited the Pacific coast, and on his return had a severe attack of illness, and was advised by physicians to seek a warmer climate. This resulted in his accepting a call to become pastor of the Lutheran congregation at Newberry. He came to Newberry in January, 1873, and continued in the pastoral office until August, 1883, when he resigned to accept a call to a pastorate at Westminster, Md.

He was married in 1860 to Miss Charlotte J. Hay, the daughter of Dr. Michael Hay, of Johnstown, Pa.

Dr. Kuhns is a man of uncommon energy and perseverance. He works indefatigably at whatever he undertakes. From the beginning, he threw himself heartily into his work in Newberry, and by his attractive style of preaching and his social disposition soon became one of the best known and most popular preachers of the town. He was the first pastor in Newberry to come directly from the North, and naturally brought with him some ideas and introduced some methods which were new to the people. Among other things, he introduced and kept up during his stay, an annual "Harvest Home" festival or celebration in his Church. His style of preaching was too practical to be called sensational, It was, however, somewhat novel and peculiar. He made much use of passing events in enforcing the lessons of his sermons. His conduct as preacher and citizen was characterized by a spirit of kindliness worthy of high praise.

It will be remembered that shortly after the recent war the property of Newberry College (the buildings having become a wreck) was sold, and the institution (in 1868) removed to Walhalla, S C. In 1876 efforts were made to secure the return of the college to Newberry, and in 1877, propositions having been made to the synod for its removal and relocation, by Newberry and other towns in the State, that of Newberry was accepted.

Mr. Kuhns was deeply interested in having the college brought back to Newberry, and his indomitable energy and perseverance contributed largely to the success of the movement. Newberry College conferred upon him the title of D. D., and he was elected by its Board of Trustees professor of natural science, but he declined to accept the chair.

REV. ROBERT A. FAIR.

Rev. Robert A. Fair, formerly a pastor of Aveleigh Church, though not born in Newberry, may in some sense be claimed as one of her sons. He is the son of James Fair, and the grandson of William Fair, who was one of the most worthy citizens of Newberry County.

Few men were ever more honored by the success in life of a large family of sons, than William Fair. Among them were Col. Simeon Fair, a distinguished member of the Newberry Bar, Dr. Samuel Fair, of Columbia, S. C., and Dr. Drury Fair, of Alabama, both successful physicians, Gen. Young Fair, of Alabama, a lawyer and at one time United States Minister to the Court of Belgium, Archibald Fair, a prominent citizen of Florida, and James Fair, the father of Robert A., who spent most of his life as a successful planter in Abbeville County, and was honored by that County with a seat in the State Legislature for a number of years.

Robert A. Fair was born in Abbeville County, on the 12th of December, 1820. He was graduated from Erskine College in 1842, was admitted to the Bar in 1843, and began the practice of law at Abbeville. He was married on the 19th of November, 1844, to Miss Mary Amanda Allen, of Abbeville. In 1845 he formed a law partnership with the late Judge Thomas Thomson, at Abbeville, which continued until 1871.

In February 1861, he was elected Lieutenant-Colonel of the 7th Regiment South Carolina Volunteers, Confederate Army, and served with that regiment until April 1862, when he resigned on account of his health, which had became too much enfeebled for longer service in the field.

In the autumn of 1862, he was elected a member of the House of Representatives of South Carolina, from Abbeville, and re-elected in 1864.

Having been thoroughly convinced of his duty to preach the Gospel, he gave up the practice of law and was ordained to the full work of the ministry by the South Carolina Presbytery at Roberts Church in Anderson County, in June 1871.

His case came under "the exception" in the Presbyterian form of Church government which authorizes a Presbytery, "in extraordinary cases," to ordain to the ministry without a regular course of theological study.

After his ordination he preached to Churches in Abbeville and Anderson Counties, until April, 1873, when he was appointed Evangelist of the Presbytery of South Carolina, then embracing eight Counties within its bounds. He continued in this work until 1874. In May of that year he accepted an invitation to supply the pulpit of Aveleigh Church, at Newberry. During the summer of 1874, he received a call to the pastorate of Aveleigh Church, and in October following was installed into that office. He resigned his pastorate and left Newberry in October 1885.

He is now residing with his son, the Rev. James Y. Fair, at Richmond, Va. His health which was quite feeble when he left Newberry, does not permit him to engage in active ministerial work.

Mr. Fair inherited many of the sterling and noble features of the characters of his ancestors. He is a faithful, conscientious, preacher; who in looking back over the eleven years of his ministry in Newberry, may well say: " I have not shunned to declare unto you all the counsel of God." He does not indulge in mere oratorical displays, or flights of the imagination. His style of preaching is simple, earnest, and scriptural ; he clings closely to the Bible and draws his arguments and illustrations chiefly from that book. He is highly esteemed for the purity and uprightness of his character.

CHAPTER XIV.

BIOGRAPHICAL SKETCHES—CHIEF JUSTICE O'NEALL—
CHANCELLOR JOHNSTONE—CHANCELLOR CALDWELL.

"A Biography sketched in outline is often more true and more useful than one which occupies itself with minute detail. We do not in reality know more of a great man because we happen to know the petty circumstances which made up his daily existence, or because a mistaken admiration has handed down to posterity the promiscuous common places of his ordinary correspondence. We know a man truly when we know him at his greatest and his best; we realize his significance for ourselves and for the world when we see him in the noblest activity of his career, on the loftiest summit, and in the fullest glory of his life."—CANON FARRAR—*Life and Work of St. Paul.*

CHIEF JUSTICE O'NEALL.

JOHN BELTON O'NEALL was born on the 10th of April, 1793, near Bobo's Mills, on Bush River, in Newberry District, S C.

He was the son of Hugh O'Neall and Anne O'Neall; both of his parents were members of the Society of Friends. His ancestors, both paternal and maternal, were Irish. His paternal great-grandfather belonged to the ancient House of O'Neall, of Shanes Castle, Antrim, Ireland. His maternal grandfather, Samuel Kelly, was of Kings County, and his grandmother, Hannah Belton, was of Queen's County, Ireland.

When he was five years of age, he was sent to a school about one and a half miles from his father's house, taught by James Howe, who was familiarly called "Master Howe."

How long he attended this school is not known, but he attended long enough to acquire a love for reading, in which he was encouraged by the teacher, who had a small library of good books.

In 1804 a Library Society, of which young O'Neall's father was a member, was formed in Newberry, and a good library of several hundred volumes were selected and purchased in Boston for the Society, by Elijah Hammond, the father of Governor Hammond. Free access to this library afforded young O'Neall opportunities for reading which he diligently improved.

In 1808 he entered the Newberry Academy, which he continued to attend for several years, first under the tuition of Rev. John Foster, and afterwards under that of Rev. Charles Strong. In February, 1811, he entered the South Carolina College, and in December, 1812, was graduated from that institution with the second honor. In 1813, he taught for six months in the Newberry Academy. At the end of that time he entered the office of John Caldwell, Esq., at Newberry, and began the study of law. While pursuing his law studies he received much valuable instruction from Anderson Crenshaw, Esq., (afterwards a Judge in Alabama,) who then practiced law in Newberry. In May, 1814, he was admitted to the practice of law and equity, and entered into a partnership with John Caldwell, Esq., who, at that time, resided in Columbia, S. C. O'Neall opened an office in Newberry, and was soon honored with a large practice.

In 1816, he was elected a member of the House of Representatives of South Carolina, from Newberry District At the December session of 1817 he voted for an increase of the Judge's salaries. The consequence was that at the elections of 1818 and 1820 he was left at home. This period of rest from political pursuits he afterwards regarded as more of a benefit than a misfortune, as it enabled him to devote more time to the law, thereby increasing both his business and his reputation.

On the 25th of June, 1818, he was married to Helen, eldest daughter of Capt. Sampson Pope, of Edgefield District. In 1820, he removed to "Springfield," (about two miles west of the town of Newberry,) which he had inherited from his grandmother, Hannah Kelly, where he continued to reside until his death. His wife survived him several years, and remained at Springfield until the close of her life. Since the death of Mrs. O'Neall the property has passed out of the possession of the family, and the old family residence, so long associated in the minds of the people of Newberry with the name of the distinguished Chief Justice, has been destroyed by fire.

In 1822 Judge O'Neall was again returned to the House of Representatives, and continued to be a member of that body until the close of the session of 1827.

At the sessions of 1824 and 1826 he was elected Speaker of the House without opposition. In this office he first displayed that remarkable executive ability for which he was so distinguished ever after. During the four years in which he held the office of Speaker, only one appeal was made from his decisions, and on that occasion his decision was sustained by the House.

At the session of 1827, the Legislature of S. C., made an appropriation of ten thousand dollars for the relief of Mrs. Randolph, the daughter of Thomas Jefferson. The Speaker did not vote but was known to be in favor of the measure. In consequence of this, in 1828, a majority of the voters of Newberry District refused to vote for his return to the Legislature.

In thus expressing their disapprobation of an act of their Representative, which at most could only have been considered a mistake of judgmen:—for no one doubted his patriotism or integrity—a majority of his constituents seemed to loose sight of the honor which had been conferred upon him, and through him upon the District he represented ; by his elevation to the Speaker's chair, and of the additional honor which awaited him if he had been sent back to the Legislature; for that body would undoubtedly have testified again, its appreciation of his talents and great executive skill by calling him to preside over its deliberations.

On the 20th of December, 1828, he was elected an Associate Judge. This office he continued to fill until December 1830, when he was elected a Judge of the Court of Appeals.

In 1834, in the midst of the Nullification agitation, he delivered an opinion in the celebrated cases of The State *ex-relatione* McCrady *vs.* Hunt, and McDaniel *vs.* McMeekin, in which he decided that the oath of allegiance to officers of the Militia prescribed by the Legislature, (Act of 1833), was unconstitutional and inconsistent with the allegiance of the citizen to the Federal Government.

In order that the reader may understand the significance of the opinion just mentioned, I will give a short history of the events which led to it.

The Legislature of South Carolina, at an extra session on the 26th of October, 1832, passed an Act to provide for the call of a Convention of the people of the State. A Convention accordingly assembled at Columbia in November following, and passed an Ordinance, "To Nullify certain Acts of the Congress of the United States, purporting to be laws laying duties and imports on the importation of foreign commodities." Congress having afterwards, by an

Act, provided for "such a reduction and modification of the duties on foreign imports, as ultimately to reduce them to the revenue standard," the Convention again assembled in March 1833, and repealed its Ordinance of November preceding ; but at the same time passed an Ordinance " to Nullify an Act of the Congress of the United States, entitled : An Act further to provide for the collection of duties on imports ; commonly called the Force Bill." A separate Clause of the Ordinance is in the following words :

" *We do further Ordain and Declare*, That the allegiance of the citizens of this State, while they continue such, is due to the said State ; and that obedience only and not allegiance, is due by them to any other power or authority, to whom a control over them has been or may be delegated by the State ; and the General Assembly of the said State is hereby empowered from time to time, when they may deem it proper, to provide for the administration to the citizens and officers of the State, or such of said officers as they may think fit, of suitable oaths or affirmations, binding them to the observance of such allegiance and abjuring all other allegiance, and also to define what shall amount to a violation of their allegiance, and to provide the proper punishment for such violation."

By an Act of the Legislature of December, 1833, entitled " An Act to provide for the military organizations of the State," it was among other things enacted, that " In addition to the oaths now required by law, every officer of the militia hereafter elected, shall before he enters on the duties of his office, take and subscribed before some person authorized by law to administer oaths, the following oath : I, A. B., do solemnly swear (or affirm, as the case may be), that I will be faithful, and true allegiance bear to the State of South Carolina."

On the 28th of February, 1834, Edward McCrady was elected Lieutenant of the Washington Light Infantry of Charleston, and applied to Col. Hunt the Commanding officer of the Regiment for his commission. Col. Hunt refused to grant it unless he would take the above oath. This McCrady refused to do, but tendered the oath prescribed in the Constitution of the State, and applied to Mr. Justice Bay for a rule to show cause why a writ of mandamus should not issue, commanding the defendant Hunt to deliver to the relator his commission.

Judge Bay on hearing the case, sustained Col. Hunt, and dismissed the motion for the mandamus. McCrady the relator appealed from this decision.

One James McDaniel had also been elected Colonel of the 27th Regiment of Militia, and had applied for a commission to Genl. McMeekin commanding the Brigade, who tendered him the oath required by the Military Act of 1833, and on his refusal to take it, refused to grant the commission. McDaniel therefore obtained a rule to show cause why a mandamus should not issue. The case was heard at Lancaster, Spring Term, 1834, before Judge Richardson, who held that the oath required by the Act was unconstitutional. The defendant appealed.

Both cases depending on the same principles and making the same questions, were carried up to the Appeal Court together.

After hearing able arguments by some of the most distinguished counsel in the State, and mature deliberation, the Court consisting of Judges David Johnson, (President), John Belton O'Neall and William Harper,—each of whom filed a separate opinion — decided that the oath of allegiance to officers of the militia prescribed by the Act of 1833, was unconstitutional and void—Judge Johnson holding that the

State Constitution (Article 4), having prescribed the form of the oath of office, the Legislature had no authority to change, add to, or alter it; and Judge O'Neall as already noticed, that the oath was contrary to the Constitution of the State, *and inconsistent with the allegiance of the citizen to the Federal Government.* Judge Harper dissenting, held that it was neither repugnant to the Constitution of the State, nor inconsistent with any obligation of the citizen to the Federal Government.

In his report of these cases, the reporter Mr. Hill, makes the following foot note:

"Since this decision, the 4th Article of the Constitution of this State has been amended to read as follows, viz.. 'Every person who shall be chosen or appointed to any office of profit or trust, before entering on the execution thereof, shall take the following oath: I do solemnly swear (or affirm) that I will be faithful, and true allegiance bear to the State of South Carolina, so long as I may continue a citizen thereof; and that I am duly qualified, according to the Constitution of this State, to exercise the office to which I have been appointed; and that I will to the best of my abilities, discharge the duties thereof, and preserve, protect and defend the Constitution of this State and of the United States. So help me God.' Judge Harper's opinion being in favor of the constitutionality of the oath even previous to the amendment, and Judge Johnson, in the conclusion of his opinion having said, that 'if the people should think fit so to amend the Constitution (of this State), as to authorize the administration of an oath of allegiance in the form prescribed by the Act of the Legislature of the last Session, there is nothing in the Constitution of the United States opposed to it;' the constitutional obligation of the oath of allegiance as now incorporated in the Constitution of this State, may be regarded as having the sanction of a majority of the Court."

The report of these cases, including the complete arguments of all the counsel (with one exception), who appeared before the Court, can be found in the 2d volume of Hill's S. C. Law Reports, and constitutes a very interesting part of the political and legal history of South Carolina.

The decision of the Court, especially the opinion of Judge O'Neall, greatly increased the prevailing political excitement, and so displeased the dominant political party that at the Session of the Legislature in 1835, the Court of Appeals as it then existed was abolished, and an Appeal Bench consisting of all the Circuit Judges and Chancellors was established in its stead. Judge O'Neall was assigned to the Law Bench, and Judges Johnson and Harper to the Equity Bench. This arrangement, with some changes made in 1836, continued until 1859.

Judge O'Neall continued to discharge the duties of Law Judge from 1835 to 1859. The Legislature having at its session of 1859 again created a separate Court of Appeals, to consist of a Chief Justice and two Associate Justices, he was elected Chief Justice, with Chancellors Job Johnstone and F. H. Wardlaw as Associate Justices. In this office he remained until his death.

At the time of his election to the office of Chief Justice, Judge O'Neall had nearly completed his "three score years and ten," but the vigor of his mind was unimpaired, and his physical health almost perfect.

We have seen that on two occasions during his career as a member of the Legislature, Judge O'Neall had incurred the censure of a majority of his constituents, and that on a memorable occasion his independence and boldness had cost the life of the Court of which he was a member. Yet the people did not long remember these things against him. And his election to the office of Chief Justice affords the strongest proof of their appreciation of his ability, and honesty, and his long and faithful public services.

One of the most discriminating estimates of his character ever published, appeared in the Columbia *South Carolinian* just after his death, from which I make the following extract:

"The Chief Justice of South Carolina has been gathered to his fathers, full of years and honors. The State has reason to hold his memory in grateful remembrance. Prompt to engage in every useful work, all the energies of his vigorous intellect were devoted to the discharge of his duties, whether in public or private life. He courted labor, and shrank from no task which duty demanded.

"Judge O'Neall's talents were of high order. If he was not *primus interpares*, yet, his great success in life, from early manhood to the close of his career, demonstrates the vigor of his intellect, his untiring industry and his devotion to duty; the more especially when it is remembered that this eminence was attained amidst the severest competition with the ablest men of a brilliant age. His mind was marked by this peculiarity, that he arrived at his conclusions with extraordinary rapidity, however complicated the question. The moment a proposition was distinctly stated, his judgment was formed, almost always right, and rarely shaken when wrong by the most elaborate argument. In this prompt judgment, he resembled those rare individuals of whom it is related that such was their remarkable aptitude for mathematics that they were able to announce the result of a great array of figures at a glance, without apparently pausing to compute their values. It seemed to be rather an intuitive process than the exercise of the reasoning faculty. His apprehension was quick, and his determined will carried itself into all his intellectual processes. His convictions were so absolute and his temperament so nervous, that it may be inferred that he was somewhat impatient of any difference of opinion. He was a successful lawyer an admirable speaker of the House of Representatives, an able and upright Judge, who dispatched business with a facility without a parallel."

Judge O'Neall was deeply interested in every enterprise which had for its object the development of the physical resources of the country, or the elevation and improvement of the moral and intellectual condition of the people. He was the first President of the Greenville and Columbia Railroad Company, and to his enthusiasm and indomitable perseverence the completion of that enterprise was largely due. He was for many years the President of a flourishing Agricultural Society in Newberry.

In 1833 he joined a temperance society at Head Spring Church, in Newberry District, of which he afterwards became the president. From that time until his death he was an earnest and untiring advocate of total abstinence from all intoxicating drinks. He filled, at different times, the highest positions in the various temperance organizations of the day both State and National, and made innumerable temperance addresses. He also delivered many addresses on education, agriculture and other subjects, and before the celebration of the "Fourth of July" fell into disuse he was often called upon to deliver orations on that day.

He was regarded—especially in his early and middle life —as one of the great orators of the State. His elocution was not ornate, but earnest and impetuous, sometimes boisterous. His speeches were generally somewhat disjointed, and showed a lack of painstaking preparation, but such was the fervor of his eloquence that, like a torrent, it swept everything before it. His commanding presence, his clear, ringing voice, and his earnestness of manner, combined to make him a speaker of unusual power. His attitudes and gestures, though entirely unstudied, were easy and striking.

In his early manhood he was enthusiastically fond of the military, and passed through all the gradations of office in the militia from captain up to that of major-general.

In 1859 he published "The Annals of Newberry" and "The Bench and Bar of South Carolina."

These works, valuable when published, will become more so, as time elapses. They contain a record of information gathered mostly from the treasures of his wonderful memory, which can be found nowhere else. It is to be regretted, however, that he did not pay more attention to the graces of style in their preparation.

Judge O'Neall's reading did not greatly extend beyond his profession. His professional and other duties left him very little time for general reading, for recreation, or for social intercourse with his friends. He was one of the busiest of busy men. He delighted most in history, books of travel and biographies—especially those of celebrated generals. He never lost his taste for military life. His speeches were frequently illustrated by scenes from the lives of his favorite military heroes.

Judge O'Neall was elected a Deacon of the Newberry Baptist Church on the 22d of March, 1834, having united with that Church on the 20th of January, 1833. He continued in the office of Deacon until his death, which occurred on the 27th of December, 1863.

Judge O'Neall was remarkable for his amiable disposition and christian humility. The humblest persons could approach him without apprehension. He was the friend of the widow and the orphan, and was at all times ready to encourage by counsel and substantial aid young men with laudable ambition, struggling against the ills of poverty and those in maturer life who were oppressed by misfortune and disappointments He was constantly exposed to demands upon his well-known liberality; and it is not too much to say that he expended a moderate fortune in responding to such appeals.

CHANCELLOR JOB JOHNSTONE.

[Authority for that portion of the following sketch which relates to the birth, parentage, education and professional life of Chancellor Johnstone, is chiefly derived from a brief biography (in manuscript) of him found among his papers after his death, a copy of which was kindly placed in my hands by his son, Silas Johnstone, Esquire. The author of the manuscript is unknown.]

Chancellor Job Johnstone, was born on the 7th of June, 1793, in Fairfield County, South Carolina, about three miles below Winn's Bridge, on Little River. Both his parents were Scotch-Irish. They were born and married in the County of Londonderry, Ireland. Emigrating to South Carolina, they landed at Charleston on the 4th of September, 1787, and proceeded immediately to Fairfield.

John Johnstone the father of the Chancellor, was one of nine sons of David Johnstone, and Sarah Meek, his wife. The family was honest and respectable, and of the class of small farmers. Though originally Scotch, they had been settled in Ireland as early as the contest between William of Orange and his father-in-law, James II. Being Presbyterians, they took sides with William, and a sword is still in the family, in this country, which was worn by Thomas Boyd, the maternal grandfather of David Johnstone at the siege of Londonderry. His mother (the wife of John Johnstone) was Mary Caldwell, the daughter of Job Caldwell, of the County of Londonderry, Ireland, from whom his own Christian name (Job) was derived. The family of Caldwell to which Mrs. Johnstone belonged, came originally from Scotland.

The Caldwells were a most respectable family Portions of them emigrated to Pennsylvania as early as 1700-1710, from which, by successive removals, numerous branches became scattered over Virginia, North Carolina, Kentucky and Tennessee. Hon. John C Calhoun's mother was one of the Virginia branch.

Mrs. Johnstone, the mother of the Chancellor, was well educated. Her mind, which was of no ordinary stamp, had a particular tendency to arithmetical calculations, in which she was very expert; and it is remembered that it was her constant habit to run out difficult questions of this description by a merely mental process; and often to attain the results in advance of her children, who happened to be working out their lessons by the ordinary methods.

Her husband, John Johnstone, though not so well educated, possessed an uncommonly strong mind He had judgment, wit and an unusual command of language, and being of a cheerful temper, amounting to gaiety, his social qualities were quite attractive. These two parents, who were successful in life, used all opportunities within their reach, for the intellectual as well as the moral and religious training of their children. All persons possessed of attainments were made welcome to their home, and thus at the fireside and the hearth, their rising offspring were given the advantages of oral instruction, administered in a way to make it impressive. They were taught to be attentive listeners, and in the course of conversations, sometimes practical, sometimes speculative, sometimes spiced with wit or seasoned with humor, and sometimes mellowed with sentiment, or chastened with the grave and more awe-inspiring truths of religion and its obligations, they caught much that no vicissitude in after life could deprive them of. When no company was in the house, or when the company was such as permitted its being done, the invariable habit of each evening was for some one of the family to read some instructive or entertaining book, while the rest listened, and to intersperse the exercise with pertinent inquiries and replies for the better understanding of the author.

The primary schools of that time were not good, but his father used his influence to procure the best teachers that could be had, and placed his children at school, as soon as they were able to go. His rule was to obtain the friendship of the teacher and to support his authority. The effect was that his children were always among the most obedient in the school, and were seldom the subjects of coercive discipline.

In 1799 his father removed to Chester. From that time until 1806, he continued to attend school either at Chester or Winnsboro. In the fall of 1806, his father having removed to Newberry, he was taken to that village and placed under the Rev. John Foster, who taught a classical school there. Mr. Foster was an indolent man, a poor scholar, and a sorry teacher. After remaining under his care until the end of 1808, he (Johnstone) entered the Junior Class of the South Carolina College. The class was a good one, containing such names as Dellet, Bull, Starke, Warren R. Davis and others, and though the youngest boy in it and spoiled by the idleness of Foster's school, he in a short time placed himself on a level with the best of them. But his attention was rather directed to general reading—and that without aim or system—than to the text books and the regular course of studies. This habit of desultory reading he had acquired—or rather confirmed, for he was always, even in childhood, a great reader in that way—while at Foster's school.

There was a library of some 400 or 500 volumes belonging to a library society and kept in the office of the Clerk of the Court at Newberry. Mr. Y. J. Harrington, the clerk, having found that this lad was fond of reading, and that he took good care of books, with a benevolence and judgment worthy of the man, gave him free access to the library, and there he spent every spare moment.

The same habit, as has been said, followed him to College. But still at his graduation in December, 1810, he took the third honor in a class of about forty-five in number, and was at the time—with two exceptions—the youngest boy that had ever taken a diploma in the South Carolina College.

In the spring of 1811, he entered the office of Mr. John Hooker, one of the best lawyers in the State, at York, as a student-at-law, or rather as he has been heard to say ; he entered his name in the office. He had some associates who were fond of hunting, and he hunted with them. He read novels and smoked cigars, and at the end of the year had not finished the first volume of Blackstone. Becoming discouraged he went the next year into the office of Mr. Clark, at Winnsboro But there he was equally idle. When the 4th of July came—as he sometimes observed—he delivered a speech to a company of artillery, and two companies of cavalry, and having done that much in the year, he declared his independence and quit.

His father having purchased and removed to a body of valuable land in Fairfield, he went home and spent two years in general reading. His morals were irreproachable, his character was good, and he had a general reputation for talents and acquirements. But no man can be idle and happy. Equally impossible is it for him to retain his own self-respect and remain a drone. Happily for this young man, his conscience troubled him, and drove him from his pernicious inactivity.

After spending a short time in Columbia as the deputy of Mr. Brown, the Secretary of State, he resolved to try an entirely new profession, and entered the office of Dr. Davis, then an eminent physician of Columbia. This was in the close of 1814. Here he read diligently, and in October 1815, went to New York, and took a course of lectures in the College of Physicians and Surgeons of that city. The next year, he still pursued his studies with diligence and obtained a very general reputation for his acquaintance with the theory of his proposed profession. In 1817, he came to Newberry with a view to entering upon the life of a physician ; but fearing to encounter the practice, he was induced in a short time to abandon the design.

In the fall of 1817, he renewed the study of law, and in the winter of 1818, was admitted to the Courts of Law and Equity, and at once entered into partnership with John Belton O'Neall, with whom he had studied. His progress in his profession was not rapid, but it was sure. He was esteemed an excellent lawyer, and argued his cases with ability and generally with success. He was never known to mislead a client by flattering advice ; but gave a true representation, according to his sincere conceptions of the case ; and it was never known that a client who had tried him deserted him. In the preparation of his business he was diligent and skillful, and such was his care and skill in pleadings that he was never non-suited at law for inaccuracy in pleading, but once, and in that instance, the pleading had been put in, in his absence by another person. Nor was any bill ever filed by him dismissed for insufficiency.

As an advocate, he had no pretensions to mere oratory. His style of address was earnest, fervent and argumentative, in cases demanding exertion. In the management of intricate causes, he showed uncommon skill, and his manner of unfolding the claims of his client when he came to the argument was marked for clearness of method, precision of statement both as to law and fact, and for chasteness and perspicuity of language. He devoted himself exclusively to his profession. He was never a candidate for military office, nor for the Legislature, but gave his undivided energies to the Courts and the interest of his clients.

In 1826, he was elected Clerk of the Senate of South Carolina; an office, the duties of which he continued to discharge until the 3rd of November, 1830, when he was elected Chancellor in place of Chancellor Harper, who was transferred to the Court of Appeals. His colleague in office was the venerable Chancellor DeSaussure.

The practice of the Court had been extremely loose and imperfect, and he set himself to reform it. As in all such cases, he was misunderstood or misrepresented by that part of the profession whose indolence was disturbed by the strictness of his discipline. But he conceived that the rights of the suitors were involved; and he persevered until he accomplished, at least to a great degree the reformation he designed.

When he came to the Bench his duties were confined to the Circuit Courts. In 1835, all the Judges and Chancellors were constituted an Appellate Court, both in law and equity. This system lasted but one year; and in 1836, the Chancellors—increased to four—were required in addition to their Circuit duties, to perform appellate duty—except in specified cases—only in equity.

Chancellor Johnstone's powers of argumentation were proved in the case of Picket *vs.* Picket, (2d Hill, Ch. 470). This case was brought before the whole of the Judges and Chancellors by appeal from his circuit decree. By the structure of the Court at the time he was not permitted to sit upon the appeal. On a conference the majority of the Court were for reversing the decree. At the request of the minority, Chancellor Johnstone wrote a dissenting opinion for them. After the majority delivered their opinion by Chancellor Harper, the dissenting opinion was read; and its effect was to change the judgment of the Court. It was adopted by the major part of the Judges and became the law of the case, and what had been intended as the leading opinion became the dissenting opinion.

Another instance alike creditable to him occurred in Field *vs.* Pelot, (McMul, Eq., 369). That was an appeal from Chancellor Harper. Upon conference after argument, Chancellor Johnstone brought the Court, and among them, Chancellor Harper, to agree to a reversal of the decree; and the case was put into his (Johnstone's) hands to deliver the opinion of the Court. In preparing to deliver it, he became convinced that his positions were untenable, and he brought the matter to the view of his brethren. But he could not bring them over. Chancellor Harper was chosen to deliver the opinion, which his brother Johnstone was to have delivered. Johnstone dissented and his dissenting opinion has been since adopted as the law of the case. Here was a remarkable specimen of judicial candor in both the Judges named.

At the organization of the separate Court of Appeals, (under the Act of the Legislature of December 1859), Chancellor Johnstone was elected an Associate Justice of that Court, and continued in that office until his death.

Other decisions of Chancellor Johnstone's might be referred to, but the scope of this sketch will not admit of it. Indeed it is not necessary. His published decrees and opinions are everywhere recognized as an important part of the judicial history of South Carolina, and they will ever stand as a monument to his honesty, ability, and great professional learning. He was almost divested of pride of opinion. His statement of causes carried up by appeal from his decisions was full and clear ; affording full opportunity to the appellant to detect whatever errors might have existed in his judgment. There was no superficial statement or covering over of the facts, but a full and even minute disclosure of every particular, so that the legal inferences might be subjected to the severest scrutiny. And he often joined in the reversal of his circuit opinions.

He was spontaneously elected a member of the celebrated Convention of 1832, and being on a Committee with Chancellor Harper, drew the Ordinance of Nullification reported by that gentleman and adopted by the Convention. He also drew and proposed the Ordinance or Allegiance ; but owing to the Convention being too much divided to render its passage expedient, in his judgment, he voted against it. It was however carried.

Chancellor Johnstone's habits were simple. He was naturally retiring and diffident. Shrinking from publicity he confined himself to the performance of his duties, and to a limited social circle.

He was an extensive planter and an experienced pomologist and horticulturist. When at home, he devoted much of the time set apart for recreation to overlooking the cultivation of his orchard and garden. Through a system of thorough trenching, he had brought his garden into an extraordinary condition of fertility. It was pleasant, and refreshing to look upon its luxuriant growth of plants. His table was never without an abundant supply of vegetables and fruits in their season.

My intimate acquaintance, with Chancellor Johnstone began rather late in his life. I soon learned however, to approach him without hesitation and was always kindly received by him. I found him especially interested in the welfare of young men, and can never forget his willingness to impart instruction and advice, from the rich stores of his accumulated knowledge and experience, nor the delicacy and tact with which he did it. He was in a broad and comprehensive sense an educated man. In addition to the law of which he was master, his researchess in other departments of human knowledge were varied and extensive. No one could listen to him without being impressed by the thoroughness and accuracy of his information on general subjects, and his practical acquaintance with the common affairs and occupations of life.

His reading—in addition to the law, and medicine—embraced the Latin and Greek Classics, science, theology, history, poetry, and about all that was worth reading in English light literature, from Fielding and Smollet down to Dickens and Thackaray. He especially admired Sir Walter Scott, and in common with all lovers of genuine literature regarded him as the prince of all novel writers. He had a high appreciation of humor, and especially treasured up and enjoyed the humor of Dickens and Burns. In social intercourse he was affable and engaging; he had the happy faculty of pleasing and interesting every one with whom he conversed, and was peculiarly gifted in drawing others out. In the language of another: "No man ever left his house without being a wiser man than when he entered it, and had to confess that there had been drawn out of himself more knowledge than he could have believed was lying dormant within him."

Chancellor Johnstone was twice married. His first wife, to whom he was married on the 14th of November, 1816, was Miss Eliza Meek Johnstone of Fairfield County. She died on the 23rd of January, 1843. His second wife, who survived him and died on the 3rd of December, 1870, was Miss Amelia De'Walt of Newberry, to whom he was married on the 7th of August, 1844.

He was at the time of his death,—and had been for many years before—a member and Ruling Elder in the Aveleigh Presbyterian Church of Newberry. He died on the 8th of April, 1862. His benefactions during his life were liberal, and in bestowing them he observed the Scripture injunction, " Let not your left hand know what your right hand doeth."

CHANCELLOR JAMES J. CALDWELL.

Chancellor James J. Caldwell was born on the 13th of January, 1799, within a few miles of Cannon Creek Church, in Newberry County. His father Dan (not Daniel) Caldwell was a farmer, a younger son of John Caldwell who emigrated from County Antrim, Ireland, in 1770 or 1771.

Dan Caldwell was born in 1769. The chancellor's mother's maiden name was Jeannette McMaster. None of her name have lived in Newberry for many years past ; and it seems that none of her near relatives live even in Fairfield County, where most of them appear to have settled. Dan Caldwell was a member and elder in the Associate Reformed Presbyterian Church, and a man of exemplary piety. Judge O'Neall speaks of him in his," Annals of Newberry," as "a man without spot."

Chancellor Caldwell often spoke of the careful religious training he received from his father, and of the frequency with which the latter, during their walks through the fields and woods, knelt down and prayed for him, his only son. Though the father died when the son had just entered his eighteenth year, it is propable that the religious character of the son was largely formed by such training and example. His father and mother both died in January, 1816.

Chancellor Caldwell received his school education principally at the Mount Bethel Academy in Newberry County— then an excellent and celebrated school. He studied also for a time at Newberry Court House. He entered the junior class of the South Carolina College in December 1815, and graduated in December 1817, taking high honors among such men as Senator A. P. Bulter, William McWillie (afterwards Governor of Mississippi), Judge Thomas, W. Glover, Solicitor Alexander A. M. McIver, Robert Dunlap and others of distinction. He taught school the year after his graduation at Edgefield Court House. Among his pupils there, were Professor LaBorde and Chancellor Carroll. He studied law with Judge O'Neall, and was admitted to the Bar in 1820. He at once entered the practice at Newberry Court House. He married Miss Nancy McMorries, eldest daughter of James McMorries, of Laurens County, in 1825 or 1826. He remained and continued to practice law in Newberry until the autumn of 1843, when he removed to Columbia, S. C. He at first had little taste for the practice of law; indeed it is said, that for several years he found great difficulty in forcing himself to comply with the requirements of the profession. Some of his friends have expressed the opinion, that it is quite probable, it would have been better for him if he had yielded to his inclinations; for successful as he was at the Bar and on the Bench, his talents lay decidedly more in the line of literature and military science, than in that of the law. He applied himself however, most laboriously to the study of his profession in all its details

Mr. John S. Carwile, who probably witnessed the trial of every important cause in the Courts of Common Pleas and General Sessions for Newberry, from 1820 to 1850, had great admiration and sincere friendship for Chancellor Caldwell I have often heard him speak of his first appearance at the Bar, and how—with some misgivings, at first, as to his success—he (Mr. Carwile) saw him, gradually but steadily, overcome all obstacles and develop into one of the ablest lawyers and most successful solicitors he had ever known

He was an ardent friend of the militia system, and advanced through its grades of office to that of Brigadier General of Infantry. He was greatly chagrined by his failure to secure a Colonelcy of a regiment in the Seminole war in Florida.

He was first elected to the State Legislature in 1830. He was a candidate before that, but was defeated, it has been generally conceded, on account of his refusal to treat voters to liquor. He was not a total abstainer, nor was he ever a member of any temperance organization, but he resolutely opposed the then almost universal custom of setting out free drinks at musters, barbecues and other occasions of public assemblings, as injurious in its immediate effects on the voter and dangerous in its tendencies. It was predicted that he would fail in his encounter with so time honored a custom. And he did; for he came out at the foot of the list of candidates. He persisted, however. in opposing the pernicious practice, and at the next election headed the ticket. He continued a member of the House of Representatives until December, 1835, when he was elected Solicitor of the Southwestern Circuit, consisting of the Districts of Abbeville, Newberry, Edgefield and Lexington. Under the Act of 1842 the arrangement of Circuits was changed, and he was allotted to the Middle Circuit, embracing the Districts of Newberry, Lexington, Richland, Kershaw and Sumter. He continued in this office until his election to the Chancery Bench in December 1846. He remained upon the Chancery Bench until his death, which occurred on the 11th of March, 1850.

His term of three years was too short to fully develop his capacity as a Chancellor; and he was subjected to very trying comparison by being placed by the side of Chancellors Harper, Job Johnstone and Duncan, each of whom had already had many years of experience on the Bench; but his decrees were seldom overruled by the Court of Appeals, and he delivered several of the most important opinions emanating from the Court of Appeals in Chancery during his term of office.

The difficulties under which Chancellor Caldwell labored, in consequence of his ill-health, would have appalled any but the most indomitable will. He had always been very delicate, and when he went upon the Bench he was worn down by the unremitting toil of upwards of twenty-five years practice at the Bar. Yet he, with his constant feeble health, never lost time from his work. His estimable widow stated, soon after his death, that except the four last days of his life, he had never, from the time of their marriage, spent a day in bed.

It was as Solicitor that he most distinguished himself; for in that office, his pains-taking in their preparation of cases and his fluent and earnest oratory, produced the most striking effects. He did not endeavor to secure convictions at all hazards; on the contrary, as his successor, Col. Fair, used to say of him, he insisted that as the representative of the State, the Solicitor must guard against persecuting any citizen. But once convinced of the guilt of the accused, he pressed the prosecution with all the zeal of his ardent temperament.

The following extract from a communication addressed to one of the Chancellor's sons, many years ago, by the Rev. Thomas Frean, of Columbia, sets forth in strong light the Chancellor's oratorical powers, and the thorough sympathy which he always felt for the unfortunate and oppressed:

"You will often hear when you grow up much of your honored father's eloquence. Permit me to give you an instance of its powerful influence; and I will do so as nearly as I can, in the language of my informant Mr. — Wilson of Union Court House.

"An action was brought for a poor widow by a member of the Union Bar, against the executor of her deceased husband, who had defrauded herself and her children of their rights. The case came on, but whether from inattention in the preparation, or from some other cause, the defendant evidently had the best of it in the trial.

"When the widow's counsel closed, the Bench was inattentive, the Bar regardless of what was passing, and the jury almost nodding. Counsel felt 'it was a gone case with him,' and taking his seat requested your father to say something, as he felt he had not done justice to the case, for wind and tide seemed to be against him.

"Though your father was not employed, and knew no more of the case than had just transpired, he arose and in five minutes the whole audience was listening in breathless silence. He sketched with a master hand the rapacity, the ingratitude and the injustice of the executor, the destitution and want of the poor widow and her suffering children. The widow drew closer and closer to him, while the big tears rolled down her cheeks. She involuntarily put her hand in her bosom and pulled out her little pocket book, and during one of her gifted advocate's bursts of eloquence in her favor, laid it down with hysteric sobbings before him on the table. The Bench was agitated, the jury moved to tears, and the Bar and the audience alike melted down. The Judge gave a strong charge for the widow, and the jury, retiring under a high state of excitement, returned in a few minutes with a sweeping verdict in her favor."

Chancellor Caldwell's study was by no means confined to his profession. He constantly read history, biography, poetry, physical science, the Latin and Greek Classics, medicine, fiction, theology—indeed almost every kind of science and literature. He went so far as to study both French and Spanish, without a master, for he had no time for lessons. He accumulated a large and varied library, and it is probable that he read every book he ever owned. Doctor Carlisle of Wofford College, has frequently spoken of the copious marginal notes which he had observed in a good many of his books on various subjects, which he purchased after his death. It is scarcely an exaggeration to say, that he was consumed with an insatiable thirst for knowledge of all things knowable among men.

He was cut down in the prime of his manhood, and just when fields for enlarged usefulness and opportunities for greater distinction seemed to be opening before him; and has left behind him the record of a life of earnest manly toil and a reputation for integrity, honor, and a just recognition of the rights of others, rarely if ever surpassed.

I have obtained the following facts with reference to his religious views and his death, from one who knew him most intimately. He was not a member of any Church, but was from his youth thoroughly religious, and a constant and thoughtful student of the Bible. His observance of the Sabbath was most strict, his reading was largely of a religious character; and he disciplined his children in the Bible and Shorter Catechism with unflagging care and regularity. For the last two or three years of his life, he was in constant expectation of death, and appeared at all times prepared to meet it. He passed away in the full possession of his faculties, conscious of the great change taking place and evincing that cheerful serenity which only a perfect assurance in regard to the future ever inspires. His body was buried in the Baptist Church Yard in Columbia, where three years later his devoted wife was laid beside him.

CHAPTER XV.

BIOGRAPHICAL SKETCHES CONTINUED—SIMEON FAIR—THOMAS H. POPE—JAMES M. BAXTER—A. C. GARLINGTON.

COL. SIMEON FAIR.

MY acquaintance with Col. Fair extended over a period of nearly forty years. During all that time—as a lawyer, solicitor, member of the Legislature, and in the years just preceding and during the war of Secession, and in the disastrous years which followed, as a leader of the people,—he occupied a conspicuous position in Newberry.

Very little is known of his early life and education. He was not a graduate of any college.

Quintillian observes that "We ought at first to be more anxious in regard to our conceptions than our expressions—; we may attend to the latter afterwards." Col. Fair always conceived well, but he paid too little attention to the latter part of Quintillian's judicious advice. He never acquired a free and graceful use of language in public speaking or in writing. Yet he conducted himself with dignity and self-possession everywhere. He possessed in a high degree that quality which modern writers call magnetism. In the whole course of my intercourse with him, I never found him dull or uninteresting. Whatever of grief or pain he may have felt, or however he may have been harrassed by the cares of life, he was always calm and cheerful, and never obtruded his private affairs upon the notice of his friends. What a useful and important lesson he taught us in this!

His reading did not extend beyond his profession. His books were the men about him. His powers of observation and memory were wonderful. He was a close student of human nature, and was familiar with the characters and personal history of all the prominent men of his own State, and of many in other States, and had treasured up in his memory, beyond all others, the traditions of his native County.

I shall always revere the memory of Col. Fair, not only because he was an eminently useful and patriotic citizen, but because, although a much younger man than himself, I was honored by his confidence and friendship. One of my greatest pleasures, while he lived was to drop into his office, when he was not at work, and listen to him as he unfolded the rich treasures of his memory. I have often wished that it had been possible for some one—especially in the latter years of his life—to have played the part of a Boswell to him, and thus to have preserved a record of much of the history of Newberry which, I fear, passed away forever when he died.

At the Bar Col. Fair was the most imperturbable man I ever knew. Nothing could throw him off his guard. He never betrayed his name; he was always fair; but like a skillful General he would sometimes make a feint, and lead his opponent into a mode of attack or defense which would baffle and cause him to lose his self-control, while he (Col. F.) would remain cool and collected, and thus secure great advantage of position. But he never resorted to subterfuge or trickery.

Col. Fair was married on the 23d of December, 1840, to

Miss Mary Butler Pearson, of Newberry. This marriage proved to be a very happy one. In addition to unusual personal attractions, a bright intellect and engaging manners, Mrs. Fair possessed that excellent virtue which we call common sense. Her husband's duties as Solicitor, required him to be absent from home much of his time Mrs. Fair displayed great energy and practical judgment in the management of the domestic affairs of the family, and also of the farm and other private business of Col. Fair's during his absence. She was a true and faithful helpmeet to her husband. She died on the 31st of December, 1867. Col. Fair died on the 15th of July, 1873, at Glenn Springs, S. C.

I shall now introduce an admirable address, made by J. F. J. Caldwell, Esq., before a memorial meeting of the Bar and citizens of Newberry, on the 1st of September, 1873, and published in the *Newberry Herald*, which gives a more faithful and discriminating estimate of the life and character of Col. Fair than I could possibly produce.

Mr. Caldwell spoke as follows :* " I feel that I should not only neglect an attention due our distinguished dead, but that I should be wanting in common gratitude, if I failed to join my voice in this act of public reverence and lamentation for one, who, in addition to his claims upon me as a public benefactor, had the more pressing claim arising from frequent and considerable kindnesses bestowed upon me individually. It is not necessary that I should recount those kindnesses; and it would be immodest in me to assert that I have been greatly profited by them, for that would

---

* Mr. Caldwell's address is given in full, with the exception of one or two paragraphs referring to certain important causes in which Col. Fair was engaged, and which would not be of special interest to readers, other than members of the Bar.

imply that I consider myself to have attained to something; but I mention them as one of my reasons for occupying the time of this meeting, and one of my reasons for endeavoring to show to those who did not know him as I did, and to remind those who did so know him and appreciate him, how excellent a man he was.

"I do not wish to use the language of idle, fulsome eulogy; if my own sense of propriety did not forbid it, my knowledge of his character assures me how he abhorred it while living, how he must have deprecated its utterance when dead. But I do wish to do him the honor he deserves, and, for our sakes, so to describe him, as shall in some measure bring him again before us, and cause him to live in our minds and hearts, although the grave has forever hidden his mortal part from our eyes. If I, or any of us, shall succeed in this, however imperfectly it may be, we shall have cause to rejoice over our assembling here, for we shall then have done the noble work of restoring and perpetuating, for the emulation and delight of those here and those to come, the image of patriotism, and usefulness, and virtue.

"Simeon Fair was born in Newberry District, on the 17th day of November, 1801. His ancestry were Scotch-Irish, his father, William Fair, being born of one of the families which came from Ireland during, and just before, and just after the year 1770. I have not been able to learn whether William Fair was born before or after the settlement of his parents in this country; but he must have been born within two or three years of it. The Fair's were of that well-known and worthy people who settled in large numbers in this county, during the four or five years just preceding and just after the date last mentioned—the Presbyterians of North Ireland. These men were not the adventurers the majority of European emigrants then were, and now are. They were mostly farmers, or hand-crafts men, of good condition. They all brought something with them; and some of them good sums of money, hoarded from the toil of years, or else realized from the sale of their valuable leases. They were a sturdy, brave, patient race; quiet and peaceable, yet obstinately tenacious of their rights; cool-headed and calculating, yet burning in their hearts with the very fire of volcanoes; rigid and abstemious in their habits of life, yet not without an excellent humor and a proper appreciation of all rational enjoyment. They were eminently religious—eminently moral. They had ever a clear, positive doctrine, which permeated all their opinions and habits; and to this they clung with a tenacity which no argument—and no misfortune could ever shake.

"Coming of such an ancestry, and reared in such a pure school of morals, it is not difficult to see how Col. Fair early learned the necessity and dignity of labor; how he learned to value men only according to their intellectual and moral worth; how he learned to estimate actions according as they were right or wrong, without recourse to the base and pitiful subterfuge of justifying the means by the end; how he learned on the one hand, that man is nothing so worthy in himself as to warrant vanity or arrogance, and on the other hand, that there is nothing, or almost nothing, which an earnest, patient, laborious man may not accomplish.

"I mention these things because I am sure that in having such training, Col Fair was more fortunate than in the possession of his fine intellect, and because I am sure that his noble success in life was but the legitimate, the inevitable result of such sentiments and such education.

"Col. Fair, as I infer, spent a good portion of his youth in labor, on his father's farm as was the case with the sons of our Scotch-Irish ancestors. We hear nothing especial of his school-days. He was not one of that bright, superficial class known in the colleges as "first honor men." He not only had no bent towards the languages and the belles-lettres, but he had rather an excessive indifference for them. Indeed, it is in this that we find the one thing to be regretted in his whole intellectual life; for his deficiency in language prevented him from putting his communications, whether oral or written, with his fellow-men, in such shape as would have displayed to the world the full strength and nobility of his mind, and the extent of his legal learning.

"He was admitted to the Bar in 1824, and he soon established himself as well worth a place amongst a band of giant minds. Immediately upon, or soon after his admission he was taken into partnership by John Caldwell, who was then in the full tide of fame and success as a forensic orator. The combination was a happy one for both parties. Mr. Caldwell, like almost all men whose eloquence gives them command over juries and spectators, appears to have relied upon that gift, somewhat to the neglect of his legal studies in general, and the serious neglect of the department of pleading. Col. Fair's clear, accurate mind naturally led him to that department, and the deficiency of his senior forced him to make it his specialty. And like the man of the fable, whom the fairy rewarded for the kindnesses he had shown her, while she inhabited an unsightly form, he received a noble bounty from this science for his devotion to her, through all the dry and tedious details of technicality, and apparently arbitrary rules. He soon had the satisfaction—alas, how much more rare in the profession than the world believes!—of bringing his cases properly and safely to their trial.

"He rose rapidly until the times of Nullification, as they

are commonly termed. Then he experienced some difficulty from his Union opinions, which were opposed to the prevailing sentiment of this District. But his fearlessness commanded so much respect, and his subsequent readiness to abandon what appeared a fruitless and parricidal opposition to the action of his people, evinced such a willingness to devote himself to those people, however wrong he might consider their theory, that it was not long before his error, as it was deemed, was entirely overlooked, and himself restored to favor.

"He practiced law without intermission, until the war in Florida, in 1836, then he volunteered into the military service, and in the capacity of Lieutenant served until the close of the war. I have scarcely ever heard others speak of his military career, and in all my acquaintance with him, I never heard him mention it a dozen times. He seems however, to have conducted himself with fair credit, in that least intellectual of occupations. At all events, he gave satisfaction to the people of the District, for on his return home, he was elected to the Legislature by a very flattering vote, and he received large accessions to his business. And from this time forward, he enjoyed the confidence of a large majority of our people, with less variation and for a longer period, than probably any man that ever lived in the District.

"Although he was in the State Legislature during the greater part of the time until 1846, his career in his profession is mainly interesting to us.

"Col. Fair and Thomas H. Pope, Esq. formed a copartnership about 1833, which continued until 1838, when the latter was elected Commissioner in Equity. During that period, it is impossible to say what part either one of them performed in their cases. No doubt, however, each bore his share of the labor, each contributed to their triumphs, each deserves his half of our applause.

"Col. Fair was elected Solicitor of the Middle Circuit in 1846, and continued in that office until October 1868—a period of nearly twenty-two years. In this office he was eminently successful in his prosecutions, eminently punctual and industrious, eminently just and conscientious. He carried out perfectly the design of the office ; he prosecuted every real criminal with skill and energy, no matter what his wealth, descent or social rank, yet extended all the liberality to the accused which the frailty of human nature could reasonably demand. Of the great number of cases which he managed, I may be permitted to mention three.

"The case of the State *vs.* Brown, (3 Strob Law, 508,) called forth what was then a leading decision in the organization of juries in criminal trials, and what is still a leading decision on the competency of an accomplice to testify against his fellow criminal.

"The case of the State *vs.* Bowen, which he successfully prosecuted against a master for not providing his slaves with proper food and clothing, and that of the State *vs.* Boozer, and others, by which he enforced the laws against patrols improperly disturbing slaves at an entertainment, have this importance, that they show, despite the slanders of our enemies, that we had laws which jealously protected our bondmen, and that in Simeon Fair we had an officer, who, in the face of all personal opposition, had the laws carried out in favor of that humble class.

"Of the many cases which he conducted in his latter years, I need not speak—partly because they are so fresh in the minds of many persons here, and partly because I might, in some instances, touch a wound which would excite feelings other than those the sadness and solemnity of this occasion demands.

"He was an excellent lawyer. He prepared his pleadings with great skill and accuracy. He collected every fact at all important to his case. He possessed himself, before argument, of every available statute and decision upon his points. He examined a witness with rare ingenuity—sometimes, indeed, forcing from him, with great display of wrath, what he was reluctant to testify, but usually conciliating him and gently—almost imperceptibly— drawing from him what was needed in the cause. He was no rhetorician, gilding or blackening the facts with the hues of his own imagination, and stealing men's hearts, to the blinding of their judgments. He seized the one or two real issues in the case, and spoke right to them, regardless of the snares and quibbles set by an adversary to entrap him. He construed the evidence, he unfolded the law, he appealed to the common sense and common justice of men. And he seldom failed. His memory was astonishingly accurate and retentive, his appreciation of legal principles, most thorough and his discrimination of statutes and decisions almost unequaled. He was every inch a lawyer, and he loved his profession with his whole soul. For nearly fifty years he toiled with almost incessant energy ; in health and in sickness, in affluence and in comparative poverty, amid the riot and tumult of war, and the ruin of a more disastrous peace, he labored steadily and valiantly, and death found him, as he said it should, 'with harness on his back.' I have known him, when stretched upon a bed of sickness, to be laboriously employed in the preparation of a case ; and on one occasion, I knew him to struggle out of bed, and travel a hundred miles in the most inclement weather, and, then though barely able to stand upon his feet, engage in one of the most delicate and difficult trials I ever witnessed. But the intricacy and seriousness of the case seemed to warm him into new life. He followed the mass of testimony from first to last; he caught every point of his able opponents seven hour argument, and in his own reply of two hours length, construed the evidence, unfolded the great principles of law involved, and fortified every foot of ground with the decisions of the Masters of Equity, both in England and America. And this was a cause in which, from first to last, he positively refused to accept even a contingent fee.

"Col. Fair's political career requires but a brief description at my hands. He was a Democrat of the true Jefferson and Calhoun school, a friend to the Union so long as his State had her rights in it, but giving his first allegiance to his State. He was not a separate State action man in 1850 and 1851; but he was a Secessionist in 1860, and as a delegate from this District he signed the Ordinance of Secession. After the war, his course, although not quite successful, was as wise a one as seemed possible under the circumstances. He was the great conservator of the county—preserving as far as possible the ancient tone of our society, protecting us as much as one could from the aggressions of our adversaries. Yet preventing undue violence on the part of a well-nigh desperate class. In these efforts he was nobly conspicuous in the Reform Movement in 1870 and the Presidential campaign in 1872. And I believe I state but the naked truth when I say, that although his conduct was not universally appreciated, it commanded the affection and confidence of his own party, and, wrung a reluctant tribute, even from those whose incendiary schemes he baffled.

"We should be chary of the epithet, but I think upon a review of his life, we may safely say, he was a good man. He was a philanthropist in the noblest sense of the term. He was kind and amiable, he was just and generous, he was honest and true. No man but the evil-doer need fear him, for while he was

> 'Lofty and sour to them that loved him not,
> To those men that sought him he was sweet as summer.'

We loved and honored him while he lived—how shall we adequately express our grief at his loss:

> 'Oh good gray head which all men knew,
> O, voice from which their omens all men drew,
> O, iron nerve to true occasion true,
> O, fallen at length that tower of strength
> Which stood four square to all the winds that blew!'

I do not say that our loss is irreparable—I do not say that, even in our generation, we shall not look upon his like again, for surely, He who was able to raise up children unto Abraham, can, of the noble material in this people, rear up another equal to him we here lament. But for the present, I must say, we are in some sense an orphaned community—bereaved of our head and leader, and knowing not if his mantle shall descend on any one of us.

"But we have great matter of consolation, even in these first hours of our affliction, and our predominent feeling should be one of thanks. For his sake we should be thankful that he enjoyed so long and happy a life, that he acquired honor and the affection of his people, that he enjoyed all the pleasures of friendship and those of domestic life, and that he had the felicity—enough to make his lonely death-bed a place of comfort and repose—the inexpressible felicity of knowing, in his last hours, that he had served his family and his friends, that he had served his country, that he had befriended the poor, the friendless, the widow and the orphan. And for ourselves we should be thankful, that we for so long a period enjoyed his services and his society, and that now and henceforth, although his visible, mortal form is taken from us, we have his example before us, to guide, to admonish, to strengthen and to comfort us all the days of our life."

THOMAS H. POPE.

Thomas Herbert Pope was born in Edgefield County, S. C., on the 12th of November, 1803. He was the son of Capt. Sampson and Sarah (Strother) Pope. He was educated in the best schools and academies within his father's reach, and was for a short time in Yale College. He read law at Newberry, with Judge O'Neall, (who was his brother-in-law,) was admitted to the Bar in 1825, and settled at Edgefield. He was married on the 19th of January, 1830, to Harriet Neville Harrington, the second daughter of Young John and Nancy (Calmes) Harrington, of Newberry. He removed to Newberry in 1832. He was elected Commissioner in Equity for Newberry District in 1836, and served until 1840, when he resigned. In 1840 he was elected a member of the House of Representatives of South Carolina from Newberry.

In 1850, an effort was made by a strong party in the State, led by the Hon. C. G. Memminger, of Charleston, to abolish the Bank of the State, which had existed for a great many years; the parent institution being located in Charleston, with branches at Columbia and Camden. There were "Bank" and "Anti-Bank" candidates brought out in all the Districts of the State. Mr. Pope, being opposed to the Bank, was induced to run upon the Anti-Bank ticket in Newberry, together with Genl. James H. Williams and Col. James W. Duckett. The candidates of the Bank party were Genl. A. C. Garlington, Maj. John P. Kinard and Col. Robert Moorman.

As the people nearly all belonged to the same National political party, elections were usually merely personal contests. But at this time the result of the election for members to the Legislature hinged upon a well defined political issue, and all other considerations were lost sight of. The Anti-Bank party contended, among other things, that it was unjust for the State to enter into competition with Banks that she had chartered, and over which she exercised control to some extent; that the Directors of the Bank of the State often used that institution to advance their private ends, and extended undue accommodations to a privileged few.

The Bank party maintained that by the profits of the Bank the revenue of the State was increased, and taxes correspondingly reduced; that planters and other non commercial classes of citizens received assistance and accommodations from the Bank of the State, which they could not obtain from the other banks; and that the Directors of that institution were as free from blame as those of the chartered banks.

The canvass which preceded the election was very exciting, but conducted with courtesy and freedom from personal invective. The people flocked in great numbers to the places of public assemblings to hear the discussions.

Mr. Pope and General Garlington were the recognized leaders of the opposing parties in Newberry. General Garlington, by the power of his eloquence and acknowledged ability as a platform speaker, always produced a strong impression upon his auditors. But in Mr. Pope, "he had a foeman worthy of his steel." Mr. Pope, though always logical and impressive, was not an eloquent man in the common acceptation of the term. His style was colloquial, earnest and argumentative. He addressed himself chiefly to the reason and judgment, and made very little effort to please the fancy of his hearers; but he never failed to arrest and hold their undivided attention. He had made a thorough study of the question at issue, and supported his arguments by a masterly array of facts and figures.

At the election, the Bank party triumphed in Newberry, as it did in a majority of the Districts of the State

While a member of the Legislature, Mr. Pope easily took rank among the foremost members of that body. By his talents, sound judgment and independent and honorable bearing, he commanded the respect and confidence of the House. He possessed many of the qualities which enter into the character of a wise and practical legislator, but his natural temperament and feeble physique, unfitted him for the exposure and excitement of electioneering campaigns, and the turmoil of political life.

The Law was his mistress, and how well she repaid him for his devotion to her! He achieved success and distinction at the Bar amid the severest competition with men of great ability and legal learning. The Equity side of the Court was his fort. He had few, if any superiors in that branch of the practice, and would have made an able and successful Chancellor. His legal papers were models of neatness and good English. He was a prompt man of business, an excellent accountant, and applied himself closely to both the study and practice of his profession. He was seldom seen outside of his office during business hours. When preparing for the Court of Appeals, he usually came to his office very early in the morning, and taking a seat near his library—with writing material at hand—would remain until the close of the day; leaving off work just long enough to partake of a simple luncheon which he had brought with him. He had a curious habit of constantly twisting the forelock of his hair which he wore rather long, around the forefinger of his right hand while reading. He had a high appreciation of the dignity of his profession, and looked far beyond its material benefits for his reward. His disposition was sensitive and his temperament nervous. He felt keenly any indignity or injustice offered him, especially at the Bar, but was never betrayed into doing an ungentlemanly act, or using an undignified expression. He died on the 4th of February, 1851, in the forty-eighth year of his age.

The writer spent nearly three years in Mr. Pope's office, and while there, began under his supervision and direction a Digest of the Law Reports of South Carolina, beginning where Rice left off. A considerable amount of work had been done, but it was far from completion at Mr. Pope's death, and unfortunately after his death the manuscript was lost.

The following extract is from a "Preamble and Resolutions" adopted by the Bar of Newberry, just after Mr. Pope's death, and presented to the Court of Common Pleas for Newberry, at Spring Term, 1851:

"Our friend and brother, Thomas H. Pope, who for upwards of twenty years has been engaged in the practice of law, departed this life at his residence in this town, on the morning of the 4th instant.

"He had a laudable ambition to excel in his profession, and during his whole life assiduously and untiringly devoted himself to its duties. To a mind both penetrating and discriminating, he united an industry and perseverance that enabled him to surmount obstacles from which others less ambitious would have retired. He put forth all his powers in behalf of his clients, and in his profession tasked his ability to the utmost. Of feeble frame and small physical strength, yet such was his desire of success and distinction, that he never permitted himself to flag under any labor required of him.

"In his intercourse with his professional brethren, he was honorable and fair, and always willing to rest the cases in which he was engaged, upon their merits."

The Presiding Judge—the able and distinguished Judge Withers—before ordering the Preamble and Resolutions to be entered upon the Records of the Court, expressed a high opinion of the legal ability of Mr. Pope, and in closing his remarks said: "While I had not the pleasure of an intimate personal acquaintance with Mr. Pope, yet, from what I saw of him on the Circuit and before the Appeal Court, I had learned to look upon him as a model lawyer."

Mr. Pope was a diligent student and his reading embraced a good many subjects, beside the law. He had good literary taste and delighted to refresh his mind, occasionally, by reading the works of the great masters of English literature.

He was very happy in his domestic relations. He had been most fortunate in his choice of a life companion, and was never so happy as when surrounded by his family. His wife inherited much of the energy and self-reliance of her father with the gentle patience and winning manners of her mother. She had a love for all that was beautiful in nature. The first flower garden ever seen in Newberry was planted and tended by her, and as long as she lived, she found time amid all her domestic duties and cares to beautify and render more attractive the family home. Nor did she neglect the cultivation of her naturally bright intellect She was an admirable type of the Southern matron, devoted to her husband, her children and her home.

Mrs. Pope died on the 22d of December, 1860.

MAJOR JAMES M. BAXTER.

Major James M. Baxter, was born in Laurens County, S. C., on the 7th of September, 1825. His parents came from Ireland, and belonged to that class commonly known as Scotch-Irish, which furnished so many of the honest, thrifty and intelligent early settlers of South Carolina

Judge McGowan, of the Supreme Court of South Carolina, in a letter addressed to the writer in relation to the ancestors of Major Baxter, and himself, says: "Our forefathers passed over from Scotland to the North of Ireland, and at the close of the last century, were living in County Antrim, protestant, old-school,—'John Knox'—Presbyterians. They were all followers of Robert Emmet, and were 'out in 1798.' Grandfather McGowan was arrested and punished as a rebel, but his life was spared, and he, with his family (wife and four children) in 1800, emigrated to South Carolina, and came up from Charleston to Laurens County, where the children grew up and married. William, the only son, was my father, and his sister Nancy, married William Baxter, also an emigrant from County Antrim, Ireland, and their only child was our lamented friend, James M. Baxter."

Major Baxter received his academic education in his native county, and then entered Erskine College, Due West, S. C., from which he was graduated. After his graduation he studied law under General Albert C. Garlington, at Newberry, and was admitted to the Bar in 1849. Soon af er his admission to the Bar, he opened an office at Newberry where he continued in the pursuit of his chosen profession until his death. He was for some time, during the earlier years of his professional life, the law partner of Col. Simeon Fair, and for several years just preceding his death, was associated in the practice of law with Silas Johnstone, Esq.

He was married on the 17th of May, 1860, to Miss Frances Nance, the daughter of Drayton Nance, Esquire, of Newberry.

Upon the breaking out of the war of Secession, he promptly dedicated himself to the service of his country. He was elected Major and subsequently promoted to the rank of Lieutenant Colonel of the Third Regiment South Carolina Volunteers, which was one of the earliest corps mustered into the service of the Confederate States. He followed the fortunes of his regiment, doing faithful and efficient service, during the time of its original enlistment. At the end of that time, he was assigned to the "Conscript Department" in which service he remained until the close of the war.

Subsequent to the war, he was, for several terms, elected Mayor of the town of Newberry. This office he filled with efficiency and success. During his administration, more attention than ever before, was paid to the sanitary condition of the town.

But the practice of his profession may be said to have been his life work; and to that we will now direct the readers attention.

Major Baxter died on Saturday, the 5th of February, 1881. The Court of Common Pleas and General Sessions met at Newberry the following week, and continued in session until Saturday, February 19th. During a recess of the Court on the 18th, the members of the Bar met to take some appropriate action on the death of Major Baxter, Maj. L. J. Jones, the senior member of the Bar presiding: Messrs. Suber, Pope and Caldwell, a committee appointed for that purpose, reported appropriate resolutions, which were unanimously adopted. On the 19th, Major Jones, as the chairman of the

Bar meeting, presented the resolutions to his Honor, Judge Hudson, in open Court.

I am sure that I could not in any other way give a more satisfactory presentation of the character of Major Baxter, both as citizen and lawyer, than by introducing the following extracts from the speeches made on the occasion just referred to. They are the testimony of his professional brethren who knew him well. They are judicious and discriminating, and free from fulsome adulation.

In presenting the resolutions of the Bar, Major Jones spoke as follows:

"May it please your Honor: I hold in my hand a preamble and resolutions adopted at a meeting of the members of the Newberry Bar, in commemoration of the death of our friend and brother, Major James M. Baxter. As chairman of that meeting and as the oldest member of this Bar, I am charged with the melancholy duty of presenting them to your Honor, with the request that they be spread upon the Minutes of the Court Before I present them it is proper that I should say a few words.

" Major Baxter's death was a great loss to this Bar, where his masculine intellect and discriminating mind, and devotion to the true interest of his clients, gave him great prominence. His mind was too broad and comprehensive to be trammeled with forms and technicalities, but easily mastered the strong points of his cases, and seized and applied with a masterly hand the broad principles of law and equity upon which our judicial system is founded, and which embodies the united wisdom and experience of ages. It was his comprehension of and devotion to principles, that gave him great power before the jury and compelled a respectful attention from the Judge to what he said. As your Honor well knows, the contests of this forum are often exciting and worrying, and it is sometimes difficult for the best of us to avoid saying and doing things, under the excitement of the moment, which should not have been said and done; but it is a notable characteristic of the members of the Bar not to let these things mar their friendship. No man was more ready to forgive and forget things said and done under such circumstances; no man was more ready to atone for things said and done by him under such circumstances than our friend and brother. His faults (and who of us have not our faults?) were faults of the head and not of the heart. He knew it was human to err, and hence he was always ready to forgive and forget. In the expressive language of another: 'He was a man of large heart and head, kind and courteous to all, a most pleasant and entertaining companion, and a true and steadfast friend. Those who knew him best admired and loved him most.' He was a kind and provident husband, an affectionate and tender parent—a steadfast, devoted friend—a patriotic citizen, alive to all the best interests of his State and county—a sincere, conscientious Christian It is therefore fitting that we, his companions at this Bar, should perpetuate and transmit to those who may come after us our high appreciation of his master mind, and his high moral, social and religious character, by spreading upon the Minutes of this Court the preamble and resolutions which I now present for that purpose."

Major C. H. Suber, in seconding the resolutions, said: Major Baxter was gifted with rare intellectual powers—endowed with faculties which eminently fitted him for the profession he adorned so highly. He was not what might be called a popular speaker, abounding in the graces of oratory and possessing the power to sway the thronging multitude. He seldom attempted flights of fancy, but always spoke in language unadorned, but pure and chaste. His style of speaking was logical and argumentative, never failing to impress upon those who heard him the conviction of his own earnestness in the cause he advocated His perceptions were clear and exact and his reflective faculties acute and vigorous. As a lawyer he was earnest and zealous in whatever business was committed to his charge, and he exhibited a devotion to his profession and an untiring industry in the cause of his clients, such as is rarely equalled. He was thoroughly grounded in the elementary principles of the law, and whenever, in the preparation of his cases he had occasion to investigate a legal principle, he always resorted to the fountains of the law for his information, instead of relying upon the reports of recently decided cases. He believed that 'the reason of the law was the life of the law,' and he searched for it in the writings of the sages of the law. He was no 'case lawyer,' but rather depended upon his own native intellect and strong reasoning faculties to guide him in the arguments of his cases. A formidable adversary at the Bar under any circumstances, but most dangerous when his case appeared most hopeless—he gathered new strength and rose to the emergency as his case trembled in the balance. He knew no such word as fail.

"But he is gone from amongst us, never to return. No more shall we hear his voice; no more shall we see his genial face in this forum. Life's fitful fever is o'er, he sleeps well."

George Johnstone, Esquire, said:

"I rise for one moment to lay a garland on the grave of our deceased comrade. This much is due to him with whom I began the study of law, and from whom I have derived more information than from any one else. This is due to one who possessed more ability than was necessary to raise him to any position in his profession to which he might have aspired. His social life was as striking and as brilliant as his professional life. That part of his character which appeared to me most lovable and the most admirable manifested itself in social intercourse. There were few men to whom the pleasures of social life were dearer, and few who contributed more to the pleasure of others. He has left us a legacy we can not forget, and has pointed out to us a career that we should diligently follow. His life was without malice and enmity, and in his death he has left neither malice nor enmity."

Mr. Silas Johnstone, Master in Equity, said :

"I would add a few words to testify my high regard for our deceased brother. More than thirty years ago I met him for the first time, and I was struck with his wonderful conversational powers. After his admission to the Bar he soon gained a practice alongside of the best lawyers of the day; and for the last fifteen years he has been the most eminent member of the Bar of his Circuit. As one who was for years his partner, I might be permitted to speak of him as a counsellor in his office. He was a safe lawyer; being well grounded in the principles of the law he came at once to his conclusions. He was not eloquent in the usual meaning of the term; but he was logical, clear and forcible. He knew his case and the principles that governed it. He possessed in an eminent degree one other quality, without which no man can ever become a great lawyer,—a love of justice. He was a man of too much brains and heart to take a back seat in any company. His life was a most useful one. Wherever we turn we miss him, and will miss him at all times. In thinking of him now I recall the lines of a poem that he so often repeated :

'The leafless tree, when Spring shall come,
May feel its warm reviving power,
And put forth many a lovely bloom,
When moistened by its genial shower;
But sun nor shower can ere restore
The friends whom now we see no more:
And birds may sing, and zephyrs blow,
These tears can never cease to flow.'"

Louis Simkins, Esq., said: "There is one aspect of the character of Major Baxter, that impressed itself deeply upon my mind, and that I now recall with grateful feelings: It was his universal consideration and kindness towards the young men of the profession and towards all young men. He took a deep and abiding interest in their welfare, and was always ready to extend to them kind advice and assistance."

Judge Hudson said: "Your deceased brother, while not known to me as intimately as to you, was amongst my most valued acquaintances. I first met him in Columbia in the Court of Appeals just after the war, where I was associated with him in an important case. I was impressed then by his open, frank manner, and the courtesy and courage that he displayed in the management of his cases. He impressed me as a strong man, and as possessing to an unusual degree that high quality of which the Master has spoken, without which no man can become a great lawyer, the love of justice. Since that time I have met him frequently at Columbia and elsewhere. I have been with him often at the Bar and in the social circle, and never without being both pleased and instructed by him. He was full of useful information outside of his profession. He thoroughly loved his profession. In preparing to argue cases before the Supreme Court, I would always consult him whenever the opportunity offered, because I appreciated and valued his knowledge of the principles of the law, and I never consulted him without profit. Not long ago I met Major Baxter in Columbia, and the thought passed over me then that this man is destined to a long life of usefulness; he was the picture of health, vigor and animation. I then thought, that of all those who had made a reputation at their profession, Major Baxter would be one to enjoy a green old age.

"It becomes us to profit by this dispensation of Providence, and to learn lessons of usefulness from the life of our deceased friend. He fought the battle of life courageously, and achieved success. The occasion is a sad one, I can add nothing more, except to endorse the resolutions. Let them be spread upon the Minutes of the Court, and let the Court stand adjourned."

In his letter (to which I have already referred), Judge McGowan says: "In his profession he, (Major B.) was especially devoted to the doctrines and practice of Equity, and I have always thought would have made a good Chancellor."

Major Baxter was very domestic in his tastes and habits. He loved his family and his home, and often sought recreation in superintending the cultivation of his farm, his orchard and his garden. His generous and abounding hospitality, in which he was most heartily joined by his excellent and devoted wife will never be forgotten by those who enjoyed it. He was benevolent without ostentation, many of his deeds of kindness were not known except by those upon whom they were bestowed, and a few of his most intimate friends.

Mr. Johnstone, Master in Equity, has alluded to his excellent conversational powers, and Major Suber to the purity and chasteness of his language. His facility in the use of his native tongue was remarkable. He never used a "big word;" yet he rarely failed to use the best word in conversation, in speaking or in writing. If young members of the Bar who may read these pages, will allow a laymen to offer them a suggestion, it is this: that they should go frequently to the Clerk's office at Newberry, and study Major Baxter's legal papers on file there. They cannot fail to be pleased with the simplicity, vigor and clearness of his style.

"Of Scotch-Irish parentage he was early grounded in the doctrines peculiar to Presbyterianism." He was admitted to the membership of Aveleigh (Presbyterian) Church at Newberry, October the 12th, 1855, and within one month thereafter was elected to the office of deacon. He served the Church as deacon for a number of years, until vacancies occurring in the bench of elders, he was elected and installed into the eldership on the 9th of July, 1865. In the latter office he served his Church until his death.

GEN. A. C. GARLINGTON.

Gen. Albert Cresswell Garlington,—who was the most eloquent and polished speaker of his day at the Newberry Bar—was born in Oglethorpe County, Georgia, on the 9th of June, 1822. He was the son of Christopher and Eliza (Aycock) Garlington. His father removed to Laurens County, S. C., when he was quite young. He received his education at Laurens, S. C., and at Athens Ga. After his graduation he read law, and was admitted to the Bar. He was married on the 12th of December, 1846, to Miss Sallie L. Moon, the daughter of the late Dr. Peter Moon, of Newberry. He died on the 25th of March, 1885, survived by his devoted wife, one daughter, Miss Octavia Garlington, (who is an accomplished and successful educator, and at this time the Principal of Newberry Female Academy,) and three sons.

His eldest son, Ernest A. Garlington, is an officer in the United States Army, (holding the commission of First Lieutenant of the 7th Cavalry,) and was assigned to the command of the expedition sent out by the United States, to the Arctic regions in 1883, for the relief of Lieutenant Greely.

At the first session of the Court of Common Pleas and General Sessions for Newberry, held (July 1885) after Gen. Garlington's death, Major C. H. Suber presented appropriate resolutions, which had been previously adopted by the Newberry Bar, relative to his (Gen. G 's) death. Major Suber's address delivered on that occasion will present to the reader a short but comprehensive sketch of the character and career of Gen. Garlington.

He said: "May it please your Honor, it is my painful duty to announce the death of a member of this Bar, that occurred since the last meeting of this Court.

"Gen. Albert C. Garlington is no more. He died at his home in this County, on the 25th day of March last. At a meeting of the surviving members of this Bar, held soon after the sad event, for the purpose of paying a proper tribute to his memory, a committee of five was appointed to prepare resolutions expressive of our feelings, and as chairman of that committee, I rise now to present the resolutions for such disposition as to the Court may seem meet.

"May it please your Honor, the kindly relations that existed between the deceased and myself, commencing in our youth and continuing without interruption to the day of his death, and our long association as partners in the practice of our profession, would seem to require that I should say something, a few words at least, on this melancholy occasion. I would do violence to the better impulses of my heart if I remained silent.

"Gen. Garlington possessed intellectual endowments and accomplishments such as are rarely found in any man. It is not often that we encounter in life a man who can speak so fluently, correctly, tersely and vigorously as he did. The legal papers drawn by his hand in the cases in which he was engaged, (many of which are on file in the Clerk's office below), will compare favorably with the pleadings prepared by the ablest lawyers who ever practiced at this Bar, and Newberry has not been unprolific in able lawyers and skilful pleaders. His arguments in the Supreme Court were models of forensic eloquence. His contributions to the Press, both as editor and correspondent, were marked with eloquence of diction and vigor of thought, as were also his speeches in Legislative halls, which won the applause of listening Senates. In times of high political excitement he was singularly apt in his speeches on the hustings, where he held sway over the minds of his hearers by the magic of his eloquence. They never tired of listening to his impassioned utterances, they would not lose the faintest words that fell from his lips. As orator, statesman, lawyer and journalist, he made his impress upon the times in which he lived.

"He enjoyed the advantages of early education and study, and well did he profit by them. He did not allow a golden opportunity to pass by without gasping it, and by perseverence and close study in his early days, he laid the foundation for the brilliancy of mature manhood.

"He was graduated from the University of Georgia, in the town of Athens, in that State, in 1843, carrying off the highest honors of his class, (as did his brother, Robert Garlington, two years later, in the South Carolina College.) Returning to this State, he entered immediately upon the study of his chosen profession, in the office of the Hon.

Charles P. Sullivan, at Laurens, and by unremitting application mastered the prescribed course in less than twelve months. He was admitted to the Bar and enrolled among the attorneys of the State in December, 1844. Immediately after, he commenced the practice of law at Laurens, S. C., under the most favorable auspices. Encouraged by the companions of his youth and his influential relatives, his success seemed assured there. But he soon led to the altar a daughter of Newberry, who loved to share with him his joys and sorrows, and now mourns his untimely end. Becoming thus identified with Newberry, he made his home amongst us, as a member of the Bar, in the early part of 1848.

"The road to success at the Bar, under the most favorable circumstances, even when a young lawyer is sustained by influential friends and relatives, is full of obstacles difficult to surmount. It is indeed a stout hill to climb, and it requires a stout heart to climb it. But to our friend the ascent was comparatively easy With his brilliant talents he sprang as it were *uno saltu* into the front rank of the profession, and that position he maintained as long as he was actively engaged at the Bar.

"It was not long before he was allured by the voice of flattery into the political arena to contend for the glittering prizes there. He came before the people of Newberry for the first time as a candidate for a seat in the House of Representatives, in the year 1850, (only two years after he had become a citizen of the County), at a time when the whole County, yea, the whole State was ablaze with excitement over the question of the re-chartering of the Bank of the State of South Carolina, which was to come before the next session of the Legislature. There was an excitement in this County such as, I learn, had not been experienced since the times of Nullification. The party lines were strictly drawn and the ablest men were chosen to represent each party. Gen. Garlington espoused the side of the Bank, and was at once accepted as the leader of that party in this County. He was elected—after discussing the question with his able opponents, at the head of the ticket, by a large majority. He went to the Legislature and at once took his stand in the front rank of the debaters there. His constituency re-elected him again in 1852. In 1854 he was not a candidate for re-election, but became a candidate for Congress in opposition to the Hon. Preston S. Brooks, who was then serving out his first term in that body. Brooks was elected. Gen. Garlington became a candidate for the State Senate in 1856, and was elected after a most heated contest. Serving four years in the Senate, satisfactorily to his constituents, he was re-elected for another term, which embraced the exciting period of the recent war between the States. He was one of the Executive Council appointed by Governor Pickens, under the Ordinance of the Convention in session at that time. He was elected Adjutant-General of the State during the war, which office he filled most satisfactorily. He was also elected Major of the Holcombe Legion, went into the field and served several months with that body of troops, when his services became needed in the Adjutant-General's office, and he was called back again.

"After the close of the war, in 1865, he was called by the people of Newberry, under the attempt of Andrew Johnson, to reconstruct the government—to again serve them in the Legislature, this making three terms in the House of Representatives, and with two in the Senate, fourteen years in all, of his legislative service.

"In the wreck which followed the war he shared the fate of his neighbors. His practice was swept away with that of others. He was left poor. His fortune which was ample for the support of himself and his family, was swallowed up ; and looking about for a wider field in which to seek the recovery of his losses, he determined to leave the State and cast his lot among the people of Atlanta, in the State of Georgia. Having graduated at the University of that State, he was not without friends and acquaintances there, and upon his arrival was greeted as a valuable acquisition to that people. He remained there several years, in the pursuit of his profession, with his heart still turning to South Carolina, the State that had delighted to do him honor. Not content with his new home he turned his face hitherward, and came back amongst us to find at last his resting place in the sod of the State he loved so well.

" His earthly career is now ended, and he has gone to his long home, where human voice no more can reach him, where the cares and sorrows of the world will not disturb him again. And may a gentle spirit preside over and preserve the quiet of his deep repose, for his must have been a gentle spirit that had drawn around him such a large circle of affectionate friends."

Gen. Garlington was gifted with a fine imagination. His speeches were often illumined by the play of a poetic fancy, and enforced by apt quotations from the great writers of the world. He made occasional contributions of verse to the Press.

Two of his shorter poems ; pathetic in their simplicity, and revealing the tender and affectionate side of his nature, are here introduced :

> The blushing Rose, at early morn,
> In dewy freshness greets the eye ;
> But ere another day shall dawn,
> Its drooping leaves will fade and die.

The glowing clouds that skirt the sky,
    Along the track of parting day,
With rapture fill the gazer's eye,—
    How soon to melt and pass away!

The queenly Moon, through starry skies,
    With silvery train leads on her way;
When from her couch Aurora hies,
    She flees before the brighter day.

But sweet Spring-time will come again,—
    The rose again will lift its head,
And 'neath the genial sun and rain,
    Will bloom as if 'twere never dead

The bright Sun, too, will rise again,
    And shed its beam of golden light,
To gild the clouds, and hill and plain,
    As though they ne'er were hid from sight.

And the Moon's sweet face, seen from afar,
    Will shine again o'er land and sea,
As on she moves, from star to star,
    In robes of light and majesty.

Thus life is chequered o'er its way,
    With flitting shades of dark and light—
The lesser and the brighter ray,—
    A shifting scene of day and night.

The blushing Rose, the Moon, the Cloud—
    Fit type's of mortals here below;
The smile, the sigh, the tear, the shroud—
    And then to mother Earth they go.

But another scene will open soon,
    Where neither eve nor night shall be;
And a glorious and cloudless noon
    Will shine throughout eternity.

O, sing my love, that song once more,
It falls so sweetly on my ear,
Though at the sound my heart runs o'er
And bids my eyes let fall a tear.

It tells of days, long, long, gone by,
When first we met in youthful prime;
When love and hope lit up our sky,
Like radiant stars in Southern clime;

Of sorrows, too, of sobs and sighs,
Of death—the little ones asleep,
Whose spirits from the upper skies,
O'er loved ones here their watches keep.

Of faded youth, like autumn's hue,
That tells the winter winds are nigh,
To break the leaf from where it grew,
And dash it on the ground to die.

But sing the song my love again;
What though its notes excite a tear;
I'll ne'er forget the melting strain,
To me so sad, but still so dear.

"Gen. Garlington was one of the most gifted of men. His mental faculties were not only brilliant, but strong and well balanced His acquirements were varied and solid; and whether in the political arena, or at the Bar, or in social life, he was a man of marked ability. As an orator, either as an advocate at the Bar, or in the halls of legislation, he had few equals. With a mind severely trained to reason and stored with information, and possessing all the graces of oratory, he had the power to move men by his eloquence, and his speeches were always effective, especially so on important occasions calling for his best efforts.

"Gen. Garlington was one of the men who spoke and wrote with equal ease and force. As a writer his style was vigorous as well as graceful. He wrote much for the press, having been at one time editor of one of the leading daily newspapers of Atlanta, and afterwards editor of the Greenville *Daily News*. During the last years of Gen Garlington's life, he devoted much time to the study of the history of South Carolina, with a view to publishing a history of the State, and had gathered from various sources a great deal of valuable material for this purpose, which we hope will be preserved and utilized by some one capable of pursuing the subject so ably begun by him."*

*Newberry Observer, (Newspaper) Editorial.

CHAPTER XVI.

BIOGRAPHICAL SKETCHES CONTINUED—Y. J. HARRINGTON—JOHN S. CARWILE—F. B. HIGGINS—DRAYTON NANCE—COL. J. D. NANCE.

Y. J. HARRINGTON.

YOUNG JOHN HARRINGTON, was born in Union District, South Carolina, on the 5th of April, 1784. He was the son of John and Frances (Burt) Harrington. His parents came to South Carolina from Virginia. His father died when he was quite young. His mother, who afterwards (in 1795) married Col. Robert Rutherford, of Newberry District, was a devout member of the Methodist Church, and distinguished for her domestic virtues and exemplary piety. At her request, Col. Rutherford, before their marriage, promised that he would never punish his step children, but would in all cases of disobedience, allow her to admonish or correct them. This promise he faithfully kept, and through his forbearance and her excellent management, much of that unpleasantness which sometimes comes into families where there are two sets of children was avoided.

Col. Rutherford was a man of great energy, and required from all under his authority, habits of industry and close attention to their appointed work. He was one of the first persons in South Carolina who planted cotton extensively.

Previous to 1796 cotton was cultivated in Newberry District for domestic purposes only, and the lint was separated from the seed by the fingers. In 1796, Col. Rutherford purchased one of Whitney's cotton gins.* This is believed to have been the first cotton-gin put in operation in upper South Carolina.

The people for miles around soon began to carry their cotton, in small parcels, to Col. Rutherford, to be ginned. Young Harrington, then about twelve years of age, was put in charge of the gin, and required to receive and deliver the cotton and keep an accurate account of the toll. This required unremitting attention on his part, and he succeeded in managing the business to the satisfaction of every one interested.

Very little is known of Young Harrington's school life. It is believed, however, that he did not attend school more than three years altogether. He came to Newberry village (then a mere hamlet) in 1799, and was employed as a clerk in the store of Major Fred. Nance, who was then conducting an extensive mercantile business. And although only in his sixteenth year, he soon secured—by his industry and efficiency—the confidence of Major Nance and became the general manager of the business.

In February, 1805, he was married to Nancy Calmes, the daughter of William Calmes, of Newberry. After his marriage, he was associated with his step-father in mercantile business at Newberry, until 1807, when he was appointed Clerk of the Court of Common Pleas and General Sessions

---

*Whitney, the inventor of the Cotton Saw-Gin, was a Yankee. Great as was his invention, it benefited him little; his patent was violated and justice denied him every where, except in South Carolina, where he was paid by the Legislature for his invention, and his patent made free to the people.—"*O'Neall's Annals of Newberry.*'

for Newberry District, which office he held—until a week before his death—a period of nearly forty-three years.

It is probable that no one in South Carolina ever filled the office of Clerk with more ability and success than Mr. Harrington.

If there was a prisoner to be arraigned, a jury to be impanelled, and application for citizenship by an alien to be heard, or any other duty to be performed in open Court, he was always prepared, and never found it necessary to resort to printed or written directions. He could repeat all the oaths and other forms required in the discharge of his duties from memory. He was prompt, efficient and obliging; a man of unusual self-reliance and self-possession. He could put his hand upon any paper in his office at a moment's notice; and never permitted a record to be carried out of his office, except under an order of Court. "He was often required, as ex-officio Commissioner of Special Bail, to decide difficult legal questions, this he did with singular promptitude and accuracy for one not educated as a lawyer."

Promptness and love of order were prominent traits of his character. If at any time an appointment was made for a meeting of citizens, or a committee of which he was a member, he was invariab'y the first man to arrive. His love of order was apparent in everything he did. He was one of the original members and a deacon in the Baptist Church at Newberry, and by common consent became conservator of order in that Church. He was a devout worshiper, but no disturbance either in the congregation below or among the colored people in the gallery ever escaped his notice. He had a great aversion to dogs, and with one exception, would not allow them to remain in the Church under any circumstances. His life-long friend, Mr.

John S. Carwile, who always occupied the same pew with him, owned a little pet dog named "Trusty" which always followed his master to Church and would take his place on the pulpit steps—for a nap during the services. If, however, any other dog came into the Church and began to wander around, Mr. Harrington would very quietly take up his walking cane, and with Trusty's assistance, expel the intruder forthwith. Trusty seemed to understand that he was "at Church" and under Mr Harrington's eye, and never made any disturbance himself*.

There was nothing especially striking in Mr. Harrington's appearance, but there was in his manner a courtly grace and ease very unusual and attractive. He was a "born gentleman." It is related of him that when he was a lad at school, he surpassed all his school-fellows in politeness and gallantry. He would walk up to the door of the school-house with a little girl and hand her up the steps with the ease and grace of a cavalier.

---

* The dog-knowledge or instinct (whatever you may call it,) of "Trusty," was very remarkable. He had very high notions of gentility and good morals. He would not tolerate, in his presence, an uncleanly or shabbily dressed person, or a drunken man. He took very little notice of other dogs, except to show his contempt for them. Whenever his master was away from home he would, at the sound of the Church bell, start off, without waiting for the family, and be found on their arrival at the Church, in his accustomed place, on the pulpit steps. If, at any time, a visiting preacher occupied the pulpit, he would as soon as he heard his voice come down into the aisle, deliberately seat himself on his haunches, and take a good look at him. Having satisfied himself (I suppose,) that the preacher was not an intruder, he would return and resume his nap. How he turned these things over in his dog-mind we may not know. But I am persuaded that if he had survived his owner, only the severest treatment could have made him leave his old haunts, and that he would have continued, if possible, to attend his master's Church during the remainder of his life.

At one of the schools he attended there was a blue-eyed, brown-haired little girl to whom he was particularly devoted in his attentions. One day he carried a bright red June apple to school, in his pocket, which he intended to present to this little girl at noon-time. But, during the morning hours, while she was standing with her class before the teacher reciting a lesson ; the graces of her person, and her proficiency in the lesson, so charmed him, that forgetful of his surroundings, he walked across the floor and placed the apple in her hand, in the presence of the teacher and the whole school. His sweetheart blushed deeply and trembled as she contemplated the probability of his punishment by the teacher, but strange to say, the stern man only smiled and allowed the matter to pass without further notice.

This little incident and the subsequent history of these children should convince the most skeptical that "marriages are made in heaven." The little girl afterwards became the wife of the gallant little fellow, who gave her the apple, and through a long period of years the fires of love and affection, which must have been kindled then, continued to burn with undiminished brightness, until they were extinguished by death.

Mr. Harrington's devotion to his wife, his thoughtfulness of her comfort, and his tender and respectful manner towards her were remarkable. She was as much admired and beloved by him, the day he died, as she was the day he led her to the marriage altar, and it is but the simple truth to say that she deserved and returned it all.

Mr. Harrington was an enterprising and a liberal citizen. He erected several of the best buildings in Newberry, among them—in connexion with James Farnandis—the Newberry Hotel, (destroyed by fire a few years ago,) which was, at the time of its erection one of the largest brick edifices in the upper part of the State.

"The simplicity of his character must have impressed any one on the slightest acquaintance. All his words and actions were marked with a candor so evident, as to make it impossible to suspect him of concealment and disguise. His mind was exempt in no small degree from obliquity of motive, in all that he did his course was a straight-forward one, guided by 'the fear of the Lord.' He was distinguished a'so for the singular kindness of his disposition. He was always ready to relieve the destitute and comfort the distressed. * * * * * * *
The uniform cheerfulness of his temper was very remarkable—a disposition of mind quite inconsistent with the idea that religion shuts up its votaries in a gloomy seclusion from all enjoyment, and condemns them to bear the burden of sombre thoughts and feelings."*

On the evening of the 11th of November, 1850, after conducting family worship, he retired to rest. In one short hour afterwards he died from a stroke of apoplexy.

His wife, Mrs. Nancy Harrington, was sixty-four years old at the time of his death, and her sympathizing friends as they looked upon her bowed form and grief-stricken face, standing beside her husband's grave, supposed that her earthly pilgrimage was nearly ended.

But how inscrutable are the ways of Divine Providence. Mrs. Harrington lived on nearly a third of a century after Mr. Harrington's death. She saw nearly all the early friends of her husband and herself, with many members of her own family, pass away. She heard the distant mutterings

---

* Sermon on the death of Y. J. Harrington, by John J. Brantly, D. D., 1851.

of the war cloud, and saw it break in all its fury upon the country in 1861, passed through the vicissitudes of that eventful and appalling time, and amid its darkest hours witnessed the destruction by fire of the old family mansion, around which clustered so many happy memories of her long married life. Old age, manhood and womanhood in all their strength and beauty, joyous youth, budding childhood and prattling infancy were alike cut down and borne to the grave. Yet the summons which she looked for constantly and often longed for did not come. Through many of the closing years of her life how truthfully she could, with the poet, have said .

"So I am watching quietly
    Every day,
Whenever the sun shines brightly,
    I rise and say :
'Surely it is the shining of His face,'
And look unto the gates of His high place
    Beyond the sea ;
For I know He is coming shortly
    To summon me.

And when a shadow falls across the window
    Of my room,
Where I am working my appointed task
I lift my head and watch the door and ask
    If He is come?
And the angel answers sweetly
    In my home,
'Only a few more shadows
    And He will come.' "

Calmly, patiently and cheerfully she waited her Master's call until it came. On the 29th of May, 1879, at the house of her grandson, Gen. Y. J. Pope, she peacefully and quietly passed away in the ninety-third year of her age.

Mrs. Harrington was a lovely and amiable woman, modest and retiring in disposition. Beneath her apparent shyness of manner, there lurked a warm-hearted, generous frankness, and a rich vein of refined, delicate humor, which gave a nameless charm to her conversation ; and there was a magnetism in her voice which can never be forgotten by those who came under its influence. Like the odor of the orange blossom when inhaled in its native clime, its sweetness lingered always in the memory.

The writer knew Mrs. Harrington well for nearly half a century, and amid all the ordeals through which she passed—as a member of society, and as a Christian, does not remember to have ever heard an unkind criticism upon her conduct.

JOHN SCHUYLER CARWILE.

[" Manhood begins when we have in any way made truce with Necessity ; begins even when we have surrendered to Necessity, as the most part only do; but begins joyfully and hopefully only when we have reconciled ourselves to Necessity ; and thus in reality triumphed over it, and felt that in Necessity we are free."]—THOMAS CARLYLE.

John Schuyler Carwile was born on the 17th day of February 1786, in Laurens County, S. C. He was the son of Zachariah and Mary (M'Mahan) Carwile. His father was a soldier of the Revolution, and fought under Cleveland at the battle of King's Mountain. His paternal ancestors came from Wales, and it is supposed, (but not definitely ascertained), that his maternal ancestors came from Scotland. His parents were possessed of very little of this world's goods. They were honest, intelligent and respectable, and esteemed for their integrity and moral virtues. Mr. Carwile's early advantages were very limited, the whole period of his school education did not embrace more then two years. He spent the greater part of his youth in laborious occupations; chiefly in farm work. At one time he undertook to learn the carpenter's trade, but as he has been heard to say: He did not possess sufficient mechanical ingenuity and skill to make even a respectable journeyman carpenter.

He did not take pleasure in his work. Not that he was indolent. On the contrary he was full of energy, and was too honest and conscientious to neglect any of his appointed tasks, but he felt that he was born for something beyond the life he was leading. He had a burning thirst for knowledge and had already caught glimpses of a world beyond the confines of the limited sphere in which he moved, where men were fighting their way up to positions of honor and usefulness In the intervals of his work by day, and by the light of flaming pine-knots at night, he practiced writing, studied arithmetic and read everything he could lay his hands upon. His reading was necessarily limited; books were luxuries then enjoyed only by a few; but his eager desire to inform himself attracted the attention of the more thoughtful neighbors, who lent him such books as they had. He soon became an expert penman, a good reader, and an authority in arithmetical problems; and by the time he had reached his majority, was looked upon as the best informed young man in his neighborhood.

Newspapers were very seldom seen in the country then. At musters, estate sales, or barbecues in the neighborhood, if any one was so fortunate as to have a newspaper he (Mr C.) was generally called upon to read its contents to the assembly. This he usually did, in summer seated beneath the spreading branches of some venerable tree, or in winter, on the sunny side of a barn or some other convenient building, with his listeners seated around him.

In his early manhood he came to Newberry District and opened a school in what was known as the "Pitts Settlement." He continued to teach school successfully for ten years. The venerable Mrs. Higgins,* widow of the late Hon. F. B. Higgins, late of Newberry, is probably the only one of his scholars now living. Following the custom of the times, he enforced rigid discipline in his school, and punished with the rod every offender. He has been heard to say that he had often "dressed off" young fellows as large and strong as himself for disobeying the rules of his school. Mr. Carwile, when a young man, had a splendid physique and robust health. He was interested in everything that concerned the industrial and social life of the people, and entered with keen enjoyment into all the primitive and simple recreations and amusements of the day. But he did not indulge in idleness and dissipation himself, nor encourage it in others. Nor was he unmindful of his personal appearance. He always dressed in good taste and as well as his circumstances would permit. In fact he was considered a rather stylish young man. I have heard him relate that he and a young friend once rode on horseback, from their homes to a place near Spring Hill, in Lexington County—a distance of probably more than thirty miles—to leave an order for a fur hat for each, to be made by a celebrated hatter who lived there.

It is to be regretted that he did not talk much about his early life. He seldom alluded to his early struggles or his successes. Even in his latter years he did not fall into the almost universal habit of dwelling upon the past in his conversation.

He was married on the 20th of December, 1810, to Elizabeth Williams, the daughter of Stephen and Catharine

---
*Mrs. Higgins died (since this was written) on the 2d of May, 1889.

(Cole) Williams, of Newberry County. Shortly after his marriage, he settled on a farm in the western part of Newberry County, about ten miles from the village.

On the 9th day of November, 1811, he united with the Bush River (Baptist) Church. In 1831, he was dismissed at his own request from that Church, in order to unite in the organization of the Baptist Church at Newberry, of which in some sense he may be said to have been the founder. He was the first Deacon elected by the Newberry Church, and continued in that office until his death. As a Christian, he seemed to prefer that his deeds rather than his professions, should speak for him, and it is perhaps not undue praise to say that in this he succeeded.

In December, 1815, he was elected by the Legislature, Tax Collector for Newberry County. At that time there were no banking facilities in the State outside of Charleston and Columbia. The tax collector was compelled in making his rounds, to carry the money collected about his person, and finally to carry it to Columbia in order to make a settlement with the Treasurer of the State.

In one of his annual trips to Columbia, Mr. Carwile traveled in a spring wagon, generally known as a "Yankee wagon." In undertaking to cross a swollen stream somewhere between Newberry and Columbia, the current carried both horse and wagon down the stream. Although encumbered with a heavy overcoat and with his money about his person, Mr. Carwile plunged into the stream, and with difficulty swam ashore. Fortunately his horse and wagon were rescued uninjured, and he spent the night at the house of an honest German, who assisted him in spreading out his bank bills before the fire to dry, and in watching them until morning

Mr. Carwile continued to reside on his farm (with the exception of four years during his first term as sheriff), until 1828; when he removed to Newberry where he remained until his death.

He devoted himself with energy to his farm, and by reason of his good judgment and practical knowledge soon became the leading man of his neighborhood. "He possessed to the full that 'business' faculty so frequently despised, but which out of ordinary material often makes a clever man; and without which the cleverest man alive can never be altogether a great man." He was called upon to settle disputes between neighbors, to adjust matters of business, to write wills and deeds of conveyance, to administer upon estates, to act as guardian for orphan children and to protect the rights of widows. He accepted these trusts cheerfully, and discharged them with fidelity and strict integrity, and in many cases without compensation. He was grateful for the confidence reposed in him, but it did not make him vain. He worked for the love of work and encouraged others to do so.

His farm lay in one of the fairest portions of Newberry, and he added to it from time to time, other lands purchased chiefly from his neighbors who—contrary to his advice—were enticed away by stories of the wonderful richness and fertility of the lands in newer States.

The same process was going on all around him, so that in after years the lands of that part of the County fell into the hands of a few persons. It was inspiring to ride over their extensive fields of grain and cotton, but the picture had its sombre tints. Here and there could be seen standing in the midst of these farms, groups of venerable apple trees, and as you drew near to them you could discover the debris of a chimney or a solitary hearth-stone—the silent witness that there once stood on the spot a human habitation in which had lived, perhaps a happy family, who had long since gone to seek another home. On Mr. Carwile's farm of about one thousand acres, there had once lived five or six families. He was devoted to his adopted County; the stories of fertile lands elsewhere could not move him. He always insisted that there could not be anywhere a more delightful country than Newberry County; there was to his eyes a beauty in her streams and forests and hills and valleys which could not be found elsewhere, and under the influence of patriotic emotions, he would often declare, that beneath her generous bosom he desired that his body should find its last resting place.

In January, 1820, he was elected Sheriff of Newberry County, and served his term of four years. In 1828, he was re-elected to that office and served another full term.

Judge O'Neall in his Annals of Newberry, thus speaks of him: "The writer has had occasion to notice carefully for thirty-eight years, the manner in which sheriffs perform their duties; and he has no hesitation in saying Mr. Carwile is the best sheriff who has ever come under his observation His books are in the Sheriff's office at Newberry, and they are worthy of any counting-house in the State. Every transaction can be traced without difficulty. He never used the money of a party; he never was told to collect money and failed to do it. If he chose to befriend a debtor, he paid the money to the creditor and thus was both kind and just.

"After he ceased to be sheriff he became the assistant of Mr. Y. J. Harrington as Clerk and Register of Newberry County. This office he filled until November, 1850, when he was called to follow the remains of his friend, Mr. Harrington, to their last resting place. Subsequently he was appointed by the Governor, Clerk pro tempore. He steadily refused to be a candidate for the vacant office. In discharging his duties as assistant Clerk, and Clerk pro tempore, it is but justice to say he was fully equal to his friend, Y. J. Harrington, who was "*primus inter pares.*"

Mr. Carwile was a clear-headed, sagacious man of business, a wise counsellor and a faithful friend. He filled many positions of public and private trust, and it can be truly said of him that he seldom failed in any of his undertakings and never disappointed the expectation of his friends. They key to his success was his courageous and unflinching devotion to duty. He was decided and outspoken in the expressions of his views upon questions of public interest, but was never an unreasonable or bitter partisan. He was fair and just towards those who differed from him. He was always on the side of virtue and good order. Though deprived of the benefits of a thorough school training in his youth, he became in the best sense of the term an educated man, his education having been secured by diligent reading and observation, association with cultured people, and the constant exercise of his naturally strong intellect. One might have inferred from the purity of his English and his excellent conversational powers, that he was a college-bred man. His temper was naturally quick, but he had it almost completely under his control. He had occasional seasons of depression of spirits, from the effects, chiefly, of bodily infirmity; but he was generally cheerful and hopeful. No one enjoyed more than he social intercourse with his friends, or relished more a really humorous story or joke, even if it was at his own expense. His laughter was hearty and contagious. He was a man of striking appearance and pleasing address. He usually wore—in the latter part of his life—a black suit with a white cravat of soft muslin folded twice about his neck, after the style we see in pictures of Gen. Washington and others of the "*old regime.*" His style of dress gave him somewhat the appearance of a clergymen. Indeed, on occasional jaunts which he made to Columbia and other places, ferrymen and toll-bridge keepers would sometimes decline at first to receive the money he offered them, saying : " that preachers were allowed to pass free." He also received many letters with the title "Revd." prefixed to the address. This rose no doubt from his having for a long time conducted the correspondence of Bible and other religious societies of which he was a member, and often secretary and treasurer.

He achieved honorable distinction among the men of the community in which he lived so long, and succeeded in surrounding himself and his family with the comforts and refinements of life ; but he never forgot his early struggles, and was always ready to extend his sympathy and aid to the needy and suffering, however humble or obscure they might be. While he never harbored malice in his heart against any one, he heartily despised all hypocrisy and double-dealing.

He died on the 8th of November, 1852. His body is sleeping by the side of his wife, (who died in 1848,) in the cemetery at Bush River Church, where six of his children and many of his beloved friends have found a resting place.

<blockquote>
" No life can be pure in its purpose or strong in its strife,
And all life not be purer and stronger thereby."
</blockquote>

Y. J. Harrington, and John S. Carwile, "*par nobile fratrum.*" The names of these two men are inseparably connected. The friendship which existed between them was as rare as it was beautiful. They became warmly attached to each other in early life, and their devotion continued to grow with increasing years. They were associated in various kinds of business, and occupied the same office for more than fifteen years.

They were both men of decided opinions, and sometimes differed from each other in their views of political and social questions. But their opposing views were never allowed to interrupt for a moment, the steady flow of the current of their friendship. From the time of their first acquaintance until they were separated by death, an unpleasant word was never spoken between them.

Mr. Carwile survived Mr. Harrington's death about two years. It is believed that he never recovered from the shock of that event, and when the sad tidings of the departure of his life-long associate, and steadfast friend were brought to him, he could doubtless have exclaimed, in the language of David, in his touching and pathetic lament over Jonathan, "I am distressed for thee, my brother, very pleasant hast thou been to me, thy love to me was wonderful, passing the love of woman."

FRANCIS BERNARD HIGGINS.

Francis Bernard Higgins, was born in Newberry County, near Higgins' Ferry, on the Saluda River, on the 22d of October, 1794. He was the son of Francis and Sarah (Coxe) Higgins. When he was three years old his mother died, leaving beside himself another son, nine years old, and a daughter six years old. The daughter afterwards became the wife of William Wilson, who was for many years, the Judge of the Court of Ordinary for Newberry. After the death of his mother, his sister was sent to friends in Edgefield, to be taken care of; the two boys remaining on the plantation with their father. As the eldest boy was attending school, Francis naturally had a lonely life, and eagerly looked forward to the time when he would be old enough to go to school himself; his father having promised that he should begin when he was six years of age. But he never enjoyed the pleasure of attending school with his brother, who died before the long wished for time had come. His father, mindful, however, of his promise, carried him when he was six years old to the school of "Master Howe," a celebrated teacher, who taught near the Quaker Meeting House, leaving him in the care of Col. John Summers, who lived in the neighborhood. He remained at this school about two years, and until Master Howe's death. He then attended a school in Edgefield County, taught by Gillson Yarborough, boarding during the time at the home of Gen. Butler, the grandfather of Gen. M C. Butler, present United States Senator from South Carolina.

He seems to have had a happy life at this school, and in Gen. Butler's family, and he entertained a strong affection for the people of Edgefield as long as he lived. Another thing which endeared Edgefield to him was, that his stepmother who came to his home two years after the death of his mother, came from that County. The coming of his step-mother, whom he always spoke of as one of the kindest and gentlest of women brought back the absent sister and thus his vacations were rendered brighter and happier. It so happened that by reason of his attendance at school and college, and the study of his chosen profession, he never lived at home a whole year at a time after he was six years old.

In 1806 he entered the Newberry Academy, which had just been opened, and continued to attend that school about six years, boarding in the village, with the exception of one spring and summer of the time, when with a view to the improvement of his health, his father required him to attend school from home, riding eight miles on horseback and arriving in time for roll-call each morning.

He had prepared himself to enter the South Carolina College in October, 1811, but for some reason did not go there until January, 1812. He then applied for admission into the Junior Class, for which he had prepared himself. As three months of the session had already past, he was informed (after examination) that he would be received provided he could get some one to hear him recite, out of regular hours, in order that he might make up for the time lost. Mr. James Gregg, then a tutor in the college, kindly consented to hear his recitations, and he was allowed to take his place in the Junior Class. This kindness on the part of Mr. Gregg, Mr. Higgins always remembered with gratitude. Years afterwards, when they were both members of the Senate of South Carolina, and some matter of importance was suddenly brought up and earnestly debated, Col. Gregg—then suffering from a temporary aggravation of deafness—said to Mr. Higgins: "You must pay me now for helping you forward in college, by keeping me informed as to the discussion going on, so that I may know how to vote." And frequently afterwards Col. Gregg would notify Mr H. that "he must be ears for him."

He was graduated from the South Carolina College in December 1813 standing third in a class of thirty three; Governor McDuffie being first.

In 1814 he read law at Edgefield Court House, under Eldred Simkins, Esq., and in 1815 continued the study of law at Newberry under Anderson Crenshaw, Esq. After being admitted to the Bar, he settled at Spartanburg, where he remained only a short time and then returned to Newberry.

Upon the organization of the Court of Equity, in 1817— and within two years from the time he began to practice law—he was elected by the Legislature of South Carolina Commissioner in Equity for the District of Newberry. He continued in that office until December, 1826, when he resigned, and at the same time retired from the practice of law. His health had become enfeebled, and he resolved to devote himself to his planting interests and land surveying, in order that he might enjoy the benefits of out-door life.

On the 12th of October, 1820, he was married to Elizabeth A. Caldwell, the daughter of William and Elizabeth (Williams) Caldwell, of Newberry District. His venerable widow, in her eighty-fourth year, is now living with the family of her son-in-law, Dr. James McIntosh, at Newberry, in the house that has been her home for more than sixty-five years.

He was elected to the State Senate in 1832, while away from home on a visit to the States of Alabama and Mississippi, whither he had gone to inspect the country, with a view to removing from South Carolina. His election to the Senate, under such flattering circumstances, decided him to remain in his native State. He continued to be a member of the Senate for three successive terms. In 1844 he declined a re-election, and retired from public life.

As Commissioner in Equity, he was prompt and efficient. His administration of the business of that office was highly commended by the Bench and the Bar.

During the twelve years of his service in the Senate, he was a laborious, faithful and efficient member, and was always a member of some of the most important committees. In all things relating to the statistics of the State, he was regarded as high authority. He once published an interesting and exhaustive statement, giving the comparative population and wealth of the different Counties of the State.

He made no pretensions to oratory and seldom made speeches. He was always at his post, and kept himself fully informed as to every measure brought before the Senate. His retirement from that body was much regretted by his fellow-Senators, as well as his constituents.

He was an excellent mathematician, and as a land surveyor—both as to the accuracy of his surveys, and the beauty and correctness of the delineations of his plots was never surpassed.

He was possessed of a naturally vigorous intellect which he had greatly improved by study and observation, was always a reader of books, delighting most in the Bible, standard historical works and the ancient classics. He had a wonderful knowledge of words, and could give at once the chief definitions of almost any word in the English language. His conversation was entertaining and pleasant. Having a good memory, he had treasured up much that he had read, and many traditions of the past. He was very domestic in his habits and tastes, and fully enjoyed the pleasures of home and the family circle. His manners were courteous and engaging. He was kind-hearted and generous and singularly free from malice or injustice, in his intercourse with his fellow-men.

In the afternoon of the 29th of December, 1863, he attended the funeral services of his life-long friend, Chief-Justice O'Neall, (who had died suddenly,) and occupied, on that occasion for the last time, his accustomed seat in the Baptist Church at Newberry, of which he had been a member since 1831. In the evening, after his return from the funeral, he read to the family the 14th Chapter of the Gospel by John, and in commenting in a familiar way upon it, said: "That he had, in his earlier life, often expressed the wish that he might not die suddenly; but that all apprehension and concern about the manner of his death had long since passed away, and if his summons should be as sudden as O'Neall's he was willing to go. And trusted that through the atonement of Christ and the free and unmerited grace of God, he was ready for the call whenever and however it might come." In less than ten hours his summons came. On the following morning (December 30th, 1863), he was stricken with apoplexy and died in a few hours.

DRAYTON NANCE.

Drayton Nance was born at Newberry in 1800, and spent the whole of his life in his native town. He was the son of Major Frederick Nance. His mother's maiden name was Elizabeth Rutherford. He received his school education chiefly, if not altogether in Newberry, and was graduated from the South Carolina College in 1821. He read law after his graduation, and upon his admission to the Bar, entered upon the practice of his profession at Newberry. In 1826, he was elected by the Legislature, Commissioner in Equity for Newberry District. He held the office of Commissioner by successive elections until 1838, when he declined to serve longer. As Commissioner in Equity he displayed talents and ability of a high order.

After leaving the Commissioners' office he retired to private life. He had an ample estate, and from the income derived from his plantations and from other sources, was enabled to live in comfort and entertain his friends with old-time Southern hospitality.

He could have had almost any position of honor or trust, within the gift of the people of his native District; but he steadily resisted all efforts made to withdraw him from his retirement. This was very much regretted by his friends, who believed that his talents, education and sterling honesty fitted him for the halls of legislation, either State or National. But though he refused to enter the arena of politics, he kept himself abreast of the times with reference to all the political and social movements and problems of the day, and was thoroughly familiar with the political history of the country.

He was a prompt, reliable and clear-sighted man of business. In the administration of the affairs of the Commissioner's office, and other public trusts, and in the management of some large estates,—which by reason of the minority of the heirs-at-law, remained in his hands as executor, for a number of years—he exhibited sound practical judgment, and unusual financial skill. While I have no doubt that he would have succeeded in making an honorable name for himself in political life, I think it is probable that he would have succeeded quite as well if he had devoted himself to commercial pursuits. But he preferred a quiet, peaceful home life, before all the honors and enticements of a public career. He was a genuine type of the old-time planter gentleman, of whom so few are left among us.

He did not often address public assemblies, but whenever he did, he invariably secured the undivided attention of his hearers. His delivery was earnest and impressive, and not without some of the elements of true oratory.

In the year 184-, I was present at a convention of delegates which met at Greenville, S. C., to consider the practicability of building the Greenville and Columbia Railroad. During the progress of the meeting Mr. Nance delivered a speech in which, after pointing out, with great clearness, the importance and value of a railroad in developing the resources and increasing the wealth of a country, he made on eloquent appeal to the patriotic motives of his hearers, which thoroughly aroused the convention. The Hon. Joel R. Poinsett (who had once been Minister to Mexico, and was Secretary of War in Van Buren's Cabinet), was present as a delegate, and was an ardent supporter of the projected enterprise. When Mr. Nance had concluded his speech, Mr. Poinsett walked across the hall, and grasping Mr. Nance by the hand, thanked him most cordially for his admirable and timely address.

Mr. Nance was not an indiscriminate reader. He read chiefly standard, historical and classical authors, and very little light literature. "But there is one book which the study of all other literature will only render more precious, while at the same time it is so surpassing and universal in its range, that all other literature serves only for its foil or its illustration, and in which there is more wisdom than in all other books of the world put together;" which he read constantly and thoughtfully. His knowledge of the Bible was surprising, and from that Book he drew the inspiration of his life. He loved the Bible for its simplicity, its poetry, its grandeur, and above all for its Divine message of redemption to man.

I would commend the example of Mr. Nance to the young of the present time. "The indiscriminate devouring of newspapers, magazines and periodicals has much to answer for. It wastes our time, it distracts the attention and weakens the memory. Further than this, a habit of indiscriminate reading tends to foster a degraded fondness for personalities and puerilities. The diseased taste for gossip which is fostered by such frivolous reading passes readily into envy, malice and all uncharitableness."

There was no mistaking Mr. Nance's position on any important question. He had the courage of his convictions under all circumstances. There was no concealment or hypocrasy about anything he did. He had a high sense of honor, and scorned a mean act. His temper was somewhat variable; he occasionally fell into a condition of despondency, which would sometimes be mistaken by those who did not know him well for indifference. He was really a just and generous man, "who withheld not good from them to whom it was due, when it was in the power of his hand to do it." His heart was quickly moved by the story or exhibition of human suffering, and his sympathy as quickly aroused to benevolent action :

> "Pitiful he was
> To all who suffered, measuring
> By the large measure of his own deep heart,
> And by the vastness of its treasure."

Notwithstanding the high and honorable position he occupied in the estimation of the community, he was modest and unpretending, and it is not an exaggeration to say that he always underrated his own abilities.

He was married on the 3rd of April, 1827, to Miss Lucy Williams, who died on the 7th day of November, 1847. She was the daughter of Washington and Sarah (Griffin) Williams, of Laurens District, S. C.

On the 11th day of February, 1852, he was again married to Mrs. Arianna Livingston, of Florida, who survived him and died in Florida some years ago.

On the 11th of February, 1832, Mr. Nance united with the Baptist Church at Newberry, and in 1834, was elected one of the Deacons of that Church. This office he continued to fill until his death.

The last act of his life was one of self-denial and mercy.

While on a visit to his plantation, in Laurens County, he sat up all night watching and caring for some of his slaves, who were very ill. On the following morning, (September, the 13th, 1856,) he had a stroke of apoplexy, from the effects of which he died in a few hours. Thus passed away, in the maturity of his powers, a man upon whose reputation, as public officer, private citizen, and Christian gentleman, there never fell a stain nor rested a shadow.

COL. JAMES D. NANCE.

James Drayton Nance, was born at Newberry, on the 10th October, 1837. He was the son of Drayton and Lucy (Williams) Nance. From his childhood he was distinguished for his truthfulness and ready obedience to those in authority over him. But he was by no means a weakling. He was always ready to assert and maintain his rights, even among his school-fellows, and very early manifested that spirit of fairness and justice which so distinguished his life. He received his school education at Newberry, and was graduated from the Citadel Military Academy of Charleston.

He had not reached his majority when his father died, yet he seemed at once to appreciate fully the loss of his only surviving parent; especially as it affected two of his sisters who were then of tender years, and had not completed their education. His letters written to them while they were away from him and at school, reveal a thoughtful tenderness and a wisdom and discretion rarely to be found in one so young. While he did not fail to counsel them to cultivate those accomplishments which would fit them to move with ease and grace in society; he was most anxious that they should diligently pursue studies which would stimulate their intellects, elevate their thoughts and feelings, and enlarge their views of the real duties of life. So that when their school-life was ended they could look forward to something far higher and more ennobling than the conquests of mere women of society. All those who ever came in contact with these two sisters—the elder of whom married Robert L. McCaughrin of Newberry, and the younger, William Y. Fair, also of Newberry, can testify how well they repaid the brother for his affectionate care and oversight by following implicitly his wise and judicious counsel. Both of these noble and accomplished women died in 1885.

In 1859, Col. Nance was admitted to the Bar, and began the practice of law at Newberry. His prospects for success in his profession were very promising, but his career as a lawyer was cut short by the "War of Secession."

In the winter of 1860-'61, he was unanimously elected Captain of the "Quitman Rifles," an infantry company formed in Newberry, and afterwards incorporated in the Third Regiment South Carolina Volunteers. With his company he repaired to Columbia, S. C., in April 1861, and was mustered into the service of the Confederate States.

At the age of seventeen, Col. Nance united with the Baptist Church, at Newberry, and from that period until his death—amid the peaceful pursuits of his home life, as well as the fiery ordeals of his military career, was distinguished for his Christian consistency.

Like his great leader, Gen. Lee, he regarded his duty to God as above every other consideration. A member of his company relates, that having been ordered to proceed by railway to Columbia, on Sunday April the 12th, 1861, Capt. Nance, after the company had been drawn up in line, and was ready to march to the railway station, said to his men :

"While it is our duty to obey our orders to proceed to Columbia, let us not forget that this is the Sabbath day." The same gentleman relates that, the night before the storming of the works on Maryland Heights, while he lay awake, at midnight, his mind filled with deep concern and anxiety, as he contemplated the desperate character of the work before them on the morrow; he heard the subdued voice of some one engaged in earnest prayer. After listening intently for some time, he recognized the voice as that of his brave and faithful commander. "The effect of the prayer on myself," said the gentleman, "was to calm and quiet my mind, and I was enabled under its sacred influence to resign myself to sleep."

Capt. Nance, with his company was engaged in the first battle of Manassas.

On the 16th of May, 1862, upon the reorganization of the Third Regiment, (the time of enlistment of the men having expired,) Capt Nance was elected its colonel, a position for which he was eminently fitted. Though young in years his character was fully formed and widely known. Dauntless but discreet, buoyant and hopeful, yet fully alive to the stern duties of life; with a clear head and great self-possession, he was in every way reliable.

As Colonel he commanded his regiment in the battles of Seven Pines, Savage Station, Malcolm Hill, Maryland Heights, Sharpsburg, Fredericksburg, (where he was wounded,) Gettysburg, Chickamauga, Knoxville and the Wilderness, where on the 6th of May, 1864, he was instantly killed.

His body was brought home and kept in the Baptist Church all night, guarded by furloughed soldiers, and after a funeral discourse by Rev. J. J. Brantly, D. D. the next day, was buried in Rosemont Cemetery, where a chaste and fitting monument now marks its last resting place.

It is always a most difficult task to follow up and describe the life and conduct of any single soldier, throughout the campaigns and battles of a long war, such as the late conflict between the States. And it is especially difficult, if not impossible, to do so within the limits of a brief biographical sketch. I can therefore only present one or two incidents in the career of Col. Nance—as given to me by some of his comrades in arms—which may serve to illustrate something of his skill, coolness and courage, and his power to inspire his men with his own dauntless spirit in battle.

"At Sharpsburg," says Gen. Y. J. Pope, " I knew him (Col. Nance) under the heaviest fire to change direction and bring his regiment back from an advanced and wholly unsupported front, by column of fours. It was inspiring to hear his voice swell in praise of the officers and men of his magnificent regiment for their heroic conduct in this battle."

"At Knoxville, (says Gen. Pope,) his regiment was selected from the corps (Longstreet's) to drive a brigade of Federal troops from a position much coveted by the lieutenant-general commanding. To say that the fire was fierce is to describe the situation very mildly. Those who were there say it was the deadliest fire they ever knew. The eyes of the whole army were upon this band. At one time the advance hesitated. Instantly Col. Nance sprang to the flag and, seizing it, led his men so intrepidly, that they burst through the enemies' works, and the field was won. Being on my back at home while this was going on he wrote me of the conduct of the regiment in words of warmest praise, *but not one word as to the part he bore in the battle*, notwithstanding the closeness of our intimacy."

The writer of the following tribute to a brother officer is, the Hon. William Wallace, of Columbia, S. C., who was colonel of the second regiment South Carolina Volunteers.

COLUMBIA, S. C., December 2, 1886.
JOHN B. CARWILE, ESQ.,

MY DEAR SIR:—I received your kind favor of the 29th ultimo, and regret that my memory is so defective as to matters which transpired so long ago, that it will not enable me to recall in detail all that I knew of Col. James D. Nance.

I knew him well, and a more courteous, amiable, cultivated and agreeable gentleman I have never met in social intercourse. And as an officer and soldier he had not a superior, if an equal, in Kershaw's Brigade.

His education in the Military Academy had made him familiar with all the duties of the officer and soldier, and we all looked forward with pride to his permanently assuming the command of the Brigade by commission, when his bright and promising career was cut short by death, on the battlefield of the Wilderness.

I saw him once in battle; it was at Knoxville, when his regiment was ordered to carry a breastwork on a hill. And although there was a great slaughter of his men, and they could not advance for the murderous fire that was poured into them at a distance of thirty yards or less, they did not waver or fall back but with the aid of the skirmishers— who flanked the enemies' position, drove them from it after capturing many prisoners, the colonel of the regiment amongst them.

I was struck with Col. Nance's coolness on that trying occasion (a quality so essential to a commanding officer) which commanded the confidence and admiration of the Brigade.

Lieut-Colonel Gaillard was killed in the same battle (Wilderness) and I heard the soldiers say, who saw them lying together, after the dead had been removed to the rear, that it was the saddest sight that had met their gaze during the war.

Thanking you for giving me the opportunity of expressing my estimate of Col. Nance, and regretting that I cannot go more into particulars,

I am, very truly, yours,
WM. WALLACE.

The reader will observe that Col. Wallace says: "We all looked forward with pride to his permanently assuming the command of the Brigade, by commission."

It was generally understood than Col. Nance, (at the time of his death), was to be, or had been already promoted to the rank of Brigadier-General, and that he would probably have received his commission in a short time, if he had lived.

Col. Nance inherited the Roman features of his father's character, as well as the patriotic heroism of his maternal ancestors. His mother was the granddaughter of Col. James Williams, of the American Army, who was killed at the battle of King's Mountain while gallantly leading on his men.

I think it was generally admitted that Col. Nance was, at the time of his death, the foremost young man of Newberry. Although he was only twenty-three years of age when he entered the army, the people had already learned to trust him implicitly. His speeches, both in the court-room and before popular assemblies were fluent, earnest and effective. He made no attempt at mere oratorical display, nor did he make excited appeals to the passions and prejudices of his hearers, but sought, rather, to impress upon them the convictions of his own sober judgment. He very early manifested a keen interest in politics, especially national politics, and watched with eager solicitude the course of events which led to the formation of the Southern Confederacy. He was an ardent "Secessionist," and yielded up his life a willing sacrifice for the cause which he believed with all his soul to be right and just.

In person Col. Nance was a handsome man. He was of medium stature, his figure erect and well proportioned, his features regular, and the habitual expression of his face serene and pleasant. In his manners he was courteous and dignified. His general appearance was suggestive of great firmness and resolution. His engaging social qualities, his sound judgment, his transparent honesty, his unselfish pariotism, his high sense of justice, his unflinching courage and devotion to duty, and his excellent Christian example, combined to form one of those thoroughly balanced and admirable characters which appear only at long intervals in the history of a community.

The following lines, in memory of Col. Nance, were written by J. F. J. Caldwell, Esquire, of Newberry, and published in the *Columbia Guardian*, newspaper, in 1864 :

IN MEMORIAM.

J. D. N.,

Who fell in the Wilderness, May 6th, 1864.

It seemed to me impossible, though oft that dreadful day,
Came soldiers from along the lines, with tidings of the fray,
And all agreed that thou hadst fallen, death-smitten in the wood,
When first the foe was turned and driven, in terror and with blood.

Full well I knew the dangers of that dark, entangled place,
For thou and thine were thrust in front, and dashed into the face
Of massed battalions hurrying on, elate with victory,
O'er lines of men who ne'er before, were known to yield or fly.
The yesterday we met those hordes, with our own little band,
And broke their heavy ranks, and drove them back on every hand;
But now at morn they moved upon us in their full array,
And swept the bruised and wearied line, that strove to stop the way.
Lee, stern old warrior, stayed the fight, and Hill, of eagle eye—
Alas! to small effect, for't seemed, we should but stand to die;
Till Longstreet brought his close brigades, of soldiers fresh and brave,
And rushed upon the foemen like a stormy ocean wave.
The battle joined, th' opposing columns met in deadly shock,
With shout and shriek and roll of arms, that made the earth to rock;
Charging and slaying, till the foe fell back on every side,
And thou lay'st down in victory's arms, and sank, and smiled, and
    died!
Oh, for the weakness of the heart, the blindness of the mind!—
I could not feel that thou wert dead, and even dared to find
Reasons within my wayward soul, to show thy valued life
Should be preserved immortal through this long, this mortal strife.
I felt that thou should'st live to see our country free from chains—
To see the light of peace once more smile o'er her wasted plains—
To see the triumph and the power of thine own favorite cause,
And help complete the fabric of our liberty and our laws:
I felt that thou shouldst live to bless the hearts that loved thee so—
That Love and Wealth and Fame and Pleasure round thee full would
    flow;
And, finally, in good old age, thy spirit pass away,
Like summer sun in golden clouds after a long, bright day!
Yet thou art dead—dead e'er thy life had reached its golden prime—
Thou of the stainless heart and mind, thou of the soul sublime!
And we who loved to plan for thee long usefulness and fame
Are left alone to grasp a fading memory and a name.
O for thy mighty heart of steel, thy firm and steady hand!
Thy courage, truth and purity, that like the rocks did stand!
O for thy kindly voice! and O that sweet and sunny smile,
So potent every weary heart of sorrow to beguile!
Yet are these not lost, though thy mortal form has passed from sight;
We'll bear them with us through the storm of Liberty's great fight;

And they shall tell us how to brave, to battle with the wrong;
And cheer us on to seek and strive, to bear and yet be strong!
They gild the past with beauteous light, they future treasures ope,
Enlarging our contracted thoughts into a wider scope;
Till rising past our daily life, beyond our country even,
They draw us up where thou art gone, unto the blissful Heaven!
Sleep on, brave soldier! Take at length thy well deserved rest!
Light lie the sods of native earth upon thy pulseless breast!
The fragrant winds of evening softest murmurs o'er thee wave,
Spring's fairest, purest blossoms flower upon thy quiet grave!
Sleep on! secure from care and toil, from envy, pride and hate,
Beyond the reach of battle's roar, beyond the shafts of Fate!
Sleep on! and may kind Providence grant us an end like thine,
To fall at duty's post and pass into the life divine!

CHAPTER XVII.

BIOGRAPHICAL SKETCHES CONTINUED—REV. SAMUEL P. PRESSLEY—REMARKABLE SCENE IN A COURT HOUSE —STORY OF A CELEBRATED TRIAL (FOOT NOTE)—REV. LUTHER BROADDUS.

REV. SAMUEL P. PRESSLEY.

THE Rev. Samuel Patterson Pressley left Newberry in 1833. Although I had attended his school in 1832, yet being very young at the time and not under his immediate care, I have retained very little personal knowledge of him. As I grew up, however, I learned how highly he was esteemed by the community, both as preacher and teacher.

By the kind assistance, (most cheerfully rendered) of the Rev. James C. Chalmers,* a native of Newberry County, now a resident of Winnsboro, S. C., who was a pupil of Mr. Pressley's both at Newberry and at Athens, Ga., I am enabled to present the following biographical sketch :

The Rev. Samuel P. Pressley was born in Abbeville County, on the 25th day of September, 1799. He was the eldest son of John and Margaret (Patterson) Pressley. The Pressley family, from which he sprang, has been distinguished for several generations by the talents and high moral character of the men and the intelligence and great moral worth of the women. Some of the ablest preachers of the different branches of the Presbyterian denomina-

---

*The Rev. J. C. Chalmers died at Winnsboro', July 7th, 1887, aged 70 years.

tion came from this family, as did also Judge B. C. Pressley and that excellent physician and Christian philanthropist, Dr Samuel H. Pressley, who recently died at Society Hill, S. C

Mr Pressley enjoyed excellent opportunities and advantages in his early moral and religious training. His parents were both pious and intelligent. It can not be ascertained where he received his academical education, but when prepared for college he entered Transylvania University at Lexington, Kentucky, and was graduated from that institutution on the 12th of July, 1820. After his graduation he taught school (probably in Abbeville County) two years. During this time he began the study of theology under Dr. John T. Pressley, of Abbeville. He then entered Princeton Theological Seminary in New Jersey and was graduated from that institution on the 20th of September, 1824. He was licensed to preach the Gospel by the Second Associated Reformed Presbytery of the Carolinas, on the 16th of November, 1824, and was ordained by the same Presbytery at Cedar Springs in Abbeville County, on the 15th of May, 1825. In March, 1826, he was installed at Cannon Creek pastor of Head Spring, King's Creek, Prosperity and Cannon Creek Churches, all in Newberry County, and remained in charge of these churches until he removed from the State.

He was married to Miss Jane W. Todd, of Laurensville, S. C., on the 22d of December, 1825. He resided in Newberry village during the time of his pastorate, a period of about eight years, preaching occasionally to the people of the village in the Court House.

Sometime previous to the year 1830 he was in charge of the Newberry Academy for about one year. About the beginning of 1830 he organized and superintended a Classical and English High School at Prosperity Church, near the present town of Prosperity. He employed a competent teacher and visited the school frequently. This arrangement continued for two years. At the same time he supertended and partly taught a Female School in Newberry, in which he employed competent assistants, devoting the most of his time to teaching the higher branches, and to the government of the school. This last mentioned school was liberally patronized by the citizens of Newberry, and much of the time numbered among its pupils young ladies from Fairfield, Union and Abbeville Counties, in South Carolina, and from Burke and Jefferson Counties in Georgia. In 1833, he taught (unassisted) a classical and English school in Newberry village.

Mrs. M. A. Lindsay, of Due West, S. C., in a "*Memoir of Miss Elizabeth McQuerns*,* (published in 1877, gives an account of a most remarkable occurrence—as related by Miss McQ.—which took place at Newberry while Mr. Pressley was living in that village.

It appears that a very respectable man, a citizen of Newberry District, had been found guilty of the crime of murder, and condemned to death. Mr. Pressley had been selected by the unfortunate man as his spiritual guide and friend, and on the day appointed for the execution preached his funeral in the Court House, to a crowded assembly. Mr. P.'s family and pupils, (Miss McQ. being one of the pupils,) and also the friends of the condemned man being present. Dressed in his shroud, the doomed man listened

---

*Miss McQuerns was a native of Newberry County. She was born in 1802, and died in 1886, at Due West, S. C., where she spent the last thirty years of her life as a teacher. She was an accomplished educator, and a noble Christian woman, who has left behind her a long record of unselfish usefulness.

attentively to his own funeral discourse, and at its close was carried immediately to the place of execution, whither Mr. Pressley accompanied him.*

Having been elected Professor of Moral Philosophy and History in the Georgia State University, then known as Franklin College, Mr. Pressley removed to Athens, Georgia, the seat of the College, and entered upon his duties in January, 1834. This position he held until his death.

In his pastoral work in Newberry, having four congregations scattered over the County, Mr. Pressley could not often visit the families of his charge; but instead, introduced monthly Bible classes—including both adults and children—in his different congregations, which met on other days than the Sabbath. He also introduced the (then) new custom of holding special services for the colored people on Saturday afternoons, giving them the front seats in the Churches; the white people, (some of whom, at least,

---

*I have learned from the venerable Rev. M. M. Boyd, and other aged persons who were present and witnessed the scene described by Miss McQuerns, that the condemned man was David G. Sims. Mr. Boyd remembers that Mr. Pressley based his discourse on the occasion upon the words: "Lord Jesus receive my spirit."

Four negro slaves having been tried a short time before, by a Court of Magistrates and Freeholders and found guilty of the murder of Mr. Sims' father, Mr. Sims himself was subsequently (in October, 1830) tried upon the same charge before Judge Evans, at Newberry, and found guilty of being accessory before the fact to the murder. And having been refused a new trial by the Court of Appeals, was now about to suffer the extreme penalty of the law.

It appears from the report of the case as found in 2d Bailey's S. C. Law Reports, that the evidence upon which Mr. Sims was convicted, was altogether circumstantial. The law did not then, as it does now, allow persons charged with such a crime, to testify in their own behalf.

Mr. Sims' counsel, were James J. Caldwell, Esq., and Johnstone and

he always desired should be present), taking seats in the rear.

He was an attractive preacher, having few superiors in the pulpit. This was manifested by the large congregations which attended upon his preaching, from the beginning of his ministerial career to the close of his life. He was a more animated speaker than most preachers of his denomination in his day.

He was a profuse writer, and acquired considerable celebrity in South Carolina and elsewhere by his letters addressed to Dr. Cooper, the Infidel President of the South of Carolina College. These letters were published in the *Charleston Observer* newspaper, and in pamphlet form. And it is said they aided no little in intensifying the opposition which arose against Dr. Cooper as President, especially on the part of those who upheld the religion of the Bible and

---

Dunlap, (Job Johnstone, Esq., and Robert Dunlap, Esq.,) of Newberry. The prosecution was conducted by Mr. Solicitor B. J. Earle, of Greenville, and A. P. Butler, Esq., of Edgefield. Four of the lawyers engaged in this celebrated trial were afterwards elevated to the Bench. Mr. Johnstone and Mr. Earle were both elected in the winter following the trial; the former to the Chancery and the latter to the Law Bench. Subsequently Mr. Butler was elected to the Law Bench, and Mr. Caldwell to the Chancery Bench.

I have been informed by J. F. J. Caldwell, Esq., of Newberry, (ho was quite young when his father, Chancellor Caldwell, died,) that his mother often told him that his father never believed that Mr. Sims was guilty. All those who knew Chancellor Caldwell, will understand that his belief did not arise merely from any sympathy he may have felt, as counsel, for the unhappy man, but rather from the dictates of his sober judgment. I have also learned from trustworthy authority that Judge Butler, of the prosecution, entertained doubts of his guilt.

The execution took place in the winter of 1830-31. The painful duty of executing the order of the Court fell upon my father, John S. Carwile, who was the sheriff of Newberry at the time. I was only five

true morality, and which finally compelled his (Dr. C.'s) resignation.

Mr. Pressley was a close, systematic student, devoting much of his time to his books. He was fond of such games as backgammon and chess—especially the latter, as a means of mental recreation. When his mind became wearied from continued close application to study, an hour's recreation of this kind, he said, always relieved and refreshed it, so that he was prepared to resume his wonted labor with renewed energy and activity.

Possessing an active, vigorous and well cultivated mind, he was aspiring without being ambitious ; unless it was an honorable ambition to occupy more advanced and important positions of usefulness. Although he died just as he had completed his thirty-sixth year, he had already risen to eminence both as educator and preacher.

In 1834, at his own request, Mr. Pressley was dismissed

---

years old then, and do not remember anything about the scene in the court house. But I can distinctly recall some things connected with the tragedy. I remember that my father became very silent and deeply concerned about the execution as the appointed day drew near, and spent many hours at night in walking the floor of his bed chamber. We were then living in the house on the corner of Friend and Wilson streets, now occupied by Mrs. McFall. I remember that while standing at a front window in the afternoon, watching the rapidly descending snowflakes, I saw my father, on his return from the execution, ride up and hitch his handsome brown mare (I have always had a surprising recollection of horses) to a projecting limb of a damson tree that stood near the street, and come into the house, shaking the snow from his hat and overcoat. And that after addressing a few words to my mother, he sat for a long time -amid the deepening shadows of evening—silently gazing into the fire, with his arms folded across his chest, and a look of deep pity and compassion on his face.

In all the history of the Courts at Newberry, no trial ever created a more intense and wide-spread interest than that of Mr. Sims.

from the Associated Reformed Presbytery of the Carolinas, to unite with the Presbyterian Church.

He died on the 29th of September, 1836. His mortal remains lie in the Cemetery at Athens, whence—having finished his earthly labors, he entered upon his reward.

REV. LUTHER BROADDUS.

Rev. Luther Broaddus was born in Caroline County, Va., on the 16th of July, 1846. He was the son of Rev. Andrew Broaddus, D. D. He was an unusually thoughtful, but not a melancholy child. Though he was not averse to associating with other children, yet he had unusual capacity to amuse and entertain himself when alone. In his early school days he was noted for his aptness to learn, and his studious habits, and throughout his life he displayed the same readiness in acquiring knowledge, and the same devotion to study.

He was baptized by his father when he was not quite sixteen years old, and united with Salem (Baptist) Church, Caroline County, Va., of which his father was pastor.

In his sixteenth year he entered the University of Virginia, where he remained only one year, leaving that institution to join the Confederate Army, in which he continued to serve until General Lee's surrender.

Soon after the war he entered the Southern Baptist Theological Seminary, and came away—after remaining only two years—a full graduate. This he accomplished by remaining and pursuing his studies, both theological and literary, through two vacations. But this close application injured his health and he was never so strong afterwards.

After his graduation his preparation for the full work of the ministry was completed by his ordination which took place at Edgefield, S. C., in 1869, and he at once entered upon active duty as pastor of the Baptist Church, at that place. He was married on the 24th of November, 1870, to Miss Sally Eugenia Bryan, of Edgefield.

His second pastorate was at Ninety-Six, and from that place he came to Newberry.

"The first Sunday in January, 1878, will be long remembered by the members of the Newberry Baptist Church. On that day Mr. Broaddus appeared for the first time in their pulpit. Many of the members never saw his face until he arose to deliver his first sermon. But before its close all hearts were drawn to him, and his presence was felt to be a benediction. Nor can they forget his tender and pathetic words as they united with him after the sermon in commemorating the death of their Lord and Master.

This relation of pastor and people, so auspiciously begun, was continued with evergrowing usefulness on his part, and unabated love and affection on the part of his flock, for nearly eight years, and until his death, which occurred (at Newberry,) October 26th, 1885."*

His wife and two daughters of tender years survive him.

The manifestations of sorrow over his death were profound and universal. He was one of the most beloved and honored men in the community in which he lived, and was recognized throughout the State as one of the most useful ministers of his denomination.

His funeral was attended by people of every shade of religious opinion, ministers of other denominations in Newberry acting as pall-bearers. The funeral services were conducted by Rev. J. A. Clifton, of the Methodist Church.

---

* Extract from a Memorial adopted and published by the Newberry Church. Mr. Broaddus is probably the only minister and certainly the only pastor who, up to this time, (1890) has died at Newberry.

Appropriate and pathetic addresses were made by Mr. Clifton, Rev. Jacob Steck, D. D., of the Lutheran Church, Rev. E. P. McClintock, of the Associate Reformed Presbyterian Church, Rev. Manning Brown, of the Methodist Church.

I prefer that others more capable than myself should speak of the virtues and work of Mr. Broaddus. The more so, as he was not only my pastor but my most intimate and trusted friend also; and a sense of personal loss and bereavement which I have felt ever since his death, probably unfits me for writing about him, in a calm, unbiased and dispassionate manner.

I am fortunate in being permitted to present extracts: (1), from an editorial of Mr. W. H. Wallace, of the *Newberry Observer*; (2), from an editorial of Rev. W. E. Hatcher, D. D., of Richmond, Va., associate editor of the *Baltimore Baptist*, and (3), from a communication by Rev. O. M. Miller, of Washington City, to the *Baptist Courier*, S. C, which together present a faithful and excellent picture of the man. Mr. Wallace wrote : " No man ever filled his place in life more fully than Mr. Broaddus, conscientious, earnest, strong, entirely consecrated to the work of the Master; he never swerved one iota from the straight path of duty. He walked in that path with such modest demeanor, such quiet unobtrusiveness, such gentle, tender sympathy with his fellow men, that his daily life was a benediction, not only to the congregation under his special care, but to the entire community in which he lived. It may fitly be said of him, as was said of his Divine Pattern, '*He went about doing good.*' Happy is the community that is blessed with such a life; and in his death all realize and mourn a loss that is irreparable.

" It is a mysterious dispensation of Providence—a man of

such usefulness to be cut down in the prime of life. But this much is certain ; he has gone to a rich reward.

"As a minister, Mr. Broaddus came up to the full measure of his responsibilities. In the pulpit he was earnest, pointed and effective. He was always interesting because he studied his subjects closely and was thoroughly imbued with their spirit. He was never dull or common place, and yet he was as free from the sensational as it is possible for any minister to be.

"He had a bright, discriminating mind and a kind and loving heart; and these he had cultivated diligently. He was in a remarkable degree, the master of his own faculties ; always prepared to do the right thing, at the right time and in the right way. Whether in the pulpit, in the social circle, amid scenes of festivity, or at the open grave, he always said the very thing that was most appropriate to the occasion. The secret was found in this; his heart was always right.

"With a bold but gentle spirit, confident in the rectitude of his intentions and in the strength of a consecrated manhood ; he was always at his best—always the same, prepared to do whatever duty required."

Dr. Hatcher wrote : " I knew him (Luther Broaddus), in his youth, knew him when in 1863, a fair and light haired lad, he emerged from the University of Virginia, and joined the Southern army ; knew him when with his commission to preach the gospel burning in his soul, he went to the Seminary to prepare for his work, and knew him, when in 1869, he began his public career as a minister of Christ. His entire ministerial life was spent in South Carolina, but through all the passing years I have watched him with a brother's eye and cherished him with an ever deepening affection. By no act or word has he ever marred the respect which he commanded at my hands even in his youth.

* * * * * * * *
*

"The Baptists of South Carolina attested in many ways their sense of his worth. He was chosen to fill many positions of trust and honor. At the time of his death he was a Trustee of Furman University, the Sunday School Editor of the *Baptist Courier* and the Recording and Statistical Secretary of the South Carolina Baptist Convention. These positions came to him unsought, and that not from any scarcity of gifts for such work in the ministry of South Carolina, but as a tribute to his real merit.

"His unexpected death has stricken the Baptists of his State with profound sorrow, and from every quarter are coming the most grateful and admiring testimonials of his rare and exalted character. It is of his character that my heart prompts me more particularly to speak.

"Americans are afraid to identify a man's character in any decisive way with his ancestry. But no man can ignore the question of kinship and association in accounting for what a man is. Two facts lay behind the personal life of Luther Broaddus, and served to mould it. He came from a race of giants Virginia has fostered no nobler stock than the Broaddus', and that branch out of which he sprang was of the best. His grandfather was one of the most delicately strung and majestic orators of this century, and his father, if not in all things the peer of his own father, is a man of extraordinary mental force—a man whose vigor of thought is well matched by his peculiar felicity in expression. From these as well as from his sweet and thoughtful mother, Luther inherited his superior intellectual gifts. Nor was this all. He grew up in a pure atmosphere—socially, morally and religiously. His sense of propriety, his conviction of right and wrong, and his reverence for divine things were fostered in him from the day of his birth. Between him and all that was mean and debasing there was a great gulf which it would have been hard for him to cross. From his childhood he was in full accord with the lofty moral and religious tone of his home and kindred. It is not wrong to say that he knew as little of sin by actual experience as any man that I have ever known.

"Not that he was a moral weakling. By no means. He was every inch a man and tempted in every point. But he had the counterpoise of a good conscience, a pure taste and a real faith. He kept from sin because he feared God and had respect for others and for himself. His elevation of character, his transparency and integrity gave him power as a preacher. Those who could not appreciate his spirituality had to admire his virtue and uprightness. They knew he was good.

"This thorough conscientiousness of nature wrought mightily in the formation of his ministerial character. It made him true at every point. It cleared his mental forces; made him studious; gave him moral earnestness in the pulpit; quickened his sense of responsibility; caused him to be attentive to the details of his work ; taught him to be strict and honest in his transactions with men, and made him faithful in every relation of life.

"These convictions helped largely to refine his manners, With such sharp notions of what was right, he had to be a gentleman. He could not help it. There was nothing in him to suggest rudeness or discourtesy. And what a lovely Christian gentleman he was ! The sight of him was a lesson in refinement.

"And yet to a coarse eye there was nothing specially winning in his bearing. He was not demonstrative, but rather disposed to retirement. He knew how to be silent, and was not given to glib and noisy speech. He spoke only when he had something to say, and then with a modesty which some would have mistaken for timidity. Beneath his quiet mien there was a mine of courageous conviction. He knew no fear, except the fear of the Lord. The strength of his character was at the bottom, and over it hung the drapery of gentleness and sobriety. He had to be known to be admired, and only those who saw him most, saw him to the best advantage.

"I did not know him as a preacher, but what I did know of him enabled me to take his ministerial measure. He was a devout and inquisitive student; his power of analyzing was excellent; he was logical in the manner of his thinking, systematic in his plans, and ready and accurate in his statements. These qualities reinforced by his faith and his steadfast zeal, and illumined by his genial and sympathetic manner, must have made him a preacher of unusual power. This opinion is amply sustained by the popular verdict. I have heard that he was a good pastor—in the social sense of the term—and I am quite ready to believe it. He was suited to add a cheery charm to a social gathering, and yet more fitted to carry comfort into homes of suffering and bereavement. There was something helpful in his quiet step, his kindly voice, and his skill in doing thoughtful things. There was a wealth of balm in his tender soul for healing the broken-hearted. In his hopeful and sympathetic nature there was a marvellous gift for recovering those that were out of the way. Men could live better and die more easily with the help of such a man as he was, and it was of his very being to tender such help whenever needed."

Mr. Miller wrote:

"Perhaps one who had the undeserved honor of his intimate acquaintance and special friendship will be excused for adding a few personal reminiscences to what has already been written concerning him. (Mr. Broaddus.) * * * *

"It was my privilege to be one of his successors at Ninety-Six, and the people there had me in love with him before I ever saw him. It was almost discouraging to follow him, for whoever might be second in their hearts, Mr. Broaddus was first. It was hard to tell whether to love him, or be jealous of him. He had a marvelous hold on the community in general, regardless of denominations. Men of the world held him in the most affectionate remembrance. He had the rare power of making the unconverted his friends without diminishing their respect for him as a minister. He was regarded as citizen as well as preacher. Eminently practical, broad minded, and public spirited, he laid his hand on the intellectual, social and civil life of the community. He had magnetic power over men, so that he was leader. No one, even if he wished to do so, would ever dare to say a word against him there—and when he died, many who years ago had called him pastor, joined in spirit the weeping congregation at Newberry as they followed him to the grave. * * * * * * * * *

"He was cheerfulness personified and sanctified. So delightful was his companionship that his presence seemed to linger with you after he had taken his leave. How does his laughter dwell like a song in the memory of those who associated with him. Quick at repartee, fond of a joke, ready to see the ludicrous, but not in the least clownish or undignified he bore up the spirits of others without letting himself down—making men think more of themselves without thinking less of him. He was lively without levity, and keen-witted, but not cutting. * * * * * *

"He was a master of men's emotions. Often under his

quiet but earnest preaching have I seen almost the entire congregation in tears. He seemed to have the key to the back door of people's hearts, so that he slipped in on them before they knew it. And sometimes during his sweet and loving talks at the fireside you would see the handkerchiefs quietly coming out on all sides. But while he could play *on* people's feelings, he never played *with* their feelings. He never spoke for effect, but never without effect. He ever spoke the truth in love. * * * * *

"The grave holds but little of him. His life lives on in other lives. His heart beats on in other hearts. His voice, with its sweetness and individuality, will be hard to forget. His memory will be linked with many a blessed hour. His name will be a household word in many a South Carolina home, and children will wish they had been born sooner that they might have seen and heard him."

With a few additional words of my own, I shall bring this sketch to a close.

Canon Farrar (in a recent article which appeared in an American Magazine) advises students to *make a habit of reading only the greatest books*, and relates that the library of a friend of his, remarkable for his wit and eloquence, contained only some dozen volumes, besides his Bible;—a Homer, an Æschulus, a Plato, a Virgil, a Horace, a Dante, a Shakespeare, a Bacon, a Milton, a Goethe, a Wordsworth, and a Tennyson. "It may have been," he said, "a scanty choice out of the world's literature, but any youth who knew the minds of only one or two of these great authors, would be in reality far better furnished than others who might have read a thousand times as many books written by lesser men. I do not, however, mean that we should never open the books of any except the few immortals. * *
* * * * * * Still the rule remains sub-

stantially true, that if we would be wise students, the best and greatest books should be our habitual companions, and the writings of those authors who are most justly famous should be 'our earliest visitation, and our last.'"

Mr. Broaddus probably came nearer following the rule laid down by Canon Farrar than most students. He did very little indiscriminate reading; and for the most part confined himself to the reading of few and standard authors, and yet he was a better furnished man than many others who had read many more books. He did not, however, wholly avoid the walks of light literature. He read the works of the justly recognized masters of English and American fiction. He studied the Bible thoroughly and constantly, and to a great extent made that book interpret itself.

His prayers offered while leading the worship of the assembly on the Sabbath, showed how fully he carried upon his heart the joys, as well as the sorrows, of his congregation, and how deeply he sympathized with all who were struggling against adversity, or were in any way troubled or disheartened.

A very intelligent and observant lady from another town, being on a visit to some friends in Newberry, attended Mr. Broaddus' church one Sunday, and heard him for the first time. At the dinner table, after her return from the services, she said : "It was worth coming all the way from home to hear the prayer offered before the sermon this morning. Did you not all notice that among his petitions for so many different sorts of people, the preacher prayed for those who were perplexed? Well, that part of the prayer exactly fitted my case, and was very helpful and comforting to me. I do not think I ever heard any one present that petition just as he did to-day."

APPENDIX.

NEWBERRY COLLEGE.

The following historical sketch of Newberry College, (a part of which originally appeared in the "*Stylus, an Educational and Literary Journal,*" issued from the College), has been kindly furnished by the President, Rev. G. W. Holland, D. D.:

The history of the effort of the Lutherans of South Carolina to found and maintain an institution for Christian education, is an eventful one. It is a record of the faith and prayer and determination that have characterized a Christian denomination for over half a century.

It is proposed to give a chronicle of this effort and labor of love. Names of those who were prominent in this work, dates of important events, resolutions and recommendations of the Synod and Board of Trustees, will form part of the record. As we review this history, we will learn to admire more than ever the intelligence, the courage and the earnest piety of our fathers in the Church. The recollection of the struggles of the past will furnish earnests of the success that must crown present and future labors.

Inasmuch as another, at one time a student of the Classical and Theological Institute of Lexington, has been engaged to write the history of that school, only a brief mention will appear in these articles.

As early as the year 1828, Rev. Dr. Bachman, that year President of the Synod of South Carolina and adjacent States, in his annual address, recommended the founding of an institution of learning to be under the fostering care of the Synod. In the following year, 1829, a committee, of which Rev. John G. Swartz was chairman, was appointed to "receive contributions to be devoted to the establishment and support of a Theological Seminary." At the Synod held in 1830, this committee reported as follows : "That exertions have been made by the committee to obtain subscriptions to a fund for a Theological Seminary, which have been attended with considerable success. The people of our Church appear disposed to contribute cheerfully to the endowment of such an institution, and there is little doubt that a sufficient fund may be obtained in the course of four years to afford it a liberal support. It is expected that by the 1st of January $3,000 will have been subscribed." Whereupon the following action was taken by the Synod :

"*Resolved*, That in humble reliance on the Divine blessing, we now establish a *Theological Seminary*, to be conducted under the auspices of Synod, and that we by this resolution do consecrate our efforts to Him who is the great Head of the Church, the Shepherd and Bishop of our souls —God over all, blessed for ever."

"*Resolved*, That as a course of preparatory study may be necessary for many theological students, and in order to the defraying of the expenses of a theological institution, we have connected with it a *Classical Academy*, under the superintendence of the Professor of Theology, and that this Academy be open to all males over ten years of age."

A Board of Directors was at once elected as follows, to wit :

Rev. John Bachman, Rev. G. Dreher, Rev. W. D. Strobel, Rev. S. A. Mealy, Rev. C. F. Bergman, West Caughman, Henry Muller, Col. J. Eichelberger, Henry Horlbeck and

Maj. J. Swygert. Rev. John G. Swartz was unanimously chosen Professor of Theology.

Thus, in faith and prayer, was founded the institution which in 1832 was located at Lexington, S. C., and which was known for twenty-five years as the Classical and Theological Institute of the S. C. Synod.

In 1854, at the session of the Synod held in Mt Pilgrim Church, Coweta, Ga., we find that the following action was had :

"Inasmuch as our Institution at Lexington is evidently in a languishing condition, and owing, no doubt, in part at least, to local surroundings, which the future does not promise to obviate, therefore be it

"*Resolved, first.* That in the opinion of Synod there is a necessity for its removal to a more eligible situation ; and that the Directors be and are hereby instructed to take the necessary steps to effect the removal to such place in South Carolina as may promise a more eligible location.

"*Resolved, second.* That the Directors be also instructed to obtain from the Legislature of the State such amendments in the charter as to constitute it a regular College, with the power of conferring degrees.

"*Resolved, third.* That the Institution with its new charter shall be called ———— College, of South Carolina."

In pursuance of this action, Rev. J. Bachman, D. D., Rev. Geo. R. Haigler, Joseph Wingard and Rev. J. B. Anthony, were appointed a committee to carry out the requirement of Synod. As stated in the report of this committee made to Synod in 1855 : "Copies of these resolutions were transmitted to those ministers and members of our Church residing in this State where there might be a probability that encouragements would be offered to locate our in-

intended College." The committee further state : "Several offers have been handed in which we hereby present to Synod, accompanied by our fervent prayers that God would give us wisdom in our decision and crown our efforts with his blessing, so that they may eventuate in increasing the facilities for mental culture—in enlarging the boundaries of knowledge and in the extension of the Redeemer's kingdom."

At the session of the Synod in 1855, the question upon the removal of the school from Lexington being about to be considered, the following resolution offered by Rev. G. D. Bernheim, was adopted : "That, prior to the discussion of this weighty and important subject, a fervent appeal be made to the throne of Grace for the Divine aid and direction in our deliberations." Whereupon, the record reads, "the whole body arose and fervently invoked the Divine blessing to rest upon us in the discussion of this all-absorbing question."

Proposals for the location of the College from Newberry and Walhalla were read. Speeches were limited to ten minutes, and no member was allowed to speak more than twice. Evidently, the Synod regarded the question of removal as most important. The question upon removal from Lexington was first taken, the vote standing, for removal, 35, against removal 20. The ballot then had between Newberry and Walhalla, resulted as follows : Newberry 46, Walhalla 9.

Upon resolution, the vote was made unanimous, and, as a body, Synod resolved to be a unit in its endeavors to promote the best interests of the Institution.

The Synod, having resolved to remove the institutions from Lexington to Newberry, and to " found and maintain a *College*," named the institution " Luther College and Theological Seminary." This name was given in 1855. But in the following year, 1856, this action was reconsidered, and the name changed to *Newberry College*.

A charter for the proposed institution was obtained from the State Legislature in 1856.

The first meeting of the Board of Trustees was held at Newberry in the parlor of the hotel of John L. Morgan, on the 13th of January, 1857. Rev. John Bachman, D. D., was elected President, Col. Simeon Fair, Vice-President, Henry Summer, Esq., Secretary, and Maj. J. P. Kinard, Treasurer.

At this meeting the plans and specifications of the proposed college building were presented and explained by Mr. Geo. E. Walker, architect. Bids for the erection of the building were opened; and that of Messrs. W. A. Cline and Osborne Wells, proposing to erect and furnish the college building according to the plans for the sum of eighteen thousand dollars ($18,000), was accepted.

July 14, 1857, Rev. F. R. Anspach, D. D., of Maryland, was elected President of the College; and steps were taken looking to an early election to other Professorships.

The corner-stone of the proposed College edifice was laid, with imposing ceremonies, on the 15th of July, 1857. Addresses were delivered by Henry Summer, Esq., Rev. J. J. Brantly, Gen. A. C. Garlington, and Rev. John Bachman, D. D.

In the summer of 1858, one wing of the college building was so far completed as to admit of its being occupied. The Board, at its meeting in July, decided to open the preparatory department, and elected Rev. M. Whittle, a native of South Carolina and a graduate of Roanoke College, Va., as Principal. This school was opened in October following, with very flattering prospects, about forty students being in attendance. Mr. J A. Sligh, then a student, was appointed to instruct some of the classes. Later in the year, Mr. — Hara, a graduate of the College of Charleston, was chosen assistant, who remained with the College until June, 1859.

Rev. F. R. Anspach, D. D., the President elect, having declined that position, at a special meeting of the Board held in Columbia in December, 1858, Rev. Theophilus Stork, D. D., of Philadelphia, was elected President, who at an early day signified his acceptance.

At the annual meeting in February, 1858, the Board resolved to open the collegiate department at the earliest possible day. Mr. Robert Garlington, a graduate of the South Carolina College with the highest distinction of his class, was chosen Professor of Mathematics and Mechanical Philosophy.

About the 22nd of February, Dr. Stork, with Rev. J. A. Brown, who had been appointed Professor of Theology, arrived in Newberry. Prof. Garlington was also on the ground; and, in the language of Henry Summer, then Secretary of the Board, "with an alacrity seldom equalled, and never excelled, they arranged the studies, so far as they could do such a work, and assigned to each one his appropriate department."

The Professor of Theology was expected to share, for a time at least, in the duties of the college, as instructor in the Latin and Greek languages.

During the first session of the college proper, which began in February, 1859, and ended in June, 150 students were enrolled.

At the meeting of the Board, in June, additional professors were elected, and we find that the Faculty for the session which began October 1, 1859, was as follows:

REV. THEOPHILUS STORK, D. D.,
President and Professor of Moral and Intellectual Philosophy, Logic, Rhetoric and Elocution.

ROBERT GARLINGTON, A. M.,
Professor of Mathematics and Mechanical Philosophy.

O. B. MAYER, M. D.
Professor of Chemistry, Mineralogy and Geology.

REV. J. BACHMAN, D. D., LL. D.,
Occasional Lecturer on Natural History.

REV. J. A. BROWN, A. M.,
Professor of Hebrew and Sacred Greek.

CHARLES A. STORK, A. B.,
Professor of the Greek Language and Literature

REV. M. WHITTLE, A. B.,
Adjunct Professor of Latin and Principal of Preparatory Department.

A. P. PIFER, A. B.,
Assistant in the Preparatory Department.

The session of 1859-60 opened with 150 students, and during the year the number increased to 175.

Hon. Henry Summer, deceased, at this time Secretary of the Board of Trustees, in concluding a report made to the Synod at its session in 1859, says: "The College opened under very favorable auspices on the first Monday in October, 1859. * * * * * * * * * *
This shows that your body and the Board of Trustees of the College have undertaken a great work—a work which, if they are faithful in the discharge of their duties, will re-

dound to the good, not only of the community in which the institution is situated, but its influence will be felt afar. Your body, individually and collectively, should feel that this institution is to exert a power throughout the whole South. It may be regarded as the child of your prayers. The earnest and untiring zeal of the good, and the wise, and of the aged ministers of your Synod, is enlisted in this noble enterprise; and will not the young and the ardent be stimulated to redoubled exertions, not only to place Newberry College upon a permanent footing, but to make it one of the luminaries of the South? Nurture this tender plant, guard it as the apple of your eye, and you shall see the work prosper in your hands."

Earnest, noble words! And none the less appropriate to-day than they were a quarter of a century ago.

During the session of 1859-60 various changes occurred in the Faculty of the College. Prof C. A. Stork, on account of weakness of the eyes, in the early spring of 1860 temporarily remitted his duties, Rev. C. F. Bansemer being engaged to supply his place. Some time afterwards Prof. Stork returned to the College and resumed the duties of his chair; but the trouble soon re-appearing, he left the College about April, and soon after sent to the Board his resignation.

Dr. Stork, president of the College, was during part of the session, on account of sickness, unable to attend to his duties, and in April went North to recruit his health, intending to return should his health permit. Previous to the meeting of the Board of Trustees held in June of that year, he sent in his resignation as President of the College. At this meeting the resignations of Dr. Stork and Prof. C. A. Stork were accepted by the Board. In so doing the Board passed the following resolution :

"*Resolved*, That hereafter when any of the Professors or teachers of Newberry College resign their places they be required to give six months notice of such resignation."

At a called meeting of the Board, held in May of the same year, Rev. Dr. Brown, professor of Theology, was chosen to act as president of the College until the close of the session. In June following he was elected President of the College until that office could be filled.

At a special meeting of the Board in August, Rev. J. M. Schreckhise, of Virginia, was elected to the chair of Latin and Greek. August P. Pifer was made principal of the Preparatory Department and Adjunct Professor of Latin, and Rev. J. H. Bailey was chosen Assistant Teacher in the Preparatory Department.

The following resolution, adopted by the Board at their meeting in August, 1860, will be read with interest, showing, as it does, that the Trustees were fully awake, not only to the wants of the College, but also to the importance of a liberal education to the worthy poor of the community :

"*Resolved*, That Messrs. Henry Summer, Simeon Fair and A. C. Garlington be a committee to draw up a petition to the Legislature of the State, setting forth the character of this Institution, and the facilites it affords to persons in moderate and indigent circumstances to obtain a liberal education, and praying for the appropriation annually by the Legislature of a sum equal to the interest on our capital fund; in return for which the trustees of the College shall educate yearly such a number of male childen in this judicial district as may be agreed upon, who may be recommended by the commissioners of the poor of said district."

The third year of the College, 1860-61, opened with the most encouraging prospects, the number of students in the several departments exceeding the warmest expectations of the friends of the College. There were at this time three College classes, a Freshman, Sophomore and Junior. The professors were hopeful: the College seemed firmly established. With the School of Theology, as connected with it, and each aiding the other, these two institutions were the pride of the Lutheran Church in South Carolina. Nothing seemed to be needed but to plant them more firmly by largely increasing the endowment; and Trustees, pastors of churches and friends of the College were vigorously addressing themselves to the attainment of this important end. Success was crowning self-denying, earnest, prayerful effort. But, "My thoughts are not your thoughts, neither are your ways my ways, saith the Lord." Why a work so well begun, so vigorously and prayerfully prosecuted, so fraught with important consequences to both Church and State, and just now so near successful completion, should be suddenly and seriously interrupted by the hand of Him for whose name and glory the workmen were laboring, is a question the answer to which is hidden in the yet unrevealed counsels of the Almighty.

In the report of the Board of Trustees, made through their Secretary, Major Henry Summer, to the Synod at its session in January, 1862, we have a condensed statement of the operations and condition of the College up to that date. As compiler of these annals I can do no better than to reproduce this report, which is as follows:

"Since the last annual meeting of your body at Newberry, in October, 1860, the country has been involved in war, the magnitude and extent of which no man, at your last meeting, could have fully taken in at one view. This had its influence upon the College, as well as all other institutions of learning in the State. The number of students was quite large at that time, but the excitement of war and the stimulus of that excitement led many of the young men away from their studies to undergo the fatigues and hardships of a life in the camp of the soldier. We know that some of them have fallen by slow and lingering disease, and that others have fallen on the fatal field of strife.

> 'Now sleep the brave who sink to rest,
> With all their country's wishes blest!'

In January (1861) before the meeting of the Board of Trustees, Rev. Dr. J. A. Brown, the Professor of Theology and President of the College *pro tem*, left Newberry for York, Pennsylvania. On the 15th of January the Board met and consulted as to what should be done as to the election of a President of the College, and an extra meeting was appointed to be held on the 5th of February following. In the meantime the College was placed under the supervision of Prof. Robert Garlington, as President *pro tem*. The Board met on February 5th, at which Rev. J. P. Smeltzer, of Salem, Virginia, was elected President of the College, *pro tem*. On the 6th of April Rev. J. P. Smeltzer arrived in Newberry, and on Monday following commenced his duties in the College.

Up to this time the number of students had been diminishing gradually, owing to the increasing excitement in the State.

About the 10th of May a disease* broke out in town, which soon assumed the light of a contagious disease; in consequence of which it was deemed advisable to suspend exercises in all departments of the Institution about the first of June.

Prof. Pifer had signified his unwillingness to serve

---

*Small-pox.

another year, and with the session his services terminated in the College. The Board testify to his ability as a teacher, his deportment as a gentleman, and shall cherish his memory as one who faithfully discharged his duty in his situation. The Board in this connection also bear testimony to the worth and ability of Dr. Brown, in the department he filled in the College.

The Board at their semi-annual meeting in June elected Rev. W. Eichelberger, of Virginia, Adjunct Professor of Ancient Languages and Principal of the Preparatory Department.*

The untiring zeal of Prof. Garlington, who has been connected with the College since its beginning, commends him to the warm regards of this Board and your body. All the the others are exerting themselves ably and efficiently for the welfare of the Institution."

The Faculty of the College, at the opening the session, 1862-3, were: Rev. J. P. Smeltzer, President *pro tem.*, Robert Garlington, and Revs. J. M. Schreckhise and Webster Eichelberger. All the students of the previous session able to bear arms had enlisted in the army of the Confederacy. Consequently the roll was small, numbering 64 only, classified as follows: Sophomore 1, Freshmen 8, Irregular 3, and Preparatory Department 52.

Owing to serious illness in the family of Prof. Garlington during the latter part of the session, and his necessitated absence from his chair, Major Henry Summer, the Secretary of the Board, and one of its most intelligent and interested members, gave instruction from about the first of March to the close of the session in June, in Latin, History and Rhetoric.

---

*Mr.. Eichelberger, having volunteered in the army of the Confederacy, did not reach Newberry until October, 1862.

1863-4.

The number of students enrolled during the session of 1863-4 was 67, with an average attendance of 45. Prof. Eichelberger had, during the vacation, gone to Virginia as a missionary to the army; and, on account of the uncertain prospects of the College, did not return to Newberry. The remaining members of the Faculty were in their places.

At a meeting of the Board of Trustees in January, 1864, President Smeltzer was appointed financial agent of the College to solicit funds for the payment of the debts of the College, and also for its permanent endowment. President Smeltzer accepted this agency and began the work, the College in the meantime being placed in the care of Prof. Garlington, who, in the words of the Secretary of the Board, "immediately took charge of the College, and superintended the same with efficiency and success to the end of session." As stated in the report of the Secretary of the Board to the Synod, in October of this year, President Smeltzer had by June secured scholarships to the amount $39,000. This agency was continued by order of the Trustees, and resulted during the year by the sale of scholarships in providing for endowment about $46,000. That the Board of Trustees fully appreciated this work, undertaken and prosecuted under so many untoward circumstances, is shown by their action taken in June of that year:

"*Resolved*, Unanimously that the thanks of this Board are due and are hereby tendered to our agent, Rev. J. P. Smeltzer, for his untiring energy and zeal in the prosecution of his agency for the College."

President Smeltzer, in a report to the Board made early in 1865, recommended to the Board that this money be used in the purchase of cotton to be stored in the College building. But the unwillingness to do anything that would show want of faith in the ultimate success of the Confederate Government, and the fear that the storage of so much cotton in the College building might lead to its destruction should it fall into the hands of the U. S. army, led the Board to reject the recommendation. Permission was given to the Treasurer, who was then Rev. T. S. Boinest, to invest the funds in his hands in Confederate bonds. This was done.

(Note. In 1882, certain of these bonds, amounting to about $21,000, were found among the papers of Mr. Boinest, and were by his widow, Mrs. A. E. Boinest, turned over to the writer, who sold them for $105, and by advice invested the amount in the purchase of the Encyclopedia Britanica for the College library).

It is altogether proper to place in this record the testimony of the Board to a worthy and generous son of the Church in South Carolina, Robert G. Chisolm, Esq., of Charleston, whose enlightened zeal was shown in his care for the funds of the College. The following resolution was unanimously adopted by the Trustees at their meeting in June, 1864.

"*Resolved*, That the cordial thanks of this Board be presented to R. G. Chisolm, Esq., for the facilities he afforded our agent in the arrangement of our finances, as well as for his assistance in procuring subscriptions for the College."

1864—5.

The session of 1864—5 opened with thirty students. Owing to the great difficulty of procuring board, arising from the high price of provisions and fire wood, there were but few students from abroad. A committee, which had been appointed to make arrangements for boarding students who were willing to come to College, reported that they "found it utterly impossible to do so." In addition to this difficulty the condition of the College building was now such as to repel students; the general feeling was that the building was unsafe. The attention of the Board of Trustees had been called by President Smeltzer to the danger to which the building was exposed from the closing and corroding of the ducts leading from the roof to the foundation. Committees to collect funds and have the building repaired were appointed from time to time. But nothing was done. This neglect, for such it must be termed, is perhaps excusable on the following grounds:

1. The languishing condition of the College at the time.

2. The many unpaid claims now brought against the Trustees.

3. The uncertainties as to the result of the war; and

4. The intensity of interest which the war demanded for itself.

The approach of the U. S. army toward Columbia in March 1865, and the consequent fears of the destruction of that city by the troops under General Sherman, led the Confederate authorities to remove their purveying establishment to Newberry. The College building was used for this purpose. As matter of necessity, the exercises of the College were now indefinitely suspended.

The College Building was occupied by the Confederate Purveying Establishment until sometime in 1865, when the near approach of the Federal army under Sherman made the removal of said establishment a matter of prudence.

After the surrender of the Confederate armies, the building was occupied by U. S. troops for two months and more. During this occupancy great damage was done to the property. The fencing was carried off, the blinds of the windows, the doors, benches, desks, &c., were promiscuously destroyed, sold to the negroes, or used as fire wood by the troops. In fact there was a complete gutting of the building. The library which had been closed by Dr. Smeltzer, was forcibly opened and many volumes were carried off, the damage to buildings, library and grounds by U. S. troops amounted to thousands of dollars.

The building was now, in autumn of 1865, almost a ruin. The failure to effect the needed repairs upon the roof, followed by the destructive occupancy by soldiers, brought about this dire result.

In January, 1866, permission was given Dr. Smeltzer to open a boys' school in the building. At this time, Capt. A. P. Pifer of Virginia was elected tutor, at a salary of $600 a year, with the understanding that his services would not be required until further notice.

In June, 1866, the Board appointed a committee to estimate the damages done to the property by U. S. Troops, and to take steps to obtain from the U. S. Government indemnity for injuries. Claims were made, but no compensation was at any time allowed.

At the June meeting of the Board in 1866, steps were taken to open the College in October following. Rev. J. P. Smeltzer was continued as President pro-tem., Robert Garlington was made Professor of Mathematics and Natural Philosophy, and A. P. Pifer, Professor of Greek and Latin.

The exercises of the College were opened in October, 1866, and were continued till June, 1867. The patronage was small, and the income from tuition, &c. was inadequate to pay the promised salaries of the Professors. In consequence the College was becoming more deeply in debt and the embarrassment of the Trustees most discouraging.

Appeals made to the community and to the Churches of the Synod, met with indifferent success. Builders' mortgages were resting over the building, and there was little encouragement to the people to put money in property soon to be under the hammer of the auctioneer.

Notwithstanding these great difficulties, added to which was the dangerous condition of the walls and plastering of the College, the exercises were opened in October, 1867.

An effort was made to secure a loan of $6,000, with which to pay off most pressing claims, and as help towards meeting current expenses. This effort failed. One great difficulty in the way of meeting expenses, grew out of the fact that many scholarships were issued during the war, and patrons now claimed the right to send sons and wards on these scholarships.

In reading the Minutes of the Board during these three trying years from 1865 to 1868, one must admire the zeal and perseverance which marked certain men. Simeon Fair, J. P. Aull, Jacob K. Schumpert, N. A. Hunter, T. S. Boinest, Jacob Hawkins, O. B. Mayer, W. S. Bowman, L. J. Jones and others appear as always present at the Board meetings, and deeply anxious for the welfare of the College.

The last meeting of the Board before the removal of the College to Walhalla, was held on the 25th of June, 1868. The College had been continued with two professors and a tutor.

It seems that at this date, matters were most discouraging. The building was falling down,—no money could be raised for repairs—the claims of W. A. Cline and J. P. Kinard were demanding payments—and judgments had been obtained against the property.

At this crisis an offer for the College was made from Walhalla, and thither by action of the Synod the College was removed in October, 1868.

In 1876 an effort was made by the people of Newberry to bring the College back to that place. About $6,000 were pledged through the influence mainly of Rev. H. W. Kuhns. The Synod was not willing to accept this offer.

In the winter of 1876-7 greater efforts were made by Newberry to secure the College. Bids for its location were made by Walhalla, Anderson, Lexington, Columbia, Prosperity and Newberry. The Synod at a called meeting in April, 1877, accepted the bid of Newberry, which was a joint and several bond of responsible citizens for $15,000. A building committee was appointed, and in February, 1878, the present building was ready for occupancy.

The College returned to Newberry in October, 1877, and until February, 1878, held its exercises in rooms over Leavell's Furniture Store—offered to the Trustees free of rent by George S. Mower, Esq.

At the meeting of the Trustees in Walhalla, June, 1877, Dr. Smeltzer resigned as President of the College, and the faculty was constituted as follows:

President, Rev. W. S. Bowman, D.D.; Vice-President, Rev. G. W. Holland, O. B Mayer, M. D., Profs. D. Arrington, G. D. Holloway and G. B. Cromer, the last two having charge of the Preparatory Department.

The number of students the first year at Newberry was 67. At the Board meeting, in June 1878, Dr. Bowman having declined the Presidency, the present incumbent, was elected to that position.

The College has now 71 Alumni, 50 of whom have graduated since the re-location of the College at Newberry.

About 340 different students have been enrolled during the ten years at Newberry.

The President of the College in his last annual report—1887, made this statement: "A study of the roll of students and alumni for the past ten years will show, that while our entire State, and to some extent, other States, have received blessing from Newberry College, two parties have received most decided and lasting benefit, viz.: The Lutheran Church in South Carolina and the county and town of Newberry. And these are the sources to which we must look mainly, both for endowment and patronage."

The present Faculty (1887) of the College is composed of:

REV. G. W. HOLLAND, A. M., Ph. D., President,
Professor of Mental and Moral Science and English Literature.

O. B. MAYER, A. M., M. D..
Professor of Physiology and Hygiene.

REV. HOLMES DYSINGER, A. M.,
Professor of Ancient Languages and Literature.

REV. A. G. VOIGT, A M.,
Professor of Modern Languages and Literature.

REV. JUNIUS B. FOX, A. M.,
Professor of Mathematics and Natural Sciences.

THOMAS H. DREHER, A. B.,
Professor and Principal of Preparatory Department.

MEDALS.

ORATORICAL MEDAL.

(GIVEN BY MESSRS. Y. J. POPE AND O. L. SCHUMPERT.)

A gold medal is annually awarded to that student of the Junior Class who has produced the best oration, regard being had to excellence both in composition and delivery.

EDUARD SCHOLTZ, ESSAY MEDAL.

Through the liberality of Mr. Eduard Scholtz, of Newberry, a gold medal is annually awarded to that member of the Senior Class who shall produce the best essay on a subject to be designated by the Faculty The essay is a requisite for graduation.

J. F. J. CALDWELL, LATIN MEDAL.

J. F. J. Caldwell, Esq., of Newberry, offers a gold medal to that student of the Junior Class who shall produce the best essay written in the Latin Language. Subject for 1886-7, De Amore Patriæ.

SOPHOMORE GREEK MEDAL.

(GIVEN BY MESSRS. T. W. HOLLOWAY AND G. S. MOWER.)

A gold medal is annually awarded to that Sophomore who has sustained the best examination in the Greek Language.

No student will be allowed to compete for any of the above medals, except the Oratorical and the Latin Medal unless he has entered for the degree of Bachelor of Arts.

NOTE.—Since the foregoing sketch was prepared for publication, Prof. Dysinger, Prof. Voigt and Prof. Dreher have resigned.

The following named gentlemen now (April 1890) compose the Faculty:

REV. G. W. HOLLAND, PH. D., D. D., President,
Professor of Mental and Moral Science and English Literature.

O. B. MAYER, A. M., M. D.,
Professor of Physiology and Hygiene.

Rev. JUNIUS B. FOX, A. M.,
Professor of Mathematics and Natural Sciences.

Rev. A. J. BOWERS, A. M.,
Professor of Ancient Languages and Literature.

A. S. LAIRD AND W. K. SLIGH.
Professors and Principals of Preparatory Department.

W. C. SHOTT, Master of Accounts.
(Eastman College,)
Professor of Penmanship, Book-Keeping, Telegraphy, Type-Writing and Stenography.

The Chair of Modern Languages and Literature is vacant at present. The duties of the same being temporarily performed by other members of the Faculty.

www.ingramcontent.com/pod-product-compliance
Lightning Source LLC
Chambersburg PA
CBHW031906220426
43663CB00006B/796